Praise for *Seduced into*

Kudos to Carrie Ishee for writing this boo victimhood is not the end-all but can be the beginning Journey to become a Survivor, and—as Carrie demonstrates—a Thriver!

—Charles L Whitfield, M.D.
Author of *Healing the Wounded Child*

Carrie Ishee has shared a physical, emotional, and psychological journey showing us how in her words, "Trauma recovery is a spirit path toward wholeness and wisdom." Her courage to speak truth to power shines a bright light on abuse, and we are better for it. Her book should be required reading in any ethics course for healthcare professionals.

—Ann Filemyr, Ph.D.
President, Southwestern College, Santa Fe, N.M.

I was stunned when Carrie—one of the most positive, optimistic, and creative people I've known—shared this dark and twisted story of her past with me. It is a testament to her intelligence and resilience that she not only pursued justice but also used this searing life experience for her own and others' positive growth.

—Valerie Plame, Author of *Fair Game*

Carrie Ishee's compelling true story of her psychotherapist's exploitation, betrayal, and abuse follows her journey from depression and attempted suicide through survival to strength and a fulfilling life of meaning and value. The story resonates in today's environment, documenting the real-life impact of the betrayal and exploitation of patients.

—Gerald S. Smith
Former Counsel to the Pennsylvania State Board of Medicine

Carrie beautifully shares the moment of deep healing through art therapy when her image revealed with painful honesty what words hadn't been able to. What began as a lighthearted abstract led to the opening within her psyche of the harshest painful truth about what had actually happened to her. It is no surprise that she became the gifted professional art therapist that she is, now offering important healing opportunities to others.

—Deborah Schroder, ATR-BC, LPAT
Chairperson, Art Therapy/Counseling, Southwestern College, Santa Fe, N.M.

A beautiful and evocative account of how a client feels on the other end of the so-called slippery slope, the receiving end of egregious sexual exploitation. In this book, Carrie Ishee makes the path intelligible and sympathetic without recourse to angry polemics or victimology. You will hand your heart over to her and thank her for your deepened understanding of this terrain and for the knowledge that there but for the grace. . . .

—Andrea Celenza, Ph.D., Asst. Professor, Harvard Medical School, Author of *Sexual Boundary Violations: Therapeutic, Supervisor, and Academic Contexts*

As Earle Plumhoff and I walked out of our initial meeting with Carrie, I voiced what we were both thinking: How are we ever going to get her through the rigors of litigation? She seemed so fragile, and a lawsuit would involve divulging the most intimate secrets of her life in a public setting. Carrie had suffered a terrible wrong that deserved to be rectified so she could live the life she deserved. Getting through the litigation would allow her to triumph in taking back the power that had been taken from her. Carrie persevered, and through her strength, justice was done.

—Robert Hanley, Attorney at Law, Nolan, Plumhoff & Williams, the firm that tried Carrie's lawsuit against Dr. Romano

In *Seduced into Darkness,* Carrie T. Ishee shares her harrowing experiences sinking into the depths of despair and suicidal depression as a result of emotional and sexual exploitation by her psychiatrist. The book also documents her inspiring healing and transformation: Carrie not only recovers from such a life-altering trauma but also allows it to become an initiation into a greater level of consciousness and self-compassion.

Carrie's personal narrative demonstrates her amazing resilience—not only to survive but also to live beyond the trauma and tap into deep healing through the arts, especially music, visual art, and writing. Her masterful weaving of her story on many levels—psychodynamic, interpersonal, sociocultural, and archetypal—makes this a standout among personal narratives and memoirs. *Seduced into Darkness* provides a compelling and instructive read, and a helpful model for others on a healing journey.

—Catherine D. Nugent, LCPC, TEP
Executive Director and Principal Trainer,
Laurel Psychodrama Training Institute
Former Chair, Committee to Implement the Recommendations of the Maryland Sexual Exploitation Task Force

Seduced into Darkness

Seduced into Darkness

Transcending My Psychiatrist's Sexual Abuse

Carrie T. Ishee

Terra Nova Books
Santa Fe, New Mexico

Library of Congress Control Number 2019951328

Distributed by SCB Distributors, (800) 729-6423

Terra Nova Books

Published by Terra Nova Books, Santa Fe, New Mexico.
www.TerraNovaBooks.com

ISBN 978-1-948749-48-0

This book is dedicated to Mom and Dad who never stopped believing that I would be well again.

Foreword

Journeys to the underworld come in many varieties, but there are two themes especially prevalent in the mythology of all cultures across the millennia: those of abduction and those of rescue. In *Seduced into Darkness: Transcending My Psychiatrist's Sexual Abuse,* you will be witness to both journeys. While the story that Carrie Ishee tells here involves a harrowing abduction by her psychiatrist, through her telling of it, another story—one of empowering rescue—emerges.

In the ancient tales, the natural world often brought the signal that the time for a journey had come. A burning bush impels Moses toward Canaan; Odysseus finds his ship carried away by Poseidon's winds; an owl arrives in the home of Harry Potter.

In Carrie's case, the signal came from the sky. Carrie and I met for an astrological consultation in the summer of 2011. We approached the session as all good astrology does: not as an oracular revelation with the sky as cause and her life as effect but rather as an opportunity to gaze together into the mirror of the stars and planets on the day she was born, and to consider creatively how the stories they told were reflected in her life. As we did so, we followed an ancient tradition that began thousands of years ago, when human beings still recognized our connection to the natural world, and when it did not seem strange to imagine that the macrocosm of the sky might reflect the microcosm of human consciousness.

As we examined Carrie's chart of stars and planets that morning, what we saw reflected back to us was a configuration of celestial bodies associated with a famous myth of the ancient world: the abduction of Persephone. The planets and asteroids named after each of the key players in this myth were arranged in Carrie's chart in an unmistakably potent way. We saw Hades emerging from his underworld kingdom, kidnapping Persephone, taking her into his realm, raping her, tricking her into staying, and making her his queen. A precise geometric alignment known as the "finger of God" or "finger of fate" tied the characters of the story together in her chart. As we further explored this, Carrie shared how much the story was reflected in the tragedy and triumph of her own life. Even more striking, the arrangement of the planets on the day we met only emphasized the *original* configuration. The "Cave of Hades" was open once more. There was an opportunity for Carrie to make a second, voluntary journey into the underworld in order to find the abducted Persephone, reclaim her, and give her a voice.

Carrie courageously chose to make this second journey by writing *Seduced into Darkness*, and we are all richer for it. Her story clearly echoes the Persephone myth's themes of seduction and betrayal. As a psychotherapist, for me to see this myth enacted under the auspices of psychology was truly chilling—surely the touch of Hades. It may be hard for many in the healing professions to read parts of this book. The repeated violation of the healer's sacred promise to "do no harm" is painful to witness. And yet to turn away from such an assault is to be complicit in it.

As Carl Jung once wrote, "One does not become enlightened by imagining figures of light but by making the darkness conscious." And James Baldwin warned: "People who shut their eyes to reality simply invite their own destruction, and anyone who insists on remaining in a state of innocence long after that innocence is dead turns himself into a monster." Carrie's story is a kind of archaeological dig into the healing professions, one that should cause all psychotherapists, social workers, doctors, energy healers, and other healing practitioners to recognize and own the shadowy underbelly of their own work, rife with its often-hidden power dynamics and potentials for abuse. Stories like this one are more common than we wish to believe. Many of our modern-day Persephones remain silent.

Like many underworld journeyers, Carrie eventually returned to the surface world bearing gifts. To me, the gifts of this book are twofold. The story itself reveals the profound limitations and harms of an exclusively medical model of psychological healing. It pulls up the rot in the roots, points out the poison in the soil. We are forced to face the enormous shadow that looms whenever we narrow our perspective to extremes, and are reminded how easy it is to be hijacked by the very places in the psyche that we blindly exclude from view. At the same time, the very way in which Carrie's story is told embodies a more-comprehensive paradigm of healing, which in its breadth and depth has the promise to return us to the original meaning of the word *psychotherapy*: to heal (*therapie*) the soul (*psyche*).

In a profoundly personal way, Carrie has tapped into deep veins of myth and meaning that long predate our current diagnostic manuals and treatment algorithms. These deeper ways of knowing do not cancel out the usefulness of the medical discoveries and advances of the past hundred fifty years. They do, however, invite us to hold them with a much greater humility in our hearts and minds, in the much wider context of thousands of years of healing history on this planet. They invite us to enter the process of healing from a place of wonder and curiosity, relinquishing the security of authority and its seemingly infallible answers. And they remind us that to imagine ourselves as gods, as some healing professionals do, is always hubris.

Seduced into Darkness is sacred medicine for practitioner and patient, and boldly challenges all of us to explore our own heroic journey of the soul.

—Jason Holley, M.A., LPCC
Psychotherapist and Evolutionary Astrologer
Santa Fe, New Mexico

Preface

This is a story of innocence, a story of abduction, a story of in-nocence lost It is a story of soul death, of darkness, and of rescue. It is a story of hope, of growth, of divine purpose, and of transformation.

It is a story that begins with an attempt to end my life.

Though most of this book takes place in a small, American town in the 1980s, it is also a story as old as time. It is the story of Persephone.

Greek myth tells us that Persephone was a young maiden picking flowers in a springtime meadow when the earth rent in two, darkness flooded the light, and Hades, god of the underworld (and her uncle), forcibly dragged her into his lair, a place darker than she had ever known, holding her captive and forcing her into an incestuous relationship with him. Above ground, the earth turned cold. Persephone's horrified parents, Zeus and Demeter, searched for her to no avail until their divine guide, Hecate, walker between the worlds, told them where fair Persephone had gone. They rescued her, but not before Hades had tricked Persephone into eating the seeds of a blood-red pomegranate from the land that held her. In doing so, she ate the most abundant, seed-filled fruit on earth, which fortified her with life while also binding her to return to the land of the dead—for a time—year after year, but now not as a naive girl but as a wise woman and goddess, confident in the knowledge she is strong enough to descend, return, and descend again, no longer bound to the will of her captor.

It is a myth that embodies the dark journey of someone who not only survives the horror of her abduction but also transcends it.

Decades after my own abduction, I was both compelled and intimidated by the idea of writing a book about it. Seeking clarity, I made an appointment with Santa Fe psychotherapist, evolutionary astrologer (and mythology expert) Jason Holley. Together, we sat down and pondered my birth chart, my life's direction. Thoughtfully, he declared, "Yours is the story of Persephone." In that moment, the air crackled around us. I knew we had identified the ancient archetype whose journey clarified my own.

From then on, each time I sat down to write this story, I'd first close my eyes and call upon her. Help me, I'd ask. Strengthen me, I'd ask.

Speak to me, Persephone.

—Carrie T. Ishee

Acknowledgments

I want to start by thanking my sweet husband, Chris Ishee, who not only made it safe to open my heart again but who also read many drafts of this book, helped me process the pain that writing stimulated, and appropriately and protectively raged at the wrong I experienced. We have just celebrated twenty-five years of being married! You have been a *huge* part of my healing and the success and joy I now have. I love you, honey, and all the meals you've made, dishes you've washed, and laundry you folded while I engaged in this project. You've been a true partner in life and toward this effort.

To my beautiful daughter, Teslin, who brought me new life and a total renewal at age forty. It is my greatest joy to see how kind, compassionate, smart, confident, independent, and empowered you are. Seeing who you have become makes me know that, if nothing else, I've done something right.

To Mom and (my late) Dad, I am so sorry you had to suffer so much while I took this journey—the ways I pushed you away must have been excruciating. Your love and forgiveness helped me come back, and your dedication to family inspires me to keep my family first while I help other families who come to my therapy practice connect and heal.

To my siblings—Jody, Bobby, Michael, Tim, and Polly—I'm sorry for all the years I shut you out when I was overcome by darkness. Reconnecting with those wonderful memories of the farm and our childhood as I wrote this book helped me heal my soul. I hope this book helps to explain. . . .

To my wonderful writing mentors who helped me craft this memoir:

• First, to CJ Schepers, developmental editor extraordinaire, who helped me raise this tale from its murky depths to give it focus and form. You were a great collaborator and gave me the confidence to keep going in those early days of writing. Your bright spirit brought light into the dark places as I retrieved and wrote about them.

• Secondly, to the brilliant and bold Tricia Ware of Lucidity Editing who painstakingly helped me bring to life the voice of my younger self and helped make the storytelling present and powerful. Thanks to all the cups of coffee and the magic we shared as I felt the feelings I needed to feel to retrieve my young, maiden self.

To my kind, ethical, and professional attorneys, the late Earle Plumhoff and Robert (Bob) Hanley of Nolan, Plumhoff, and Williams, who helped me believe there are good men interested in securing justice. Thank you, Bob Hanley, for your support of this book. It always meant a lot to me when you called me "a compelling witness," and when you made me laugh during those tortuous days of litigation.

To Marty and Scott Gerber of Terra Nova Books. Thank you for helping me birth this book into the world after many years of incubation.

To the staff at Sheppard Pratt Hospital who helped me make sense of what had happened to me, especially to Dr. Robert Temple who encouraged me to take legal action as part of my recovery process. If I had not been believed, or not been supported in pursuing my rights, I doubt I would be where I am today. Thank you.

To the patients at Sheppard Pratt who allowed me to know your stories and be touched by your hearts and will to heal. You will never know how much your struggles inspired me. I have written this story for you as well as me to break down the stigma around "mental illness" and what happens in a psych hospital. You made me laugh and cry, and you made my heart open with compassion.

To Leslie Krohn, my wonderful feminist therapist whom I saw for many years after this violation. Thank you for working from a place of openness and care. You taught me to stop pathologizing myself and start loving myself. You had an important place in my life as you taught me how to heal myself of co-dependency.

To my thoughtful endorsers, thank you to:

• Dr. Andrea Celenza—for your deep comprehension of and work around this issue. Thank you for "getting it."

• Dr. Peter Rutter—for your book *Sex in the Forbidden Zone* which helped me make sense of what happened to me. It was healing just reaching out to you for your endorsement.

• Dr. Ann Filemyr—for your incisive understanding of power and spiritual abuse and your vision that this book be used in ethics classes.

• Deborah Shroder—for your personal support of me and your deep understanding of the power of art as medicine.

• Dr. Charlie Whitfield—for your work on healing childhood wounds and your recognition that I am not just a survivor, I am a thriver!

• Gerald Smith—for your solid legal knowledge and the work you did to help bring light to this issue back in the '80s and '90s.

• Valerie Plame—for being a fellow warrior and my friend. Thanks for seeing and honoring my light.

• Jason Holley—whose brilliant understanding of myth and astrology and whose declaration "Yours is the story of Persephone" lit a match in my soul and sparked my voyage to write this book.

• Robin Duda—my new playmate in storytelling, healing, and joy—thank you for helping me embody and share my story as part of my continued healing.

And finally, Dr. Michael Plaut, for his years of dedication to bringing awareness to this issue, helping survivors get the resources they need to heal, and working to prevent occurrences through education and rehabilitation—bravo. Thanks especially for all the hours you put into reading this book, giving feedback, writing a great afterword, and helping me make connections in spreading the message. You have been a powerful ally. Thank you.

To many friends who have cheered me on over the years: the late David Langer, Adonnah Langer, Sandy Szabat, Kate Simpson, Cathy Nugent, Susannah Garrett, Val Valentine, Sherry Young, Nancy Ingraham, Holly Skinner, and Flynn Sylvest. A special thanks to Lori Rios, the first person who helped me take the lid off Pandora's box. I know what you witnessed wasn't pretty.

To other important helpers: West Cooper, my website and book cover designer, for your amazing attention to detail, availability, and creativity in the design process. To Lynann Cimino, my business coach and angel investor, for believing in me, reading my book, and encouraging my vision and authenticity. For Lisa Kramer, my life coach of many years, who always helped me believe I am capable of anything. And to Marisol Angulo of Artotems who keeps making publicity and marketing a powerful, deep, fun, and exciting adventure!

A special thanks to artist Patricia Ariel whose artwork graces the cover of this book. Your beautiful images of healing touch the world.

To my clients past and present who have allowed me to bear witness to your stories, your hearts, your healings. I am blessed to work with all of you at such depth. Thank you for your bravery and trusting me with your sacred journeys.

To my young, vulnerable maiden self who was terrorized by all that happened—this book is for you. We made it through! And I am wiser for it. . . .

And finally, to the Divine—the mystical, magical, loving presence that runs through life itself. Thank you for providing an internal as well as eternal place to come home to. All healing journeys somehow include you. Thank you for the gifts of spirit that came to me from healing my trauma—powerful dreams, synchronicities that guide the way, the experience of oneness, and a buoyant, joyful resilience fueled by your light and grounded through your sacred earth.

I am grateful for the journey!

I share this book as a prayer for the
healing of our humanity.
Facing our shadows, challenging abuses of power,
and embracing our healing personally
and collectively is the path to a more-conscious,
loving, and compassionate world.

~ 1 ~

The elevator doors closed with a thud.

I woke to find myself strapped to a stainless-steel gurney and flanked by two men dressed in white. I felt a strange, hard object in my mouth. I couldn't speak.

Help . . . please get it out!

I struggled to lift my right hand, but it didn't budge. The gurney's restraints seemed to clamp even more tightly around my arms and legs. I couldn't move.

"Nooo!" I shrieked as best I could with the awful tube in my mouth.

Then I realized where I was. I looked up at the attendants accusingly.

Why the hell did you save me? Why didn't you let me die?

The elevator lurched to a stop, the doors opened, and a sharp draft of antiseptic hit me in the face. The men steered me down a long, white hallway. I could hear the gurney's metal wheels squeaking across the tired linoleum. Suddenly, they took a left and rolled me into a small, cold, windowless room.

One man removed the aspirating tube, and my saliva clung to it stubbornly. I gagged, and my eyes teared. Silently, the men unlatched the straps and gently lifted me from the gurney onto a sterile, white bed. No one spoke. I sensed judgment mixed with tense impatience. One of them dimmed the harsh fluorescent lights, then left and locked the door.

I'd failed again. An entire bottle of Xanax washed down with beer, plus my head in the oven with the gas turned on should have done it. I really thought I'd been determined and thorough this time. If only the exterminator hadn't found me. Vaguely I could remember him standing over me in his green jacket and plaid pants. Then a lot of people were standing over me, talking. They must have put me in an ambulance, then pumped my stomach, but I didn't have any recollection of that.

My eyes searched the room. There wasn't a single wall hanging, lamp, or chair—nothing. The only piece of furniture was my blanket-less bed, dressed in a crisp, white sheet. I was wearing nothing but underwear and a hospital gown. A series of shivers rattled my body. I tried to get out of bed, but my legs wobbled like chopsticks holding up a watermelon. At least some of the pills must have made it into my bloodstream.

My eyes shifted to the tiny, square window of the thick, steel door. For now, it was my only portal between two worlds—the one from which the hospital's staff peered in at me and the one from which I peered back.

The killer inside me still dreamed of our escape. Twenty-four years of this hopeless life were far too many. I couldn't lose my determination now. After all, hadn't I crafted this attempt only four days after release from a psychiatric unit for my previous one?

This attempt was better. The first one, I had to admit, had been haphazard, unfocused.

Three weeks ago, I was supposed to be preparing a presentation on depression as described in the *Diagnostic and Statistical Manual of Mental Disorders*, or DSM III, for my classwork as a graduate student in clinical psychology. Only I couldn't seem to finish it, because every time I tried to work on it, I felt like I was describing myself—and froze.

I thought about my coming deadline while riding the bus to the library to rehearse the presentation. The bus was crowded with passengers whose eyes looked everywhere but at each other. I felt like I was watching a movie of my life instead of participating in it. Out of nowhere, a voice whispered: Honestly, would you miss this place if you left it? I answered without hesitation: Hell, no!

A rush of energy seized me. It was the perfect solution.

I skipped the library, went home, flipped through my copy of Sylvia Plath's *Collected Poems*, and found what I was looking for: "Daddy," one of my favorites. I read it as I gulped down aspirin and sleeping pills:

At twenty I tried to die
And get back, back, back to you.
I thought even the bones would do.
But they pulled me out of the sack,
And they stuck me together with glue.

Plath wrote the poem shortly before her third suicide attempt, when she managed to successfully gas herself in her oven. She was thirty years old.

I remembered my own gas stove in the kitchen. For the past year, my depression had muffled any attempts to cook on it. Most days, I barely ate. I'd recently lost fifteen pounds, reducing me to a scant one hundred, tops. All that much easier to kill off, I assumed—plus, historically, carbon-monoxide poisoning was fairly reliable.

My head was deep in the oven when I changed my mind. I didn't want to die in this dirty kitchen infested with mice and cockroaches. Lately, I'd been setting mousetraps. In the middle of the night, I would hear them snapping as I tried to sleep. *Another one gone*, I'd think as I rolled over. Last week, I had managed to kill a mama and six or seven of her babies. Disposing of their bodies, I'd nearly vomited.

I wanted to die peacefully, beautifully. I wanted to drown. I'd take more pills and booze, swim out to sea, and just let go. I pulled myself out of the oven and headed for the beach.

I crawled into my lemon yellow 1979 Volkswagen Rabbit, the one he had helped me buy. I tried not to think about him as I flew down the highway at a hundred miles an hour on the hundred seventy-mile drive from Richmond, Virginia, to Duck Beach, North Carolina, all the while guzzling Bacardi and Budweiser to wash down more pills.

When I spun the car into the empty, gravel parking lot, it was well after 8 p.m.; the beach was empty. I left the keys in the ignition and made a slow but determined walk toward the Atlantic Ocean, its frothy, blue surf beckoning me. But a few feet from the edge, I recalled my obsessive fear of being eaten by sharks in the water at night, similar to that girl in *Jaws*. I collapsed onto the sand a little way into the water. I was a coward. I figured I'd just relax and let the pills do their job. My whole head felt tingly and really warm. I felt my heart slowing down. Surely, I would die any minute. Gradually, I lost consciousness. Then I heard a voice:

"Miss? Miss, you have to leave. It's illegal to be here."

I opened my eyes. A security guard was squatting next to me. Who knows how long he'd been waiting for me to wake up. I was still alive: soaked, shivering, and breaded in sand. It felt like early morning, but it was still dark. I thanked him. I didn't really mean it, but I'd been raised to have good manners.

The other voice inside me rose up: Tell him you're dancing with death! Tell him! Instead, I drove back to my cockroach-infested apartment on autopilot, guided by a dimly lit, hung over, and still-desperate mind. After all, I still had the oven.

I knew the word had to be out: Carrie had missed her presentation on depression. A month ago, I had actually spilled my burdensome tale, my shameful secret, to my classmate Lori. Now I wondered if she had guessed why I missed class. Like I cared! I imagined showing up for the presentation in my tattered, sand-encrusted, sea-soaked dress, reeking of beer and pills—a textbook example of a depressed, suicidal patient. How educational for my fellow psychologists in training.

Someone was banging on the door. I answered it: Lori. Her eyes widened at the sight of my sun-streaked brown hair, twisted and dirty, my eyes dark and empty, my skin as pale and cold as a wax doll's. She darted into the kitchen, and it was all there—the oven door open, oven racks pulled out, pills scattered across the floor, and a rambling hand-scrawled suicide note. Oh, yeah, I had forgotten about that.

I don't remember if Lori called my parents and told them I'd been admitted to St. Mary's Hospital or if someone else did. For years, I'd been silently pushing them out of my life. They took the family station wagon down I-95 from their home in Frederick, Maryland, a hundred fifty miles away, and found me confined in the psychiatric ward. I looked at them through the tiny window at the top of my locked door. They took turns peering in at my small, isolated world, and me. Light from the hallway filtered through it and danced around the edges of their anguished faces.

I heard the social worker fumbling with his keys. He unlocked the door to my tomb and led me and my parents down another long hallway into a consulting room. Their faces were elongated and slack with sorrow. The pupils of their eyes were enlarged like those of terrified animals. Something inside me stirred. I started to weep. Mom and Dad held hands tightly. I'd never seen the wrinkles on my father's face etched so deeply. His weary blue eyes filled with tears.

"Suicide, Carrie? Why?"

The Innocent Maiden

Persephone gathered flowers in the sunny, green meadow—roses and crocuses, irises also—when she saw a radiant, golden narcissus. Longing to possess the beauty and enlightenment it promised, she reached for it . . .

~2~

Romano, Anthony J. MD, Suite 101

I read the directory on the wall of the small, red-brick building. It was Christmas Eve, 1980, I was a senior in college, and I stood in the office vestibule of the man who might become my new psychiatrist. *Romano. Obviously Italian.* A trusted family friend had recommended him highly. I brushed the snow from my boots. Then I slowly made my way down the narrow corridor toward the open door at the end.

One of only a handful of psychiatrists in our small town of Frederick, Maryland, Romano had an office just a mile away from my parents' house, and right around the corner from the flower shop where I used to design arrangements on my summer breaks. The shop had been a refuge of colors and scents—a welcome departure from my college studies in biology and psychology. It had been one of the few places where I could immerse myself in a world of beauty and delight without any guilt. At this moment, however, the pleasures of the flower shop seemed so far away. *What happened to the colors, the smells?* Everything was gray.

"Carrie?" Dr. Romano stood before me, a slight man with graying temples and deep, warm, blue eyes. He motioned for me to sit on a tweed couch. I glanced around while he took a leather director's chair just a few feet away. The room felt pleasant, calming. The wallpaper was light brown grasscloth, and the paintings were earth-toned abstracts. I wondered what the artist was trying to express. *It's kinda easy to breathe here,* I thought. *I like this room . . . it feels safe.*

Dr. Romano studied me intently, silently. He watched my expressions. His eyes looked deeply into mine. I quickly shifted away from his gaze and continued to scan the office. A bright ribbon of sunlight streamed through two clerestory windows, drawing a line of light on the floor between us. My eyes met his.

Dr. Romano shifted in his chair. "I understand you've been having some difficulty lately, Carrie. I'd like to hear what's been going on."

I struggled to put my experience into words, unsure of what my mother might have said when she set up this Christmas break appointment. My mind reeled back over the last six months. I explained that physically, I'd been run down, had a chronic stuffy nose, and a sense of low energy that left me feeling weak and spacey. The symptoms seemed to mushroom until my emotions were out of whack too. I found myself crying often and struggling to get out of bed in the morning. Other times, I had the sensation that someone was standing on my chest and I couldn't breathe. When this happened, I felt paralyzed, terrified that I was going crazy. I had once been an outgoing young woman and a good student. Now I didn't seem to have enough energy to focus on my studies. What if I had one of my paralyzing episodes in front of other people? I would be humiliated. So I generally avoided going anywhere. There just didn't seem to be a point to anything anymore. I wanted my old self back, but I feared she was lost forever. And I knew I couldn't go on like this.

"I'm just feeling so bad lately," I said. "I've lost all my confidence."

I was skeptical that a man more than twice my age could ever understand what I was feeling, or the hell that I'd been living, even if he was a highly regarded, Georgetown-educated psychiatrist. My parents were back home praying for me right then. My parents prayed about everything. Out of pure desperation, I'd begun praying too.

Dr. Romano glanced up at me from his note-taking. "So what do you think caused this?" He leaned forward, engaged, and clearly curious, without any negative judgment.

"Well, I used to be so confident, you know . . . about life . . . boys . . . my schoolwork." I paused before adding, "I think I fell for the wrong boy."

I thought about Louie. That breakup had hurt me like no other, and I was still trying to understand why. I told Dr. Romano how at first, I was crazy about this charming guy, but after we'd been dating a while, he announced, "You know, I'll never give up other women for you." He described a future that didn't include monogamy. "My dad always says to keep 'em lined up," he said proudly. "In case it doesn't work out with one, there's always another waitin' in line."

I explained to the doctor that while I wasn't that serious with Louie, I knew I wanted a committed relationship with someone, and he obviously didn't. So I thought I had no choice but to break up with him. I'd had other boyfriends and understood the adage that "breaking up is hard to do," but Louie's reaction shocked me. He turned as red as a ripe tomato and snapped "If you break up with me, I'll never ask you out again."

I described how on the morning after the breakup, I woke with a dance in my step, feeling lighter than I had in months. Sure, my heart was still aching, but my head was beginning to clear. I skipped out of my apartment and down the stairs on my way to school.

Then I saw it. There, right in front of me, across the parking lot, was Louie's car, a blue Chevy Nova with its unmistakable rear-end dent. I sensed someone moving and glanced up at a nearby apartment window just in time to see Louie with a dark-haired woman. He paused to look at me a little longer before closing the curtains.

Mo. It was Mo's apartment. He must have spent the night with her. There were ten thousand females on campus, and he chose the one who lived across the street from me. I told Dr. Romano that at that moment, I felt my confidence draining, drop by drop.

A gentle, reassuring voice reached into my psychic cave: "That sounds very painful."

Now, as I returned to the present, I heard myself crying. It was like purging a huge chunk of contaminated waste from my belly. I felt a little lighter. I looked at Dr. Romano through my tears. *Is this therapy? Is this what will heal me? Can this really help?*

He continued. "Your mom says you've been having a hard time with your studies."

I nodded and reached for a Kleenex to clean up my soggy cheeks and snotty nose. "Yeah, I used to be a really good student, but suddenly, I just stopped caring."

I explained to Dr. Romano how I found myself breaking into tears in the middle of class. Until then, it had been easy for me to focus on school. Now it was as if my professors were speaking to me through a thick shroud of gauze. Their words couldn't reach me because I was someplace else far away—and drifting farther.

I confided that graduation was nearing, and I feared that my dream for myself was just that—a stupid dream. For nearly four years, I had dedicated myself to my career path, but I wanted a husband and family too. The media told young women like me that we could have it all, but I didn't know any real woman who did. I told Dr. Romano how a few months ago, a family conversation had captured my internal dilemma best.

I was in the car with my godmother, my aunt Mary. She was a major presence in our family, the matriarch who stood just slightly behind the patriarch, my uncle Bud, the colonel. I always saw her as a movie star figure, mostly because she resembled Elizabeth Taylor. She walked with the pride and assurance of a queen, and everyone obeyed her commands, which were lovingly but firmly directed to her eight children and many nieces and nephews. She and I were discussing what I would do when I graduated in the spring. I announced that I was considering medical school. I had excellent grades in the physical and social sciences and dreamed of helping people. My beloved Aunt Mary looked me straight in the eye with her regal authority and said, "That's all well and good, but you better be home in time to serve your husband dinner." I could actually feel my heart split in two.

Would pursuing my dream really make it impossible to have love in my life and a family of my own? And if it did, why had I invested so much of myself in my education? On the other hand, why was I worrying about marriage? It wasn't as though I'd fallen in love with someone who was husband material—only Louie who turned out to be a cad. It all felt so hopeless.

"I feel disconnected from the kind of ambition I should have," I told Dr. Romano. "I used to be at the top of my class."

"I'm hearing you say 'should' a lot," he interjected. "In fact, I just counted five 'shoulds' in the last five minutes." He showed me his marks on his clipboard.

"Huh." I felt self-conscious about being observed this closely. "I guess there are a lot of 'shoulds' in my family. I *should* marry young. I *should* always do well in school. I *should* never hurt anyone's feelings."

He looked over his notes. "I see that you were raised Catholic. Does that have something to do with the 'shoulds'?"

"Yep. And according to the church, or at least the people I've been hanging out with lately, I shouldn't be seeing a psychiatrist either. If I had enough faith, God would heal me himself."

Dr. Romano gave me a puzzled look. "Do your parents believe that?"

"No, not so much. They just want me to feel better." I paused, uncertain of how much to share. I shifted awkwardly in my seat.

"I do feel all of this has something to do with a spiritual crisis," I said. "I guess I need to know, how do you work with people who are religious?" I think I surprised even myself with this question because "religious" was a fairly new term for me, at least in the way I described myself. "I guess I need to know that you honor God's word."

Dr. Romano leaned forward. "Well, if I wasn't comfortable navigating the realms of religion and psychiatry, I wouldn't be seeing so many nuns and priests."

"Really, you see nuns and priests?" Now he had my attention.

"Yes, some I've seen for years," he said. "It can be a bit challenging to tease out what's spiritual from what's emotional."

He sat back in his chair with a smile. I liked his confidence. And his answer. Now I wondered whether to discuss with Dr. Romano the fact that he was actually the second psychiatrist I'd seen recently. The first had quickly diagnosed me as manic-depressive (what would be called bipolar disorder today) and suggested lithium. I knew I needed help, but I didn't think I was *that* crazy. Then again, I didn't know what I thought about anything anymore. I tried to act casual as I asked the question that scared me most.

"Do you—do you think I need to be on medication?"

"Well, I think we need to take a few days to finish up the assessment and then have your parents in for a conference. I'd like to avoid medication if we can."

I nodded, secretly relieved.

~3~

I returned to the red brick, four-story home of my childhood to find my mom in the kitchen. She was mixing ingredients for turkey stuffing and had pumpkin pies in the oven. The room was filled with the soothing smells of Christmas meal preparations. I breathed in all the aromas deeply, but they failed to spark the happy feelings I used to get.

"Hi, honey, how did it go?" My mother continued stirring. She seemed confident that everything would be just fine now.

"Okay, Mom. He seems pretty nice. He asked me a lot of questions. You'll like this, he says he was raised Catholic and that he treats nuns and priests."

"Hmmm . . . that does sound good. I know Dan from church speaks highly of him. That's good that he's a Catholic." Dan was one of the deacons in our parish whom my parents often shared the altar with when helping to serve Holy Communion. My parents attended church every week, often every day when they could.

"Yeah, I guess that's good," I said vacantly, not really knowing what was good or bad anymore.

"So . . . does he think you need lithium?" She set her spoon down and joined me at the kitchen's center island, its countertop the color of persimmons. I used to love the fact that my parents had chosen such a bold color, and was thankful for the way it often brightened my mood, but now it seemed gray like everything else.

"He wants to see me one more time—then with you, me, and Dad."

"All right, honey." Mom's eyes were filled with compassion. "I just know it's all going to be okay." Her fingers reached out to gingerly touch my hand, and it caught me off guard. Perhaps because she was an admiral's daughter, Mom never showed much spontaneous physical affection. I always loved it when she did, though. In fact, I ached for her affection even though I never let her know how much.

"Now come help me, will you?" she said. "I need some help setting the table, vacuuming the living room, wrapping presents. We've got a lot to do before Mass."

I wanted to please her, but my body felt like it was made of lead. Obediently, I vacantly followed her to the dining room. Mom quickly left to put on her favorite Christmas music, Handel's "Hallelujah" Chorus, and I heard her belt out "haaa-le-lu-JAH!" from the living room. She popped her head in cheerfully. "Let's use our holiday china."

I stood before the built-in china cabinet and looked at my reflection in the mirrored doors. I felt a million miles away from the girl in the looking glass. Everything about the young woman seemed to shine, except that her blue eyes looked so sad and heavy. I gave myself a little grin, hoping to reconnect with my lost self, but all I could see was a fake smile. "Why bother?" I heard myself say. I sighed and reached into the cabinet for the beautiful white lace tablecloth. As I turned around to put it on the table, I flashed back to the time ten years ago when I had used this same dining room table to lay out the cutting board and fabric to sew my first dress. My mother had told me what to do to get it set up and did her best to give me a thirty-minute sewing lesson. She took my measurements and helped me modify the pattern.

"Let's take it in here in the waist, and . . . oh my, I guess we need to let it out a bit in the bust! My goodness honey, you are well endowed," she said while finishing up the final measurements. "Just like your Grandma Josephine." My eleven-year-old self blushed, embarrassed again by my blossoming figure which seemed to draw so much attention all of a sudden.

"Mom, Mom!" My younger brother Tim appeared. "I need your help with ironing."

"Oh dear, honey, got to go. Just read the directions, and lay out the fabric. I'll check in with you in a few minutes." She rushed out the door to help Tim.

"But . . . but . . . okay," I said to myself, now in an empty room. Despite what she said, I knew my time with Mom was probably up, so I took a deep breath and jumped into figuring this out. If I wanted a nice wardrobe, I'd need to sew it myself.

Back from my reverie, I brushed the creases out of the tablecloth and placed the round, gold Advent wreath with white candles in the center of the table. As I turned to reach in the china cabinet for the gold-rimmed plates, Mom ran back in, this time with my sister behind her. "Mom, what should I wear for midnight Mass?" she asked.

"Don't forget to put out the red candles," Mom said to me, eyes bright, before scurrying upstairs to help my sister. I opened the middle drawer to find four new, cellophane-wrapped, red candles that would be placed in the wreath tonight, after midnight, after Christ was born. Tonight the festivities would begin: midnight Mass, carols around the Christmas tree, eggnog before bed, and the eating of Grandma's special-recipe Christmas bread which Mom made every year even though she complained it was too dry. Mom was always so happy this time of year. I hoped it would be contagious, but it wasn't. *What is wrong with you, Carrie? Get your shit together! Cheer up! Mom needs your help.*

I concentrated hard just to move my body, thick with darkness, into the living room and on to the next task. Mom appeared again, almost out of nowhere. "Haaa-le-lu-JAH!" she sang as she handed me the handle of vacuum cleaner. "Oops . . . I've got to check the pies," she remembered, and once again, she was gone.

I started the job, squinting to see the pine needles and specks of dirt littering the mauve carpet. I made my way to the mantel where eight hand-knit stockings hung, each with the name of one of our family members lovingly stitched by my late maternal grandmother. My eyes focused on my stocking, fifth in line from the left and fourth from the right: Carrie 1959. I lifted it to see the minute details Grandma Pauline had knitted in twenty-one years ago—the Santa Claus, the Christmas tree, the holly—they were all perfect.

My eyes scanned the row of stockings again, and I could almost hear my mother's sing-song voice calling out "JodyBobbyCarrieMichael-TimmyPolly, oh yes, Car-rie!" She would giggle with self-effacement when finally landing on the correct name of one of her brood. I always felt a bit dismissed by this habit. Even though she expressed triumph when getting the correct name, I always felt a bit sad for her and for me. Was I really that insignificant? Then again, she was pulled in so many directions. How does she do it? I wondered to myself, barely able to get through the simple task of vacuuming.

My hand reached for the ledge of the mantel as I steadied myself, weary with heaviness. My eyes fell on the manger, lovingly displayed, surrounded by all the barnyard animals. Baby Jesus was not yet in his bed, but I could see his little porcelain foot peeking out from his hiding place behind the beasts of burden. Later, after midnight Mass, Mom, Dad, Santa, or Jesus himself would put the little figure in the manger, and we would all feign surprise to find him there, touched by the mysterious hand of God and tradition.

"Oh Baby Jesus, please help me feel better," I heard myself say with complete seriousness as I flashed back on all the Christmases when the six of us kids had searched the living room for the pile of gifts Santa had left for each of us. Mom or Dad always reminded us, "Let's not forget the real meaning of Christmas" as they pointed to the manger, giving us pause from our frantic quests.

As I continued to vacuum, I arrived at the opposite side of our large living room where the glorious, eight-foot Christmas tree glistened with lights and silver icicles. I thought back to the days when the whole family would gather in this room for our weekly ritual of Black Cow Night. As we settled in before the TV, floats made with Coke and vanilla ice cream served as our Friday night rewards for getting through the week. "The Brady Bunch," "The Odd Couple," "Room 222, and later, when we were older, the risqué "Love, American Style" entertained the eight of us. Black Cow Night was as predictable a ritual as Sunday morning church.

I finished with the vacuum as the last needle made its way up into the machine. I stepped back to admire the tree and remembered when we were younger and the "elves" mysteriously decorated it the week before Christmas. Now, in my emotional funk, I pined for the days when I believed in such magic. "All I want for Christmas is to feel like myself again," I heard myself say.

From here, I could hear Dad in the vestibule fumbling with his keys while stomping the snow off his boots. I used to love going into the vestibule, between the two doors, to hear myself sing. It served as an echo chamber, enriching the sound, and in those moments, I could pretend I was Linda Ronstadt or Stevie Nicks. That little space fed many adolescent dreams of being a beloved folk singer who entertained people all over the world.

"Hey, where is everyone?" Dad called out.

"I'm in here, Dad."

"Carrie, sweet Carrie. How are you doing today, honey? How did it go with Dr. Romano?" My dad's blue eyes sparkled with concern and curiosity.

"Okay, Dad. He's nice."

"He comes highly recommended, Carrie. We're going to get you squared away. Everything is going to be all right, honey. Now let's get dressed for church! You know how your mom loves to hear the choir before Mass."

He gave me a big bear hug, a squeeze of the arm, and quickly walked away whistling, "White Christmas."

I took a deep breath, thought again about the elves, baby Jesus, and Linda Ronstadt, then went upstairs to dress for midnight Mass.

~4~

It was nearing midnight, and anticipation hung in the air as my family approached the majestic Greek Ionic edifice of St. John the Evangelist Roman Catholic Church. Bells pealed from the five-story-high tower, summoning us to Mass.

As we passed through the snow-white wooden doors, angelic voices singing Handel's *Messiah* poured over us from the choir loft above, creating the feeling that heaven was very close by. Candlelight flickered, its warm glow so welcome on this cold winter's night. We made our way down the hundred-foot-long center aisle to our usual seats near the altar. Here, an invisible cloud of frankincense lingered, heady and sweet, evoking a sense of ancient mystery. The large-scale nativity scene before us reminded me of that proud day in fourth grade when I was asked to carry the nearly life-sized baby Jesus up the center aisle and gently place him in the manger. Dozens of red poinsettias popped against the magnificent white marble interior. Though darkness still lurked inside me, I couldn't help but feel my spirits lift.

In spite of its colossal proportions, the sanctuary was nearly as familiar as my living room. We'd been coming here since I was five years old. I took my first communion here. My sister was married here. Now, as the eight of us kneeled to pray and I stole a quick glance at my five brothers and sisters, they seemed to blur together as one fuzzy ball of energy I called "siblings."

Even in my glum state, a part of me still held on to the possibility that my low emotions and loss of confidence were some sort of spiritual crisis and that God *would* be healing me soon. I turned my eyes to the ceiling and the painting of Christ ascending to heaven by the Italian artist Ferdinand Baraldi. As the choristers' voices reverberated throughout the sanctuary, I imagined each note pouring the love of God down into my body. Suddenly, I realized that I had a renewed longing to believe in a higher power. *Please God, please heal me . . .* I imagined myself rising from my knees and instantly being myself again.

As the priest proceeded down the aisle and Mass began, I reflected on my longing to feel the peace, certainty, and love of a higher source. I recalled how back at college, a particularly low day had found me wandering into the campus ministry building, where I encountered a tall, thin, pale man named Dr. Rabbe. He greeted me with warmth and presence, and called himself a "nondenominational Christian minister." Dr. Rabbe seemed glad to listen to my struggles. I was struck by his confidence that I was merely going through some kind of awakening, and that Jesus wanted to heal me. He gave me a Bible and encouraged me to read it daily.

For me, that was new territory. I'd attended Catholic school through eighth grade, and Mass every week until I went away to college, but I'd never felt any real connection with the Bible. The priest was our messenger, a sort of go-between for God. I had never understood how to speak directly to God or to have a close, personal relationship with Jesus.

As Dr. Rabbe shared his interpretation of Christianity, I found myself listening from the place of one who *wants* to believe but feels excluded from the club. I envisioned myself facedown against a white piece of gauze, arms outstretched and fingers kneading into the fabric as I desperately tried to push past the veil.

Dr. Rabbe said I must be born again in order to find my way back. He handed me a flyer with step-by-step instructions for my salvation.

Back at my apartment, I knelt beside my bed, following Dr. Rabbe's script. "I accept you, Jesus, as my Lord and my Savior. Please come into my life."

Nothing.

The battles of hope and despair raged within me. Alone in my room, I rationalized that maybe if I continued to put the word of God at the center of my life, it would fill the void.

"The Lord be with you," said the priest, jolting me out of my reverie.

"And also with you," answered four hundred voices in unison.

As I glanced around the sanctuary, I wasn't sure what I thought about my own spiritual upbringing. I loved the pageantry and mystery of the Catholic Church, but there were also times when I knew I was just going through the motions, and it seemed other people were too. I had to enter these dark, mahogany confessional booths that felt both austere and otherworldly and then confess my most private thoughts and sins (most of which I fabricated so I'd have something to be contrite about) to a priest whom I knew but had to pretend not to know. Time and again, I'd say my five Hail Marys and Our Fathers, and obediently return to the pew to kneel and ask for His forgiveness. Yet I didn't feel as though I was getting in touch with God—or myself.

I thought about how, a few months earlier, I had confided on the phone to Mom that Catholic ritual often seemed futile to me. She encouraged me to make the five-hour drive home the next weekend to try one of the Charismatic Renewal services she'd been attending of late. I couldn't remember when she'd been more alive or inspired, and I was curious about her new passion for God.

The gathering was held in the cafeteria of my Catholic elementary school. This was where I used to hand over my four pennies for a small carton of milk while doing my best not to attract the attention of the nuns who looked and acted like strange giant penguins, mysterious and distant. As Mom and I descended its steps, I was struck by how different the room felt.

Nearly twenty people were gathered, and everyone was talking. Mom explained that the group was actively engaging the Holy Spirit. I didn't doubt it because it simply felt true. Then the prayer service began. People started yelling thanks to God and making requests. I noticed a bright light in their eyes. It was very different from the sleepy, hollow gazes I'd seen during Mass.

I looked around for nuns or priests, but no, this service was led by laypeople only. Everyone seemed equal. Everyone received. My heart vibrated. I turned to my mother. She was more relaxed and alive than I'd ever seen her. The spirit of God was in everyone, and I wanted what I saw. When the service ended, Mom introduced me to Mary Ellen, who radiated a peace and love I had never seen before. *I have to have what she has.*

"Carrie, I just know that God wants to heal you," Mary Ellen said. "There's nothing that can't happen for good when God is called. We're holding a healing service in a few minutes. Please join us . . . I feel how hungry your spirit is to be connected to the love and peace of God."

I followed Mary Ellen into the library for the healing service. Surrounded by the books of my youth, which had once educated but failed to inspire, I could see everyone's colorful souls glowing against the background of these barren volumes. Mary Ellen introduced me to Kay, Bill, and other members of the healing team.

"What would you like healing for?" Kay asked, her eyes bright with confidence. She put her hand behind my head; I felt a sudden rush of warmth sweep down my spine.

"I need healing for depression," I said, sharing a brief description of my emotional descent.

"In the name of Jesus, we ask for a total healing of Carrie," Kay said. "In the name of Jesus, banish all the woes from her heart and fill her with light."

Many pairs of hands touched the back of my head, forehead, arms, and back. Waves of energy surged through me. I had never experienced anything so pure and loving.

A male voice began singing in a language I didn't recognize, but it comforted me in a way I couldn't explain. *This must be that thing they call speaking in tongues. Is this for real?* I slowly opened one eye to see Jim singing nonsense syllables like chimes blowing in the wind. Another wave of warmth hit me . . . and I felt my heart open and directly connect to what I can only describe as . . . the Divine.

"My Child, I am giving you a Crown of Joy and a Mantle of Peace. You are my little one, I love you." Kay was speaking now, but her voice sounded different, deeper and with more authority. The group continued to lay hands on me for a few more minutes. An occasional "Praise you, Jesus!" and "Thank you, Lord!" rang out.

"Carrie, you must be prepared that God wants to heal you entirely, in body, mind, and spirit. You may not need to see a therapist," Kay said. "God has big plans for you, and it is clear that he loves you."

Afterward, I happily shared with Mom that I'd felt a deep sense of healing ... and that I wanted to come back for more.

When I returned to campus, my heart swelled in my chest as I shared my first spiritual experience with other students. Their faces said it all: They were suspicious. I soon felt even more alone, strange, and adrift. My high spirits plummeted.

Tonight as I lined up to receive Holy Communion, I found myself wondering who I was and what I believed.

Things had been so much clearer when I was a little girl. In fact, some of my most spiritual experiences had happened when I was about five years old and we lived on a farm outside Frederick. It was a beautiful piece of land, some hundred-plus acres, an outdoor sanctuary.

Besides three brothers and two sisters, my playmates were the cows, ducks, chickens, and sheep, plus a pony, cat, and dog. It was a little girl's dream. I fell in love with the peach tree. Every day I'd climb its branches, my heart beating fast with anticipation of hanging upside down by my tiny legs and arms, completely nourished by the sights, smells, and sounds of the countryside. I also had the unshakeable feeling that magical fairies indeed lived in that tree. They felt more alive to me than Jesus or the saints. Maybe it was because at that age, feeling was believing.

One day, while hanging upside down in the tree, a clear, and complete truth spoke to me: "Everything that happens in your life is created by *me* as a test to see how you will respond, what you will choose. I will be watching and noticing . . . . You are not alone."

Another revelation came to me one day while I was sitting on the stone steps leading to the springhouse, watching our lamb, Bucky, graze on dewy grass. Suddenly I was struck by the grays and whites of the springhouse stones and could sense the pulsing vitality of the deep-green grass as well as the muted yellow-whiteness of Bucky's wool. I remember hearing the words in my mind, "I am an artist." This moment felt truer than all the prayers I'd raised since, or the love of my family, or the implicit trust in the sun rising and setting.

In those days, I loved sleeping just as much as I enjoyed being awake and alive. As I drifted off, I'd see the greatest fireworks show on Earth—with both eyes closed. Mom used to say I often had a soft smile on my face while falling asleep. I could remember nodding off many, many times to find myself standing in a magical room filled with brilliantly colored gemstones.

I wished I still felt like that five-year-old girl who kept her inner life to herself and didn't have anything to prove. Now I felt like I couldn't tell anyone about those experiences. Who would understand or accept me?

As I stood before Father Eckles, I opened my mouth, and he placed the communion wafer on my tongue.

"The body of Christ," he said.

How can this truly be the body of Christ? I thought as I chewed the pasty wafer. *Is my doubt a symptom of my depression, or is Catholicism a sham? Am I the only one having trouble swallowing all this?* I sipped the wine and made my way back to my seat.

~5~

"Come in please, Carrie." Dr. Romano waved his arm toward the sofa. It was December 30, and all the other offices in his complex were closed for the holidays, but there he was, waiting for me.

"How are you?" He showed a knowing concern that I hadn't felt from anyone else.

I stared at my hands. "Christmas was hard."

He waited. I looked up.

"I just don't know if anyone understands how bad I feel."

I described how I'd struggled through the past few days, escaping family gatherings to curl up in my room with my thoughts and my books whenever I had the chance. Everyone else's jovial mood often grated on me. High school friends kept inviting me to parties, but I was too self-conscious to be around anyone from my past. They were nearing college graduation too, filled with hope and happiness, which made me feel like even more of a loser. Mostly, I'd spent the holidays retreating into my journal, where I chronicled my secret prayers, wishes, and thoughts. I tried to put it all into words.

"I'm just really, really low," I said. "I keep reading the Bible and wondering why God doesn't heal me. I think he wants to . . . it's probably just a matter of time."

As I heard myself say this, I wondered if God even existed. At the same time, I also worried that Dr. Romano might deem me crazy after all. Today was my second assessment appointment, and he went on to ask what seemed like routine questions about my childhood.

"Where were you born?"

"Fort Sheridan, Illinois. We lived on an Army base."

"What is your birth order?"

"The third of six."

"How close are your siblings in age?"

"There were six of us in nine years."

It seemed like Dr. Romano just wanted to know our family history, all the fill-in-the-blanks of my upbringing. I explained that when I was a nine-month-old baby, my mother was caring for me, my four-year-old sister, and my three-year-old handicapped brother, and was pregnant with her fourth child when her husband (my dad) was deployed to Iran for a year. We had to move in with my grandparents in Washington, D.C., so Mom would have some help. Then came the birth of my fifth sibling, and the sixth soon followed. I described all the times we had to move and leave friends behind. With each passing detail, I felt heavier and heavier. Then something opened up in me that I hadn't expected.

"It feels like I never got much attention. There were always so many of us."

Dr. Romano's pen was busy. Now that I thought about it, I could rarely complete a conversation with either of my parents without another kid interrupting. I hadn't realized how much I needed to talk.

Then there was my eye surgery as a toddler. Mom said that one day she was holding me in her lap, and my left eye turned inward. I had strabismus, or lazy eye, and needed an operation to strengthen the muscle.

"The doctors put a mask on me, and I thought they were trying to kill me," I explained. "These were the days when parents weren't allowed to stay with their children in the hospital, so I thought my parents had left me there to die. The nurses were nice, but I was scared. I was mad. I think this experience changed my personality and made me more fearful of the world. That's what my mom says."

"We moved a lot from place to place," I went on. "I went to two different schools for kindergarten, another school for first and second grade, and another school for third grade . . . . I think I only felt happy once I went to public high school. I really excelled at sports . . . . I was even a leader."

I told Dr. Romano how I felt that I never truly belonged anywhere. I may have been successful in high school, but some of the girls seemed to resent me for being pretty and dating the popular boys. "Some girls seemed to envy me for doing well at most things I tried," I confessed. "That made me feel bad because I just wanted to belong."

Suddenly, I was tired and inhaled a deep, deep breath.

"I guess I've always had the feeling that everyone else is more connected, more rooted, more real than I am."

As I shared my story with Dr. Romano, I felt something inside me shift. It felt good to have someone listen so intently. I was sharing uncomfortable feelings and private memories with someone who wasn't shutting me down or changing the subject, and it made me realize how much I'd been shutting myself down. So I kept going.

"I think I've always just assumed I'd fall into something I liked. I never thought too much about the future . . ." My voice trailed off.

Dr. Romano listened tirelessly, showing compassion and concern. No one had ever listened to me like this before. Most of the time, I felt as if I wasn't being seen or heard at home or at school. Sure, I could be pretty, popular, perky, athletic—but that wasn't the whole me, even if those were the only things most people wanted to see. I felt like an actress. Tears filled my eyes as I spoke of feeling lost. Dr. Romano's prompts and my insights made me feel as if I was coming home at last. I had a loving family, but we rarely talked about stuff like this. Until now, I hadn't realized that a huge part of me seemed invisible. Talking to Dr. Romano felt as though I'd been wandering in the desert and someone had finally handed me a gallon of cool, clean water. Yes, I still felt incredibly lousy emotionally, but Dr. Romano really saw me, so now I didn't feel as crazy or alone.

"It sounds like you've been bottling things up for a long time," he said.

"Yes," I replied through my tears, "and no one seems to understand."

My friends at college were wondering what the hell was up with me. I think they assumed I had it all—and could have anything, anyone, I wanted. I could tell they didn't hear me or believe me when I talked about my desperation.

"Carrie, what's your history of other relationships? You told me about Louie. What about other boyfriends?"

I described my high school sweethearts, Marty, then Scott. They'd both been loyal, loving boyfriends. Scott even rode his bicycle some sixty miles to make it to my seventeenth birthday party. Then there was Jeff, my college beau, with whom I was inseparable for nearly two years. I'd had a blast with all of the attention and fun but never got seriously intimate with any of them.

I didn't know if I should tell Dr. Romano that I grew bored and restless with each relationship, always wanting something different. I didn't like that about myself. I was convinced that I was a bitch. My older sister had only dated one man since junior high—her husband. What was wrong with me?

"Were you sexual with these boys?" Dr. Romano gazed into me.

That caught me off guard. I squirmed in my seat; I couldn't tell which was more blunt: his question or his stare. Then there was the disconcerting fact that he was still taking notes. I felt put on the spot. My family had never discussed sexuality, except the fact that it wasn't something you'd even consider until you were married. I really wasn't prepared to talk about sex with this stranger. But I reasoned that since Dr. Romano's questions were part of my assessment, they were valid, even if they were extremely uncomfortable.

"Well I played around . . . but always stopped before going all the way."

Dr. Romano leaned forward. He was very interested in me.

So this is how therapy works. From my classwork, I knew a little about Freud's theories on how sexual impulses played a big part in the needs of the human psyche. I had to give Dr. Romano the benefit of the doubt, right? He needed the full landscape of my sexual experiences to determine what was wrong with me.

He continued to question me about my belief in God, and rattled off a checklist that I'd later discover was used to diagnose whether someone was bipolar, or manic-depressive. We talked about my moods. They swung high to the level of euphoria whenever I was feeling close to God and then plummeted into despair when I found myself doubting God's existence or questioning whether there was a larger purpose for any of us. I told Dr. Romano how the Charismatic Renewal experience had made me feel better temporarily but that the "cure" had left once I returned to campus and was struggling again to concentrate on my schoolwork.

"Carrie, it sounds like your self-esteem is so low now that you wouldn't really be able to stay focused on a goal . . . even if there was something you truly wanted."

He was right. I used to laser-focus on whatever I wanted.

Dr. Romano was relaxed and knowledgeable. He was happy to educate me on the clinical aspects of psychology: how a psychiatrist diagnoses manic depression, what "individuating" from one's family means, the importance of goal-setting, and more. I was starting to feel that working with him might make a difference. He was classy and professional, confident and wise.

My hour was almost up. He said he wanted to meet with my parents and me the next day and decide how to proceed with my treatment.

"Okay," I said nervously, feeling a bit like I was only ten years old and needed someone to guide me around because I was totally clueless. If Dr. Romano had any hope that he could help me, then maybe I could have hope of getting better.

"See you tomorrow . . . ." His kind, blue eyes poured into mine.

Back home, my parents and I confirmed the appointment: December 31, New Year's Eve, at 10 a.m.

"Well, Carrie, we're close to making a plan," Dad assured me. "Everything's going to be all right . . . okay?"

His concern was deep. We were all preparing ourselves for what this highly regarded expert had to say about my depression.

That night, I wrote in my journal: "Dear God, please let Dr. Romano know what I need for healing. Please work through him and help me recover. I want to do your will, whatever that is." I slept well.

~6~

Dad quickly drank his coffee before heading outside to start the car. "Okay, ladies, hurry it up . . . I'll be out front."

"Okay, okay!" I yelled back, "I'm coming."

He slammed the door behind him.

It was 9:30 a.m., and Dr. Romano's office was only a mile away. I could never get used to my father's intensity around time. According to retired U.S. Army Lieutenant Colonel Robert F. Tansey, a.k.a. Dad, there was no such thing as being too early. I inhaled my Cheerios and gulped my coffee. It had been three and a half years since I'd last lived at home.

Mom was behind me, also rushing. "You know how your dad likes to be prompt." We both scrambled into the car just as Dad blurted, "Goodness gracious, this is an important day. What took you so long?"

As I sat in the back seat feeling resentful as hell, all the muscles in my body tightened, the way they always did whenever he started barking orders and lecturing us on matters of time and tardiness. Ours was a military family indeed, and I often failed to fall in line with the rest of the troops.

Dad steered our green, 1978 Plymouth Volare station wagon with faux wood panels along the snowy road, taking a shortcut through the college campus by our house. Hood College had once been a women's liberal arts school. It had a formal but lovely vibe to it. It was clearly a place for wealthy students. Piles of fresh, thick snow blanketed the roofs of the red brick, colonial-style buildings. Rows of giant maple trees dressed in white hovered above us like an ice-fairy canopy.

"Do you think he'll recommend medication, Carrie?" Dad had roused me from my secret bubble.

"I have no idea, Dad."

I'd been staring at the wintery landscape, shifting my gaze in and out of focus, something I'd been doing a lot lately, using my farsighted vision problems to straddle two worlds—one blurry and somehow mysterious, the other crystal-clear and therefore tangible. Like a painter who finds beauty in something she sees in the distance, then returns to her canvas to capture it, or an astronomer who points his telescope at billions of stars light years away, then turns to his notebook to map their positions, this eye defect of mine had helped me to naturally zoom in and out of reality. I had a tiny bomb to share with my parents and held my breath before dropping it.

"Dr. Romano . . . he thinks my depression has something to do with separating from my family."

My parents didn't say a word as we pulled into the empty parking lot. It was New Year's Eve. Inside, we made ourselves comfortable in the waiting area, flipping through *Life* and *Time* magazines. Dr. Romano showed up just a few minutes before our scheduled appointment looking relaxed and ready. Dad couldn't help but eye his watch. A frown crossed his face.

"Mr. and Mrs. Tansey . . . Carrie . . . please come in."

"How are you today?" Dr. Romano sat down and eyed us all. He had an uncanny manner of watching a person's every move, no matter how slight or seemingly unimportant.

Dad spoke first. "Well, Doctor," he cleared his throat and crossed his arms. "We're eager to get your opinion on what we should do. Does Carrie need medication?"

"I'll get to that, but first I want to ask you some questions."

Out of the gate, Dr. Romano had grabbed the reins of conversation from my father's hands and hurried pace. He smoothly steered the session back to my parents, their observations of me, and their own family histories, which like most family trees, included depression, anxiety, and dalliances with alcohol.

When Dad began talking about being in therapy himself and how he had struggled with depression and anxiety for years, I was shocked. My eyes opened wider as he continued to openly share some of his struggles with alcohol; I sat on the edge of my seat as he described its dark presence. Dad seemed relieved to finally talk about his family secrets. He was savvier about psychiatrists, medications, and mental illness than I ever would have guessed.

Here I thought that we had descended from a long line of noble blue bloods and could handle things mere mortals could not. I thought back to my grandfather's funeral when I was fourteen at Arlington National Cemetery along the Potomac River. Military families move around as much as gypsies, but ours could always count on returning to at least one plot of land: Arlington, where the bones of my grandfathers—one an admiral, the other a general—now lay, along with their wives, a mere eighty yards apart.

That day, I watched awestruck as a riderless horse, a casket wrapped in an American flag, a twenty-one-gun salute, and a slate of dignitaries paid their respects to my paternal grandfather, Major General Patrick Henry Tansey. He had played a critical role in World War II as the U.S. Army's head of logistics in Europe. Grandpa Tansey was a hero and right-hand man to the legendary General George Patton. He was also close to General Douglas MacArthur, and my Uncle Mike and MacArthur's son were buddies growing up. I remembered thinking, *Wow, my people were important. They were leaders. They were powerful . . . but wait, the powerful ones were all men. The women were their supporters, nothing more.*

I wasn't sure where that left me.

Meanwhile, Dr. Romano was asking my parents lots of questions about me. As my father offered his perspective, I noticed my mother backing him up on everything. Now and then, Dr. Romano looked up from his note-taking to check in with me.

"We were so surprised when we dropped Carrie off for her junior year," Dad explained. "We were at her new apartment with her good friends, and she just started tearing up. She always seemed so eager and ready to leave home before, but then everything changed. We noticed she was more emotional and vulnerable . . . just not herself."

I listened to my parents describe me. I was on trial for my life, and they had been called as witnesses to testify to my good character. They were as strong and supportive as any defendant could hope for, but I could only conclude that the girl they were talking about had been very good at presenting herself as an image of success when, in fact, she was a fraud.

Dr. Romano glanced my way. I felt like the derelict daughter who couldn't get her shit together.

"Well, Mr. and Mrs. Tansey, I strongly feel that Carrie needs intensive psychotherapy," he said with utter authority and confidence. "And she should take a break from college. Healing needs to be her top priority right now."

The three of us sat there stunned. *Leave college with only six months until graduation? Can't a pill lift me out of this? Or some good psychotherapy?*

I sat like a flower frozen by a sudden springtime snow.

Dr. Romano continued. "I think Carrie is in a significant emotional crisis."

Dad struggled to keep his voice calm. "Doctor . . . do you think Carrie is manic-depressive and needs lithium? Like the other doctor suggested?"

"No, I don't think she's manic-depressive. I think Carrie has an agitated depression, but she's not psychotic, nor does she have a thought disorder of any kind."

Thought disorder. The words reverberated in my foggy brain. Lately, my thoughts had certainly seemed disordered to me, but I was relieved by his diagnosis. *Whew! I thought I was fucked up, but now I know I'm not* <u>*that*</u> *fucked up.*

Dad continued to probe about my future. "Doctor, how long do you think this will take?"

Dr. Romano estimated that I would need two to three years of intensive psychotherapy, two or three times per week.

"Carrie is very smart and insightful—a good candidate for insight-oriented psychotherapy," Dr. Romano continued. "I'd rather she not be on medication so she can do the deep emotional work she needs to recover."

Insight-oriented psychotherapy. Carrie is smart. Insightful. I let these encouraging words linger in my mind. I sat up straighter, and somewhere beneath the layers of fetid fog inside me, a tiny voice said, *Yes, Carrie, you are.*

"Well, does that mean we have to go get all her stuff from campus?" Suddenly Dad looked older. There was something in his face I'd never seen before: defeat, vulnerability. "Please tell us what to do, Doctor."

"My suggestion is that Carrie put her healing first in line," Dr. Romano said. "Is it all right if she lives at home for a while? Before she gets her own place or returns to college?"

My own place? Plans were being made without me. I could barely get up in the morning let alone get my own place. I was relieved to hear my parents say: "Yes, she can live at home."

Everyone stood up, and Dad reached out his hand. "Very good. Dr. Romano, this sounds like a good plan. Don't let her get away with anything. Be direct. I like the no-medicine policy. Let's all pray that Carrie can find her way through this."

"Yes, Dr. Romano," Mom smiled politely. "Thank you." She had no questions, or if she did, she didn't reveal them. I wondered if she had an opinion of her own.

"Carrie, we'll see you in the car," Dad added. They closed the door with hopeful smiles.

I sat alone on the couch feeling like a dissected frog in biology class. *Ohhh, ick!* I thought. *Look what's inside this thing!*

"So, Carrie, how do you feel about the plan?" Dr. Romano asked.

I was silent. Two to three years of intensive therapy felt like a mandatory sentence in addition to a very long probationary period. I wondered about living with my parents again. I imagined getting my things from college and the humiliation of not finishing when I was so close. I dreaded the possibility of running into Louie, especially at a time like this. I was ashamed that I couldn't take care of myself.

"I also think," Dr. Romano's voice pierced my ruminations, "we need to take a look at how uncomfortable you are with your sexuality."

I was back in the room and suddenly felt naked.

"What?" I asked.

"I think therapy can also help address your discomfort with your sexuality."

Had I heard him correctly? Discomfort with my sexuality? I let the words sink in. He had waited until my parents were out of the room to spring this one on me.

I was afraid to ask him what he meant by that. After all, he was the professional. I had enough to think about. Leaving college . . . making healing my priority . . . moving back home. And now there was discomfort with my sexuality? That last one hadn't even been on my list of worries.

While Mom and Dad waited in the car, Dr. Romano and I scheduled more appointments, beginning next week.

On the way home, Dad was turning the wheel with one hand, relaxed. "I like him, Carrie. I think he won't let you get away with anything. He's wise, seasoned, smart . . . I say 'yes' to the plan."

I'd ignored putting on my seatbelt and leaned forward, poking my head between my parents' seats. I tried to sound casual, but the words caught a bit in my throat.

"He said he thinks I'm uncomfortable with my sexuality."

There was no response from Mom or Dad. The rest of our drive was quiet, except for the squeegee-crunch of packed snow beneath the car tires.

The Abduction

She had barely touched the flower when the earth ripped in two, and Hades, lord of the underworld, rose out of the dark chasm in a chariot pulled by his immortal horses. He claimed Persephone's great heart for his own, and as he dragged her away to his realm of mist and gloom, she lamented.

~ 7 ~

It was morning, and I peered out my window at the oak tree now bursting with the bright green leaves of spring. I saw a robin's nest in the large tree and heard the mama bird screeching to keep a squirrel away from her eggs. I wasn't ready to leave the solitude of my room for the chaos that was breakfast in our kitchen.

"Carrie! It's almost time to go!" Mom hollered up the stairs.

I took one last glance in the mirror at the aqua blue sundress I was wearing which I had made the summer before. I quickly pulled out a white sweater and wrapped it around my waist in case the day cooled off later.

It was May, five months after my first meeting with Dr. Romano, and I had settled into a steady routine. Two or three times a week, I'd make my way from the boisterous Tansey home to the earthy serenity of his office, though by now, he insisted that I call him Tony.

I took our therapy sessions very seriously and strove to please him. He regularly commented on my intelligence and perceptiveness. I was curious about all things spiritual and psychological, and he treated me like someone special—someone who stood apart from his regular patients.

Outside the sanctuary of my sessions with Tony, life wasn't as easy. It was embarrassing bumping into neighbors who once knew me as the high school tennis champ and student leader. It was difficult to answer the steady stream of questions from relatives, friends, and neighbors asking why I had dropped out of college. Despite my lethargy and low self-esteem, I had taken two steady part-time jobs in our neighborhood. I was babysitting a sweet, two-year-old boy who lived across the street and handling the overnight care of a blind, frail elderly woman. At times, I found myself having to fake interest in them. But I figured that if I could just *act* like I cared about these people, then hopefully, those feelings would eventually appear. Sleep was my only escape, and I couldn't get enough of it.

A few days before, Dad had suggested that he, Mom, and I take a short trip to the National Shrine of the Immaculate Conception in

Washington, D.C., forty-five miles away. We'd tour this colossal church and tribute to the Virgin Mary in time for Mom and Dad to drop me off at my early afternoon appointment with Tony. Then they'd go to lunch.

As our green station wagon zoomed down the road toward our destination, the artist and spiritual seeker in me was tantalized by the idea of seeing the world's largest collections of contemporary sacred art surrounded by glorious Byzantine architecture. At the same time, I was nervous about my parents' dropping me off at Tony's office instead of going there myself as I usually did. My relationship with him was becoming private enough that I felt more comfortable keeping it separate from family life. *Maybe if I can say a prayer when we're inside, it will calm me down.* As the car purred up Michigan Avenue, the white stone church came into view, the surrounding lush green grass and trees making it pop in exquisite relief.

Dad opened the huge wooden door of the largest Catholic church in the United States. "Okay, ladies, we only have half an hour."

I eyed my watch. More than seventy chapels and oratories, two floors totaling 206,308 square feet, 75,545 square feet of Byzantine-style mosaics, and a great dome twice the size of St. Mark's Cathedral in Venice, and Lieutenant Colonel Tansey expects us to cover this territory in half an hour? I felt my body start to go rigid with angst.

"Actually, Dad, I think we have an hour," I said softly. But he didn't hear. Or didn't want to.

Nevertheless, as the three of us walked through the nave, I felt as if I had just entered the Louvre. My eyes were drawn upward, as if to heaven, gazing at the magnificent dome with Jesus and the disciples at the Last Supper rendered in glass mosaic. More than two hundred feet overhead, it glimmered as if it had been placed there by the Hand of God.

As a kid, I always wanted to go to museums, but we didn't do things like that as a family. I guess there were too many of us, and it probably didn't sound like fun to my athletic parents who kept us in the swimming pool or on the tennis courts all summer. Inside the church, I drank in the colors, the textures, the palpable sense of the sacred. It was such a contrast to the straight lines and Greek Ionic style of St. John's back in Frederick. This architecture, composed of circular designs, windows, and arches, felt softer, perhaps from the intention of honoring the feminine nature of Mary, the Mother of God. I felt as if I was in a sacred, precious womb.

I was mesmerized by chapel after chapel, celebrating the diverse lands and cultures of Catholic immigrants from around the world, each venerating the Virgin in a different artistic and architectural style. I did my best to take in all the multicultural richness saturating a single place. As I strolled silently from one chapel to another, I heard Dad speeding up behind me. I didn't have to look at him to know he was fixated on his watch, becoming more agitated.

Eager to get away from his intensity, I escaped into the Blessed Sacrament Chapel and sat on a pew to say a few words to God. *Please Lord, please Mary, I need your help. Lift me out of my darkness. . . .*

"Carrie, Carrie!" Dad whispered urgently. "What are you doing? We've got to go!"

I jumped up. I thought the point of being here was to drink in the glory of this place, but whenever Dad spoke in that tone, I didn't want to disrespect him. Still, we had enough time to get to my appointment. I knew we did.

Going against the grain of my instincts, the three of us rushed out of the church, down the magnificent white stone stairs, and into the car. As we drove away, I kept turning around to look at the sacred place. *I must go back. There is so much more to see . . . the exquisite rose windows, the many chapels, the Crypt Church underneath the main sanctuary. I wish I had lit a candle there. We have more time . . . I know we have more time . . .* I bristled with resentment. *Sometimes being a lieutenant colonel's daughter is a total bummer,* I thought to myself. *At least Tony is so much more relaxed. With him, I can slow down long enough to think.*

We arrived at Tony's office a full thirty minutes early. I tried not to roll my eyes. "I told you we had more time, Dad," I said, tight with anger. "I'll just go into the waiting room . . . you two go ahead." I slammed the car door a little too hard, then scolded myself. *Gosh, Carrie, you really should be more grateful.*

As I walked into the familiar, red brick office building, relief washed over me. Methodically, I got myself some tea, trying to soothe my nerves. Tony's previous client walked out his office door. Tony gave me a big smile. "Oh, you're early. Come in and sit down, I'll be right with you."

He made his way to the restroom while I made myself comfortable on the couch. I looked around the room that had become like a second home to me. *I can really be myself here. There's lots of time. I talk and he listens.*

When Tony sat down, he looked at me long and hard.

"You seem so agitated today. What is happening with you?"

Immediately, I felt relieved that he was tuning into my feelings.

"Oh, I just visited the Shrine of the Immaculate Conception in D.C. with my parents. I was so aggravated with my dad. He's so intense and impatient! I wanted to bask in the beauty of the place. It's amazing, and there's so much to delve into there. He made us leave after thirty minutes. I'm not even sure why we went."

My heart felt heavy. I wanted to share in meaningful conversations about God, architecture, culture, and art with my parents. It was so obvious that would never happen.

"Carrie, I have a great idea," Tony said. "How about if we go to the Shrine together? I often take clients on field trips, and this could be a great chance to see how differently you might experience the place while not with your family."

He looked eager, open, present. He wanted to help me, it was clear. How could I turn him down? *I can't imagine going to a church together wouldn't please Mom and Dad. He's Catholic and supporting me in my religion.*

"Sure, that sounds great," I said with a bit of nervousness in my voice. *Even if they'd approve, though, I don't think I should tell them. It's really none of their business, anyway. This is <u>my</u> therapy.*

That night I wrote in my journal how excited I was about our coming trip. But then I added: *I'm starting to wonder if Tony sees me as more than just a patient.*

The next week, without telling anyone else, I met Tony in his office parking lot. He signaled for me to climb into his sports car, a blue Fiat, and soon we were speeding down the highway. As we drove through D.C. traffic, he was chatty, telling me about all the places he had worked and pointing out landmarks. He also mentioned that he lived on a farm about sixty miles away in Virginia's Blue Ridge Mountains.

At the shrine, we spent more than an hour strolling around the beautiful space while discussing the saints, the altar relics, and all the mystical imagery. I thought, *I'm in the presence of a soul guide. He's here to facilitate both my inner and outer growth, but I'm here to help him as well.*

At one point, while roaming the church, Tony firmly grabbed my hand and quickly led me downstairs to the eerie, low-ceilinged, and cavernous Crypt Church, modeled after the early Christian catacombs. Something taboo and dark and appealing seemed to be happening as we walked down the stairs, holding hands and entering the darker place below. My face must have turned red. I didn't really want to be holding his hand, but I couldn't bear the thought of hurting his feelings. I felt a sense of excitement and fear. *I don't think he should be doing this, but hey, I'm pretty uptight, so maybe it's all okay.*

There, beneath the low, vaulted ceilings, he excitedly pointed out the iconic marble columns crafted in his home state of Vermont and proudly shared with me his humble upbringing: His parents had been blue collar and lived in rural Rutland, where they often hunted deer for their dinner. His father was a laundry deliverer. When Tony got accepted without an interview into one of the best medical schools in the country, Georgetown University, it was a huge moment for his family. They were poor Italian immigrants, and their son had finally made it. This was new and thrilling territory: Dr. Tony Romano, my psychiatrist, was opening up *to me.* I nonchalantly took my hand back while pointing to a statue that I wanted to talk about.

Whew . . . I feel a bit more comfortable back in my own space. I hope I didn't hurt his feelings. He seems so excited to share this with me.

At that moment, I felt deeply nurtured and proud that I'd managed to overcome my social anxiety. I was having a lovely educational experience with my psychiatrist, and it was a blessing. *He's getting me on a deeper level,* I happily reflected, *so he can really understand me and know how best to treat me.* We walked back upstairs, and I headed toward the exit.

"Where are you going?" Tony said. "Do you have a bit more time? I would love to take you out to lunch. I had a cancellation and have another hour before I have to get back to the office."

"Get anything you want. My treat," he said as we sat in the shrine's cafeteria selecting our food. Even though this was not a fancy restaurant, I felt happy to be taken out to eat. Going out to lunch, even in a cafeteria, was rare for my family, which was always budget conscious. I felt a bit uncomfortable sitting so close to Tony, and his eyes seemed to penetrate me even more. But I picked up on his sense of delight in being with me, and that felt so good inside. Afterward, we drove back to his office.

"What a lovely time, Carrie," he said. "See you tomorrow!"

I drove home feeling buoyed by a sense that my doctor really understood me and was teaching me to be in the world in a new way. He could heal me of my anxiety. He was the perfect guide. He was so comfortable with himself—he could teach me to be comfortable with myself.

That night at home, I ached to share this experience with my family, but I was worried that they wouldn't understand what Tony and I shared. I didn't want to lose all the beauty and meaning of the visit. I also wondered if our field trip could get him into trouble. Anyway, how could I explain it? "Hey, Mom, Dad . . . Ummm, Tony, er—Dr. Romano invited me to go to the National Shrine in D.C. to make up for what I missed with you guys last week. He says it will give us insight into our family dynamics and my relationship to God."

Uh, no.

The next day, I had another appointment. I walked in feeling a tad apprehensive about yesterday's hand-holding. Tony, on the other hand, was radiant.

"I had a wonderful time yesterday," he declared. "I was struck by how relaxed you were and how you knew so much about the saints and the architecture. I found you great company, and you didn't experience at all what you describe as uptightness or any inability to converse comfortably. How was it different with your parents?"

"You were way more relaxed than my dad," I responded. "I'm sure that's why I got more out of it. You're also so much more interested in what's going on inside—my thoughts, my feelings. Often, it seems like Dad and Mom are just going through the motions."

I basked in Tony's undivided attention. I never got such a thing from my parents. They had five other children who needed them. At home, it seemed as if I was perpetually struggling to be heard.

"Carrie, when I grabbed your hand—"

Uh-oh, here it comes.

"—did you notice that I touched your breast?"

What?!

I actually hadn't noticed *that.* For a second, the room spun, and it felt like my whole body must be flushing bright red. Certainly, I had a big bosom, and at times, I was self-conscious about it. Sometimes in public places, people accidentally bumped into my breasts. I'd just learned to ignore that kind of thing. Or was this part of what Tony called my "discomfort with my sexuality?"

Now I was more embarrassed than ever. Why did he say that? Was it part of a test? Not knowing how to respond to his question, I didn't. I didn't want to appear to be uncomfortable with anything related to sexuality. I wanted to prove to him that I was a relaxed and together kind of person, not easily freaked out. I wanted to demonstrate that I was growing up and individuating from my family, and that our work together was making a difference.

I just shrugged the whole thing off. Or at least, I tried to.

~8~

"Bob, Bob! Breakfast!" Mom yelled from downstairs. "We only have thirty minutes before we have to leave."

"Carrie, will you wake up Bob?" she hollered. "He needs to get going."

Standing before the upstairs bathroom mirror, I saw my soaped-up face fall and felt my heart drop as I prepared to heed her request, one she frequently issued to each of her four other children regarding her eldest son.

I rinsed and dried my face, then put on a bit of mascara to finish my morning ritual. Keeping my appearance in order helped me battle the cloud of depression I met each day upon waking. Reluctantly, I padded down the hallway's mauve carpeting past three doors to my older brother's room.

"Bob," I said softly, knocking tentatively.

Nothing.

"Bob!" I knocked louder, then opened the door only to get hit by a wall of odor that made my stomach turn.

My brother groaned, "What, Carrie?"

"Wake up, Bob. You have to leave soon." I looked around his room—ultra tidy, pens lined up in order on his desk, shoes and clothes neatly organized in his closet. The ambient smell of body odor did not match the scene.

"Oh God, Bob. When was the last time you took a shower?"

"Carrie," Bob growled, "just yesterday." He slowly swung one long leg over the side of the bed.

"Okay, well Bob, I don't know if it's your feet, your armpits, whatever Bob, it stinks in here. Mom says you have to leave in thirty minutes."

I walked out the door with the sick feeling I always had when trying to motivate Bob. I didn't want to hurt his feelings, but I got so frustrated with him.

Ugh. This situation with Bob is so hopeless! I am such a bitch for thinking that! I have to tell Tony about Bob. He'll know what to do.

I rushed down the two-tiered staircase and entered the kitchen where my parents were finishing their coffee. I had only a few minutes to eat before my therapy appointment.

"Well, honey, what are we going to do about Bob?" Dad said.

I sighed. I was so tired of that question. It was probably the fiftieth time he had asked me in the past five years.

"I have no idea, Dad," I said numbly. "His room absolutely reeks."

"I know this is tough, honey, but remember, we have to be there for Bob," Mom chimed in. "We're all he has."

I could have recited that line along with her; it had left such an impression so long ago when she first responded to one of my observations about him. Bob had been born almost three months premature, with a brain injury, and didn't speak until he was four years old. I was his younger sister but couldn't help but move ahead of him developmentally. Once we were in school, he was only one grade ahead of me even though two and a half years older. All my life, I had tried not to upstage him, not to make him feel bad about himself. My guilt over Bob pinned down my wings. I could never fly because my older brother, whom I adored, could not.

This particular morning, Dad had stayed home so he and Mom could accompany Bob to his appointment with a new social services person. Bob would never be completely self-sufficient. But government agencies kept denying our family any assistance because they said he functioned too well to qualify. He had done so well for a while, washing dishes for a local restaurant for nearly a decade, but he had gotten in trouble at work recently because of his drinking. At twenty-four, he could drink legally, of course, but alcohol had begun to destroy him, a toxic mixture—brain damage and booze.

Bob shuffled into the kitchen scratching the back of his head, an anxious habit he had developed in high school. Now, he had a bald patch because of it.

"Well, there he is," Dad sang out to the tune of "There She Is, Miss America," with the usual upbeat approach he took with matters of his oldest son.

Even so, I saw the weariness in Dad's eyes. The toll of raising a child who would never truly grow up was etched on my father's handsome face. This was another reason I had to grow up and heal myself. I had to keep focused on my own individuation. I mustn't cause my parents any more suffering.

"I've got to go," I explained. "I'm seeing Dr. Romano today in thirty minutes. I'll walk. Good luck. I hope it goes well, Bob," I said, rushing to close the sliding-glass door behind me. The all-too-familiar sense of futility and guilt came over me as I walked through the backyard gate and down the alley shortcut to the street, feeling as if I was abandoning a sinking ship to save myself.

I walked through the leafy Hood College campus to Tony's office, glad to move my muscles and shake off the weighty question of what to do about my brother.

It wasn't always like this. When the six of us were a teeming sea of little people with different ages, needs, and abilities, Bob's differences didn't stand out so much. There were even moments when his quirks reminded all of us to stop taking ourselves so seriously. I could remember a day in 1967, when I was seven and he was almost ten, and we were all piling into the family station wagon, a white Ford LTD with wood-grain side panels, headed to Main's Ice Cream shop in Middletown, about ten miles away. It was a big day for us. Main's was the most delicious ice cream for miles around. We were also excited about the roller coaster ride along the way as Dad would speed up and sail over road bumps, cuing us to yell "wheeee!" We'd giggle with the thrill of feeling our stomachs soar into our throats.

On this day, Mom, Dad, Jody, Mike, Tim, Polly, and I had piled in the station wagon, and I had snagged the cherished middle-seat bump. As usual, slow-moving Bob was the last to get in the car, sliding in beside me and challenging Lieutenant Colonel Tansey to be extra patient.

Years later, I still wasn't sure what happened that day. All I could gather was that Dad must have been rolling out of the driveway before Bob had completely closed the rear passenger door. Suddenly, we heard a low, droning scream. Then, Bob yelled, "Stop! Stop!"

The outburst was unusual for my introverted brother, who typically sat quietly in his own world doing things only he liked, such as memorizing facts from history books. (He was the only person I'd ever known who could tell you what year Hannibal crossed the Alps *and* how many elephants were with him.)

Dad hit the brakes.

"My foot, my foot!" Bob screamed.

A few seconds of chaos followed as the seven of us tried to figure out what the heck was happening. I leaned over to have a look. Somehow, Bob's gangly right leg was still outside the open door, and his foot was wedged between the tire and the road.

Even now, I wondered how he had managed it. I mean, how does a person's foot get run over while he's sitting face forward? Mom, neatly dressed in her blue plaid seersucker pants and crisp white T-shirt, scrambled out to inspect the situation and guide Dad as he *slowly* pulled forward, loosening the tire's grip on my brother's foot.

"Hold it, hold it . . . six more inches, Honey . . . slowly," she said calmly to her husband, hands in motion like a good patrol cop.

Miraculously, Bob was fine, and he got a double scoop of ice cream that day.

Now, I smiled ruefully as I walked. We were actually overdue for a family trip to Main's Ice Cream, I mused. It was summer, after all.

Tony was waiting for me at the entrance to the building with a huge, warm smile. "Help yourself to some tea," he said.

I took a deep breath. Despite my hopeless morning, I felt a sense of possibility just looking into his eyes. Once I was situated on the couch, I recounted my challenging morning and the pressure my parents were under, providing for Bob and helping me in addition to raising my brother Mike, who was struggling with college, plus caring for two younger children—one in college and the other still in high school. Meanwhile, my older sister was married, living in the neighborhood, and pregnant with her first child, which meant soon, Mom was sure to be helping with the new baby too. I confided that I thought my parents were stretched too thin, and started to ask what might be done, at least with regard to Bob and social services, when Tony interrupted, "My, it seems no one is getting their needs met."

That stopped me in my tracks. I'd never thought about it that way before. Were we doing something wrong? I thought families were about sticking together and figuring things out, not about "getting our needs met," but come to think of it, I guessed no one was, especially my parents who never had a moment of peace.

"What do *you* need right now, Carrie?" Tony said. "I hear you focusing on them and their needs, how about *your* needs?"

"I guess I just don't know how to deal with my brother Bob and his handicap. It's so draining on our family."

"Well, you know, part of individuating from your family is recognizing your own path, what you can control and what you can't," Tony said. "Individuating is separating from 'we' to 'I.'"

Wow. What if Bob wasn't my responsibility? Suddenly, things didn't seem so heavy.

"As I see it, Carrie, your family dynamics are such that everyone is kept in a state of dependency," Tony proclaimed. "Is Bob really this helpless, or are your parents keeping him that way so they can focus on him and stay in denial about the real issue: the problems in their marriage?"

Problems in Mom and Dad's marriage? True, I had told Tony that Mom didn't always seem so giving to Dad, and it made me sad to see him sad, but I guess I never really viewed this as "problems in their marriage." But I had to listen to Tony if I was ever going to overcome my depression.

"I think you plummeted into this depression because of your family's lack of support for your individuation," Tony went on. "Did you ever think that your parents may not only be keeping Bob in a state of dependency but you as well?"

I sat there mouth agape, listening. Tony broke through the pregnant pause.

"And I hate to say it, but your family's uptight morality around sex is holding you back from developing a mature romantic partnership."

He took the yellow legal pad on his desk, turned it horizontally, and drew something on it, then held it up to me. On the far left side, he had written "Sex & Intimacy," on the far right, "Career & Independence." In the center of the paper was an enormous X. He pointed to it with his pen.

"You're stuck right here," Tony said emphatically. "Because of your parents' taboos about sex before marriage and their own intimacy issues, it's impossible for you to move forward with the mature love and romantic partnership that are integral parts of the individuation process. At the same time, their lack of support for your separation from the family means they are holding you back from completing college, having a career, and being an independent adult."

My body felt tense with mixed emotions. I wanted to defend my parents. In so many ways, they were great at raising all six of us. Tony was a psychiatrist. Didn't he understand that Bob had been born with special needs? Mom and Dad didn't make him that way.

"Carrie, some of this sounds shocking at first, I know, because these family behaviors are unconscious," Tony went on. "You and your family aren't aware of them, but as your psychiatrist, I know. I've seen these dynamics time and time again." He nodded his head with a sense of authority.

You've seen them? You've never even met Bob! I felt like yelling, but I didn't. No matter what I thought, I had to listen to Tony if I was going to heal, to individuate, to move on with my life. Maybe I actually needed to distance myself from my family to do that.

The swirling emotions settled down into one clear focus: anger. Deep, abiding anger. I looked at my doctor. He looked back at me with the satisfied finality of an attorney resting his case.

~9~

May gave way to June. My days continued to consist of my family, work, Tony, and occasionally the meetings of Mom's Charismatic Renewal Group. Since last December, I had become good friends with Mary Ellen, the first member Mom had introduced me to. She was always attentive to my angst and depression, and confident that God would heal me. She was four years older than me and one of the few people I allowed into my inner sanctum.

I felt that I needed both Tony and religion in my life—the voice of psychology *and* the voice of spirit, but striking that balance was difficult. At Charismatic Renewal meetings, I would often hear Tony's voice in my head questioning what was *really* going on with these people, and how they needed to grow up psychologically instead of spending so much energy on useless praying. On the other hand, whenever I was in session, I would hear the women's voices asking me whether I sought God's healing, not Tony's, for my pain and worries.

I journaled my prayers daily and shared my spiritual experiences at my therapy sessions. Tony surprised me by encouraging me to tell him more. I wanted to understand everything about life and the mysteries of our existence, and our therapy time took a more philosophical turn. What did it mean to be human? What's our relationship to God? What was my purpose? Who was I really? Did God even exist? If He did, did He even care?

Outside of therapy, I felt something inside me shifting. As part of the Charismatic Renewal, I'd been laying my hands on people to heal them and had begun trying it on my own. When my older sister, Jody, had morning sickness, I put my hands on her belly. They quickly warmed, and her nausea suddenly disappeared. When my brother Tim hurt his knee playing Ultimate Frisbee, I placed my hands on the injury while we prayed. He said his pain was instantly gone. I truly believed that the healing energy that poured from Jesus flowed into my heart and through my hands. In life, there were so many things I was skeptical about, but for some reason, this was real to me. I think it was because I could feel it, and I knew that healers from many cultures had long believed that human touch could transfer healing energy.

I sensed I was on a spiritual path not unlike that of the early Christians. One day, while in a room filled with hundreds of people who had their hands high in the air praising God, I was suddenly filled with deep joy and aliveness. It was like liquid gold pouring down from the heavens, and it drenched me head to toe. I could only describe it as the light and love of God himself. I was surprised to hear myself utter a beautiful but strange sound—an unknown language. It was as if it flowed through from another dimension or time. The feeling was exhilarating, and in an instant, any sense I'd ever had of being alone and separate from others evaporated. Later, someone explained that I had experienced the Holy Spirit and had been speaking in tongues. All I knew was that it had come to me so naturally it seemed as if someone had turned on a celestial valve.

As I tapped into Christ's unconditional love, I began to experience longer periods of feeling good about myself. In those moments, I felt strangely at home. There was clarity. Peace. Whenever I was in this space, I found I could pray for everyone. In session, I shared these thoughts with Tony. He was riveted.

"Carrie, what you're talking about feels alive, not the Catholic Church's version which seems rote, formulaic."

I was so grateful for Tony's encouragement. I wished my friends from Charismatic Renewal were as supportive of my healing through psychotherapy, but they weren't. Some actually asked me if I thought all this self-exploration through Tony wasn't doing more harm than good.

Now as he and I wound down our discussion, I slipped my clogs back on, got up from the couch, and picked up my purse to go.

"Oh, Tony, I almost forgot," I said. "I have to reschedule next Monday's appointment. Third trimester just ended at Virginia Tech, so we're going to Blacksburg this weekend to get my things and may not get back in time."

"What do you mean?"

"Maybe I didn't tell you," I said apologetically. "School's out. My apartment's lease is up, and some of my stuff is still there. It's kinda depressing. When I withdrew in December, I thought I would be going back to finish college before now. I'm really dreading seeing my friends. They're all graduating, and they'll be partying like crazy. I think I'm dreading seeing Louie the most."

Tony's eyes narrowed. I felt him bristle. "You're seeing Louie?"

"Only because I loaned him my TV," I explained. I sighed and rolled my eyes at myself. Sometimes I was so afraid of telling someone "no" that I put myself in awkward positions like this one. *Honestly, why had I loaned that jerk my TV?*

Tony's voice softened. "I know leaving school was difficult, but your therapy work is going so well," he said.

As usual, he was my rock.

"Oh, I know. I just wish I could tell my friends about my individuation and self-actualization, but they'll just think I'm nuts. They'll be going to parties and having fun, and I'll be wanting to meditate," I said, trying to force a laugh. "I know this is important work for me, but sometimes, I still feel like a failure for not finishing college," I confided.

"All in good time, Carrie. You'll finish," Tony reassured me. "You're making more and more progress every day."

I tried to steel myself with a deep breath.

"When the student is ready, the teacher appears," I said looking around the room. "*This* is my education right now."

Tony's eyes looked dewy, and he shook his head.

"Louie must have been crazy," he said, staring at me with a glazed look in his eyes. Then he snapped back to reality. "But we're still on for this Friday?"

"Sure, see you then."

Friday morning, I was in the kitchen putting bread in the toaster when Mom entered and said, "Carrie, I just took a message from Dr. Romano's office. He's sick and canceled your appointment today."

Huh, I thought, pouring myself a glass of orange juice. *That's weird. He never cancels.*

"Well, great," said Dad, finishing his scrambled eggs. "Now we can leave for Blacksburg that much earlier!"

Of course this would please Lieutenant Colonel Tansey. Not that I minded. It was about five hundred miles round-trip, and I sincerely wanted to get the whole thing over with.

On campus, I muddled my way through the task of getting my things, seeing old friends, wishing them well, and trying to mean it. On the drive home, our trusty green station wagon was saddled with stuff—my Eagles and Fleetwood Mac records, my sewing machine, my diaries and photo albums, all those biology and psychology textbooks.

I gazed out the window as the sun started to set over the Virginia countryside. Then, as we passed the exit to Luray Caverns, Tony came to my mind in a powerfully visceral way. It was like the stories you hear of mothers somehow knowing that their children are in danger. I sensed Tony was in serious trouble, and found myself compelled to pray intensely for him, sending him light and love. I knew in my deepest being that he was in some kind of crisis.

The next day, I arrived at Tony's office to find him radiant. He sat me down and told me he had something important to say. I noticed that his face was relaxed, almost incandescent.

"I had a crisis this weekend, Carrie. Sometimes I suffer from intense, chronic pain due to a condition called trigeminal neuralgia, an inflammation of the fifth cranial nerve, and I have to take Tegretol whenever I have a flare-up.

"I woke up in the middle of the night feeling toxic, like I was going to die. I asked my fiancee for help, but she rolled over and went to sleep, apparently disinterested. It was at that point that I said, 'I surrender, Lord. Take me.'

"All of a sudden, a light appeared in the room," he went on. "I let go, and all the pain left me. Instantly, I said to myself, 'This must be what Carrie is talking about.' I went back to sleep and awoke with a sense of deep joy and peace with no pain."

I could barely contain myself. I had to let him know about my premonition.

"I'd been praying for you that day! I felt that something was terribly wrong."

"I knew it!" he said with the enthusiasm of someone who had just tapped into the wisdom of the universe. He leaped out of his chair and clasped his hands over his heart, as if in prayer. "I just knew it."

Time stood still. We both sat in his office basking in the feeling that God had indeed touched him, and that my prayers and intuition had been the conduit. I realized I might have something valuable to offer the world. *What if I'm some kind of healer? What if I can bring him to God, and this is the reason we've met?*

Deep inside me, the voice that came to me at age five spoke again: "Everything that happens in your life is created by *me* as a test to see how you will respond, what you will choose. . . . You are not alone."

What if leaving college and starting psychotherapy wasn't indicative of my personal weakness but part of a greater plan?

Tony seemed happier, lighter, and now he finally understood the reality of my spiritual experience. It made me trust him that much more. When our session time was up, he asked me to come back later that night to finish our talk.

After dinner, I put on my white gauze pants, a striped T-shirt, and Tretorn tennis shoes and wrapped a casual sweatshirt around my waist. I slipped out of the house, telling my parents I wanted to take a stroll around the neighborhood to see who was playing tennis, but I walked the mile to Tony's office instead. Even though the clouds were shrouding the stars, it was a beautiful night.

He met me at the door, and I took my usual seat on the couch, sitting cross-legged. I was all ears. God had truly touched him. Then out of nowhere, a jolt of skepticism penetrated my spiritual high: *Is this session for him or for me?* I wondered if he was billing my parents for this secret time between the two of us.

"Carrie, I don't know what's happening to me," he said. "I think about you day and night. I want what you have. I want a little piece of you every day."

Seeing his eyes light up that way and all the tension drain from his face made me feel enormously expansive and grateful just to be alive. I could tell that he was talking about finding a larger purpose for himself and a real connection with God. Something was happening here that felt risky and exciting. It felt so gratifying to lead someone to his own greater truth. *But what did he mean by "a little piece of me?" I'm sure he meant a little piece of God.*

~ 10 ~

After that, our sessions took a refreshing turn; they were more focused on God. Tony and I also discussed my interest in becoming a psychologist, and he enthusiastically supported it. He even offered to help pay for my education if I promised to work for him once I graduated! I was extremely fortunate. This successful, intelligent man wanted to help me navigate my life's path. He believed in me.

During one session, Tony talked about his son, Dave, also a psychology student, and how much we had in common. He wanted us to meet, so he invited me to their farm for the weekend. "It will be a good break from your family," he said. Tony assured me that his fiancee would be there so I'd be hanging out mostly with Dave, who was my age. I was flattered, intrigued, but a bit unnerved. *Am I ready to get fixed up with my doctor's son? What has he told Dave about me? Won't it be kind of weird to be around Tony and his fiancee?*

That night after dinner, my siblings had all retreated to their rooms, so I had a few moments in the kitchen with my parents. I helped Mom wash dishes while Dad emptied the trash.

"Mom? Dad? Tony ummm . . . Dr. Romano invited me to his farm next weekend. You know, he lives in Front Royal on the weekends. He thinks it would be nice for my psyche to get away, and he thinks I'll like meeting his son."

Dad froze, then put down the trashcan he was holding with a resonant thud. He glanced anxiously at Mom.

Mom shut off the faucet, quickly dried her hands, and motioned for us to join her at the kitchen table. Once we were seated, tension hung thick in the air.

"Carrie . . . wow . . . I think that is highly inappropriate," Dad said once he could find the words.

My stomach tightened. I had meant to bring this up casually and didn't want it to turn into a serious conversation.

"I think it will be okay," I said. "His fiancee and his son will both be there."

Dad's brow furrowed, and he scratched his head.

"What are his plans while you're there?"

I found it hard to look at my parents. I tried to defend my doctor.

"Well, he owns ninety acres, so I think I'll do some hiking with Dave, and we'll share some meals together."

I squirmed in my seat. Now that I heard myself say this aloud, it definitely sounded awkward. What was I supposed to say? Now this seemed like some kind of weird double date. I thought back to our conversation in his office.

"I can't promise that David won't spontaneously try to kiss you," he had said.

At the time, I had interpreted that comment as a quip and a compliment, even if it was one I didn't really care for. Maybe he wasn't kidding. I blushed just thinking about it.

Mom and Dad were staring hard at me, which brought me out of my reverie and back to the kitchen table.

"No, honey, this is highly unusual," Dad said. "We won't let this happen. I'm putting a call into Dr. Walden. She referred us to Dr. Romano in the first place. I'd like to hear what she has to say about all this."

This is why Tony says what happens in therapy should stay in the therapy room! Now I thought back to the Shrine visit and felt sick to my stomach. I had better not tell them about that.

I felt like I was straddling a vast chasm with each foot in a different world. I wondered how long I could hold out. I wanted to please everyone. Part of me was secretly relieved Mom and Dad didn't approve. I wanted to be individuated from my family, but Tony's suggestion just didn't feel right.

Mom spoke up.

"Carrie, we're worried for you given the times these days . . . and well, you know, you're so attractive," she said. At that moment, I wondered: *How does Tony see me?*

About a week later, Tony began our therapy session by telling me that Dr. Walden had called to question him, saying: "What's this I hear about you inviting a young female patient to your farm?"

Tony was angry with me as he sat on the edge of his chair, his Italian hands gesticulating wildly in the air: "Don't you know a rumor like this spreads like wildfire? Why did you tell your parents?" he said in a threatening tone, his eyes piercing right through me.

For a while, I didn't say anything. I just sat there thinking. Sure, I had been frustrated with my parents before, but this wasn't one of those times. I was grateful they'd stepped in so I didn't have to make a decision. It also occurred to me that between the insurance company and my parents, Tony was getting close to a thousand dollars a month (almost \$2,500–\$3,000 in today's dollars) to treat me. Our relationship was special, yes, but it was also supposed to be a professional one. All of a sudden, it felt uncomfortably personal, but why? It was then that I realized: *He expects me to lie. He wants me to live a double life.*

Tony continued ranting. It was painful to hear him rail against my parents for what he called their "uptight morality." At the same time, I valued my sessions with him and had no intention of jeopardizing his reputation, even if he was behaving in an unconventional manner. Without him, I'd never get my life back. True, I was touched by my parents' protectiveness, but Tony would never do anything to hurt me. What if my parents were right about one thing, though? What if Tony and I were getting too close?

Day by day, I was experiencing more emotional breakthroughs, growing stronger, and feeling more confident about my future. Some mornings, I'd wake up and not even notice the depression. I was aware, however, of the elephant in the room: I could tell that Tony longed for more than friendship, but how could I walk away from the mentor and doctor who had brought me this far? He was like my second father, a father I could tell anything to.

The moment arrived when I knew I had to just get it out in the open. I couldn't bear to upset him, but I didn't want to lead him on and ruin our special bond. One day in session, I brought it up.

"Um, I have something I need to say." I nervously glanced down at my hands. "It feels like there's a barrier keeping us from going any deeper." I slid my hands down the invisible wall that seemed to separate us.

"What do you think it is?" he asked.

I was shocked by what came out of my mouth next.

"I'm afraid I'm falling in love with you."

He scooted to the edge of his chair.

"Have you ever stopped to think that maybe I'm in love with you too?" His eyes brightened.

"Well, that's it. We can start planning to do things together. You can come to the farm. We can do things around D.C. on the weekends. I'd love to take you to the opera. . . . This is just great."

I sat there in stunned silence. *I had just said, "I'm afraid I'm falling in love with you," emphasis on the word "afraid."* And he continued talking, oblivious. He had just broken up with his fiancee, and now he was acting like a kid in a candy shop who had permission to grab whatever he wanted. *Did he break up with her because of me?*

Suddenly, I sensed a ball of light quivering in my belly, and I felt it leave my body and rush into his. Paralysis swept over me as if I'd just gotten hit with a blow dart big enough to stun a rhinoceros. *What just happened? How do I get my sense of self back?* Now that I had named my fear, the barrier between us seemed to dissolve, but so did my sense of being separate from him. The room started spinning like a top, and I could feel myself floating out of my body. I was losing it.

Wait! I silently screamed. *Wait! I thought I could say anything in therapy, and we'd explore it together. I thought we were here to examine our feelings, not act on them! I didn't mean it . . . . I don't know how to say I'm afraid <u>you</u> are falling in love with <u>me</u>. Wait! Wait! Wait!*

From my studies in school, I knew some fundamentals of psychotherapy, including that it's common for patients to feel as if they're falling in love with their therapists, but instead, what they're really experiencing is called transference. I was confused about my feelings, and wondered if I was experiencing transference too. I wanted to talk about this with Tony, not become his girlfriend, but he was so happy, so excited, I couldn't bear the thought of letting him down.

That day as I left the building, I was nauseous, and my whole body felt as heavy as lead. I could sense Tony back in his office jumping up and down with delight. I walked slowly under the weight of dread and a deep sense of foreboding.

I was finally getting better, and now this. This wasn't what I wanted. I only wanted to heal and move on.

That night at dinner, I sat like a mannequin. My family was so used to my mood swings that no one even asked me what was wrong. The wheels of my mind were spinning as I considered what to do. I had to take it back. I'd call and tell him he'd misunderstood me.

After everyone went to bed, I quietly made my way to the basement to use the phone. I couldn't think, let alone sleep. I had to get this cleared up.

Tony answered with a warm, dreamy voice, "Oh, it's you."

I took a deep breath and blurted it out. "I think you misunderstood me. I think maybe I shouldn't have said that. I love you. I really love you. I don't, however, want that kind of relationship with you. I just wanted to explore my concern that we were getting too close."

His warm tone instantly cooled. He became authoritative. "What—what? I can't believe I'm hearing you say this. What happened? How did you change your feelings so fast? You know that's impossible, don't you? We have to talk about this tomorrow, in person." He ended the call abruptly.

The next morning, I dragged myself to his office building, terrified of what might happen. I had to resolve this. I needed to salvage our friendship and my health. My hand was shaking as it slid up the stair rail. At the top, a woman was waiting for me. It was Tony's daughter, Mary Catherine, who sometimes did office work for him.

"I don't know what's wrong with Dad," she said. He's so upset. He's in pain and still sleeping."

Because his farm was about sixty miles away, Tony often stayed at the office on weeknights.

"I'll try to wake him," she said with concern and a hint of curiosity. I went in the office and took my usual seat on the couch.

My body was bristling. I knew what was wrong with him, and I hated him for it. Part of me was worried and the other part felt completely manipulated. This was supposed to be *my* therapy, *my* healing.

Eventually, Tony shuffled in and limped over to his chair. He looked like a devastated man.

"What happened, Carrie? You know that it's impossible for your feelings to shift that fast. I'm wondering if this is your fear of intimacy revealing itself."

I felt my resolve crumbling. Now that we were face to face, I couldn't think of what to say. I wanted to take it back. But what if he was right? *Oh God, I guess I really am fucked up. I must be in love with him because he's in love with me. Right?*

I loved my doctor and wanted to protect him, but I didn't want a romantic relationship with him. I just wanted him to keep being my doctor, my friend. He was clearly suffering, and it was all my fault. What I really meant was, "I'm afraid you're falling in love with me, and we need to talk about it." *So why didn't I say that before? Why couldn't I say that now?*

I sat there, paralyzed.

I just wanted things to be the way they'd been before. I was willing to say anything just to regain the peace between us. I decided to save Tony's feelings by lying about mine, "Well, I think I'm feeling that way again."

Tony smiled. He took a deep breath.

~ 11 ~

Golden sunlight bathed my room with the glory of Indian sum- mer. I blinked. As I lay in bed, my head, shoulders, and back throbbed with tension. I looked at the clock on my nightstand: 11 a.m. I couldn't believe I'd slept so late. I kicked off the covers and lay motionless, trying to gather the energy to hoist myself out of bed. A thick cloud of depression hung heavily over me as I stared at the ceiling thinking of Tony.

True to our code that what happens in therapy stays in therapy, I had told no one of his confession—or my confusion over it. That had been weeks ago, and I still didn't have clarity about it. Tony had risked so much for me. I couldn't bear the thought of hurting his career or his feelings. But how did *I* feel? A wave of nausea hit me.

I trudged to the bathroom, then brushed my teeth and looked in the mirror. Wow, I didn't look half bad today. How could that be when I felt so awful? Downstairs, I heard the front door open and male voices in the vestibule. Who could that be? Maybe my brother Mike had brought one of his cute friends home from college this weekend. I surprised myself with the thought. The girl in the mirror raised her eyebrows.

Gosh, I never saw any guys these days. Would I ever venture out socially again? Thinking about it made me feel ashamed of myself as I washed my face. I couldn't even remember how to flirt. All of that seemed stupid anyway. I had much more serious issues to deal with: Tony . . . therapy . . . God.

My stomach churned when I thought of my dilemma. I prized my relationship with Tony above all others. Now that I had resumed my education at Hood College that fall, I needed his support more than ever. I loved him because we were of like minds. But did I love him like a boyfriend? He was my dad's age. He was my psychiatrist. I shook my head trying to settle down the confusion.

"Carrie, someone down here wants to see you," Mike called.

Now I was even more curious. I dried my face and put on a little rouge to make myself look brighter. Back in my room, I dressed, slipping on my tennis socks with the bright green pompoms and Tretorn tennis shoes, then trotted down the stairs to the kitchen.

"Oh, my gosh, Carrie . . . it's so good to see you!" Jay, a cute guy who had been a year ahead of me in high school, jumped to his feet and gave me a bear hug, lifting me a foot off the ground. For a minute, I felt like the bubbly, confident fifteen-year-old girl who had met him years before. His smile lit up his face, highlighting that adorable dimple I now remembered.

Behind him, my brown-haired, athletic brother looked only slightly sweaty and barely winded in his Adidas T-shirt and shorts as he laid his Frisbee on the kitchen counter, opened the fridge, and took out two Gatorades. "Look who I ran into at the Saturday Ultimate match," he said.

"Jay, wow . . . Jay." Memories flooded back to when he had asked me out, and I had to gently decline. I had already fallen for his older brother's best friend, but Jay was always special to my heart. He made me laugh. He made me feel free. My heart felt warm and open, and my body light, the way I used to feel when I was in the presence of a guy I liked—friend or love interest.

For a moment, my cloud of depression lifted. Jay and I chatted for a few minutes, and then he asked me to a party at his house that weekend.

"I'm sure there'll be lots of people you'll know," he said. "Come on over and hang out like old times."

The weight returned to my heart and head. How could I tell him I'd forgotten how to have fun? That I was on a deep quest for healing? That I'd been depressed and had panic attacks? I didn't say anything.

"I seem to recall you dancing for hours at our high school parties," Jay prodded with a grin. "You'll be the one who gets everybody on the dance floor. Please come, Carrie."

In that moment, a wall of fog descended between the two of us, and I got sucked backward into a vortex of mounting anxiety. I wanted to say yes to Jay, yes to the party, yes to dancing, but my growing sense of panic wouldn't let me.

I wasn't that fun-loving girl anymore. I wished I was, but there was no going back. Something else called me. Couldn't he see?

"Thanks for the invite, Jay," I said. "So great to see you." I gave him a big hug and blushed. "I've got to go. I have an appointment to get to. I'll be in touch." I knew I would never call him.

I bolted out of the kitchen trying to look cool but feeling like a crazy girl divided. Half of me, the formerly healthy college co-ed, wanted to stay with him and reminisce about high school, but Tony was waiting for the other half of Crazy Girl to show up in his office. Tony understood the part of me that seemed invisible to everyone else. He was wise. He would know how to make me feel better. Besides, guys like Jay were too young for me now; something powerful was happening between Tony and me. Maybe I didn't love him like he loved me, but whatever it was felt like it was my destiny.

I shuffled the mile to Tony's office, feeling split in two and hungering to be whole.

"Hey there, Carrie," Tony said, ready to walk me from the waiting room to his office. He was such a loyal guide. Guys like Jay and Louie were fun and sexy, but Tony was a man of substance.

We took our respective seats. I studied him more closely. His salt-and-pepper hair was thinning; his mustache was somewhat wiry. Looking at his navy blue knit vest and crisp red tie, I thought of Jay's wavy brown hair, black Baltimore Orioles T-shirt, orange OP shorts, and tanned legs. Tony was a mentor, like another dad. I felt myself settle down inside. Jay might have been cute, but life with boys like him would be all about parties, crab feasts, and baseball games. Life with Tony was deep, soul-searching talks about psychology and God. Tony wanted to understand everything inside of me. Guys my own age never seemed to get past my looks.

"How are you?" Tony began, his eyes wide open and glassy.

I decided not to tell him about my encounter with Jay. Instead, I stared back into his eyes, searching them to read what Tony was feeling today and what he needed from me. He looked calm on the outside, but I also sensed some tension, some neediness on his part. If I could just calm Tony's skepticism around religion, perhaps he could better understand the role of the spirit in healing. Maybe we could even walk the path of psychological and spiritual growth together. I decided to steer the conversation in that direction.

"Well, you know how I'm curious about Christian Mysticism and Contemplative Spirituality?" I began. "I've also been listening to recordings by Father Brennan Manning, this controversial Catholic priest." I braced myself for Tony's usual rebuttals, such as the times he had questioned the mental health of my friends from the Charismatic

Renewal. Or the time he told me one of our church deacons, a friend of his, had confided that he'd been unfaithful to his wife.

Tony only nodded, encouraging me to continue.

"Actually, a lot of more-traditional types have criticized Manning for mixing Catholicism with Eastern mysticism and Jungian psychology, but I find it fascinating, and I think you would like his ideas too. For instance, Manning says self-hatred, low self-esteem, and excessive guilt are our largest obstacles to connecting with the divine."

Tony's silence made me a little nervous.

"So, um, anyway . . . Manning . . ." I paused and cleared my throat. "You once told me to let you know the next time one of these spiritual services was happening. I thought you might like to know that Manning is actually going to be speaking and leading a Mass at a church in Gaithersburg next week."

"That would be great," Tony said without hesitation. "Let me check my book."

My heart fluttered.

"Yes, I finish with patients early that night." He looked up at me. "Let's meet in the parking lot of the Gaithersburg mall so we can avoid parking two cars. Then I'll then drive you over to the church. Meet me at six, okay?

Oh. I hadn't really intended for us to drive to the service and sit together, but I guessed that was okay. Besides, since Gaithersburg was twenty-five miles away, no one would see us. I would never do anything to jeopardize Tony's career.

"Okay, sure," I said. "And I won't mention this to my parents," I added, hoping to reassure him after that debacle with Dr. Walden.

I felt warmth spread from my heart into my belly. All the anxiety about Jay and socializing with my peers vanished. Tony was open to the will of God for his life and mine. A deep sense of peace washed over me. This was the green light I needed: Bring Tony to Father Brennan Manning so he can understand my relationship with God.

~12~

I pulled on my warm fuzzy, cream-colored turtleneck, buttoned my rust-colored corduroys, and left the house by 5 p.m., telling my parents I'd be home by midnight after seeing Father Manning in Gaithersburg with a college buddy. Luckily, they didn't ask for more details.

As I cruised my way down I-270 from Frederick toward Washington, I turned on the radio and cracked open the window to feel the crisp fall air against my face.

"This is National Public Radio, and you're listening to *All Things Considered.* U.S. flags fly at half-staff as the world mourns the assassination of Egyptian President Anwar Sadat. President Reagan, along with former Presidents Nixon, Ford, and Carter will attend the funeral in Cairo next week."

I changed the station.

Now, Kenny Loggins was belting out:

This is it
Make no mistake where you are . . .
This is it
The waiting is over

A tear rolled down my cheek as an overwhelming sense of gratitude came over me.

For once in your life,
Here's your miracle
Stand up and fight

Ever since embarking on my spiritual quest, I had looked for a sign that I was on the right path toward healing. My doctor loved me and wanted to understand my spiritual path. He and I had such a special connection. Was this my miracle? I listened more intently to the song's message:

No room to run, no way to hide
No time for wonderin' why
It's here, the moment is now
About to decide

Please, God, work in Tony's life, I prayed, gripping the steering wheel more tightly. *I need a sign that he's a man of God and I'm on the right path with him.*

At the mall, Tony pulled up alongside the family station wagon in his blue Fiat, and I jumped in. It was the only time I'd been in his car except for the trip to the Shrine. Was this another therapeutic outing like that one? What was this actually? Was this it? The song lyrics echoed through my head.

Tony looked at me with his dewy, blue eyes. "You look beautiful tonight."

I felt a bit of a thrill in my bones mixed with some tension in my belly. "Thanks, so do you."

That was a silly thing to say. He looks the same as he always does after working all day. I wonder if he's gone to a service like this with any other patients?

We drove the few miles to the church without a word. I was relieved to pull up to the modern building and quickly leave the car to escape the strained silence between us.

Will he like Father Manning's message, or will he see my love for these experiences as evidence of my pathology?

The church was packed, but we managed to squeeze into a back pew. My heart was so open and eager for Tony to have his first true spiritual awakening. If this man really did experience the love of God during this service, that would be a clear sign that I was safe in his care, that he was a man who was open to God, capable of leading me on my own path to the divine. A man I could continue to grow with.

A smile came to my face when I saw Father Manning. He was dressed head-to-toe in white, and a large wooden cross hung from his neck. He looked smart and so Irish, and radiated the love of God as he made his way down the aisle to bless the parishioners in the opening prayer.

I knew this service was a good choice for Tony because Father Manning was more intellectual and less flamboyant than some other priests I had seen over the last few months. I knew Tony wouldn't go for seeing people "slain in the spirit" or speaking in tongues, so this Mass was safer, more accessible for him.

Father Manning performed the ritual of the Catholic Mass as usual; the only evidence of a deeper spirituality was that people were occasionally raising their hands in the air as if they were reaching out to God in heaven.

I joined in, raising and waving both hands. Reluctantly, Tony raised his hands too. As our eyes met, I saw in him a genuine longing for a higher power, but I could also see that he was still wearing his psychiatrist's hat and skeptically asking himself what was really going on here.

By contrast, I felt receptive, open, engaged. Tony just looked stunned. I wondered how he was really processing all this. Was he seeing it through the filter of his clinical mind? As my doctor, was he grappling with it so he could figure out how to further help me? Or was he enduring it because he was fascinated by me and wanted something more?

After a few minutes, hundreds of hands were waving in the air praising God. I turned to Tony, and this time, I was the stunned one: He was in a complete state of rapture. His hands were high in the air like mine, and there was a look of peace and joy on his face that I'd never seen before. It was as though everything inside him had been emptied and he was filled with a golden light calming every cell of his body.

Now I knew for certain that God was actually working between us. The sign I'd been waiting for had finally appeared. *Tony must be the healer who is the answer to my prayers.*

The service ended, and the crowd began to exit the church. Tony and I were quiet as we walked into the star-filled night. The sky was crackling with anticipation, and the breeze was whispering "yes."

Tony seemed to be walking on air. My stride was more grounded because I'd already had the mystical experience of what we call God. When we climbed into his car, Tony draped himself over the steering wheel as though he were made of warm honey. "This is *not* supposed to be happening," he said. "This is *not* supposed to be happening," he murmured over and over.

But there was no denying it: Something *was* happening.

Then Tony turned to me looking bewildered. "What do you want me to do now?" he asked, peeling himself off the wheel.

For a moment, I said nothing. What if there really was a God and he was working through my doctor? Could Tony's experience be the fusion of the psychological and the spiritual that I was hoping for? Could this bring forth the complete healing I craved so desperately?

I looked into Tony's eyes and felt his longing for me. I knew what he wanted. In that moment, all I wanted was to make him happy. I said, "I want you to kiss me."

He quickly leaned toward me and pressed his lips against mine. In that moment, I knew an agreement was unfolding between us, but my lips were indifferent to it. I couldn't even open my mouth. Finally, we pulled apart.

I scanned my body. I felt strange, numb.

Across from me, in the driver's seat, Tony looked enrapt. He smiled. His eyes glimmered. Normally, they were heavy with the weight of his patients' problems, but tonight, his pupils were like radiant, warm pools. I sensed his pulse quickening. This was the spark, the aliveness I had always wanted for him.

He drove me back to the mall and to my car. It was getting late, and I had to get home and not worry my parents. As I drove off, I could see his whole being glowing with happiness and wonder. I was thrilled to see my beloved doctor so happy.

As I made the twenty-five-mile trip back home, I noticed that the stars above were sparkling brighter than usual. I had done my soul's duty to bring my doctor to God. The deal was sealed. Whatever transpired next must be blessed and ordained!

The Rape of Persephone

But no one, either of the deathless gods or mortal men, heard her voice.

~ 13 ~

Two weeks after attending the Brennan Manning service, I felt breezily optimistic sitting beside Tony in his Fiat as we wound our way through the Blue Ridge Mountains headed toward his farm. The surrounding woods, not far from Shenandoah National Park, were ablaze with the reds, oranges, and yellows of autumn. In the distance, the sun sank toward the cerulean peaks, bathing the view before us in shimmering twilight.

A few days before, Tony and I had been in session, talking about the mystical realm and the transcendence of connecting with nature when he confided how much he enjoyed sitting by the bubbling stream on his farm.

"I just sit beside it, listen to the rolling water, and it's as if all my worries just float away," he said. "You really should come to the farm, Carrie. It's so beautiful. I know you'd enjoy it. It would be great to take a break from your family tension for a while. You can sleep there—I have four bedrooms—or at Mary Catherine's farm a few miles away. She'd love to take you horseback riding."

Escaping Frederick had been a cinch. I told my parents I was going away for the weekend with some college friends. After everything that had happened after his first invitation a few months ago, I didn't want to worry them—or get Tony into hot water. I met him in the Hood College parking lot after he'd wrapped up the day's appointments, and we left around 6 p.m.

I just knew I was going to love this place that Tony called "heaven on earth." I imagined a deeply, soulful experience with my doctor at his farm—long, intellectual talks about God and nature, the links between the emotional and spiritual realms, where therapy ends and God's will begins. I was hooked on sharing these deep musings with my sensitive doctor. After all, he understood what inspired me better than anyone else. I was also really excited about riding horses again. I loved horses. What a great retreat! I thought of my suitcase in the trunk and hoped I'd brought the right things. I'd packed my jean jacket, some sweaters for cool morning hikes, my old boots, and my tan corduroy blazer and plaid skirt, in case we went to church or out to dinner while we were there.

Tony and I chattered nonstop about school, my future, and his son. Then, he confided that he had sold some land near D.C. for a charming sum, which was how he could buy his large farm. A big grin spread across his face.

"Carrie, when it comes to investing, I just seem to have the Midas touch."

I thought about how I had only a hundred bucks in the bank. My family had never given much importance to making money. We seemed to do okay on Dad's military retirement and his salary as a juvenile corrections social worker. I suddenly realized how little I knew about finances, and it occurred to me that it might be good for Tony to teach me.

Night descended, and we sat in silence as the Fiat's headlights pierced the darkness. As we neared a remote turnoff, I sensed nocturnal animals stirring in the woods. I imagined the deer, raccoons, and mountain lions that must be only yards from the road. Now my stomach was queasy. Was it the winding road, the thought of the animals, or something else?

Tony turned down a back road that took us more deeply into the forest. Tree branches stretched overhead, blocking out the starlight. I felt as though we were headed to the middle of nowhere. At that moment, it struck me how much I needed to trust Tony, because now I had no choice. Next, he turned onto an even narrower road, and I heard the crunch of gravel under the tires. A rusty gate loomed in the headlights. He stopped. We were here.

Tony turned off the ignition and stepped out to open the gate as two dogs came bounding toward us, barking and desperately wagging their tails. Tony told me that Kissie and Moose were "just country dogs" that hung out at the farm while he was away.

"Who takes care of them when you're gone?" I asked, petting Kissie and trying to calm her down while she jumped on me repeatedly.

"Aw, these guys? They're survivors. They know how to fend for themselves," he said, scratching Moose's head. Moose was smiling, his pink tongue lolling as he panted. Growing up, we had had dogs too, but we cared for them like part of the family. It was hard for me to accept the idea of someone's leaving these two alone for a week at a time without any food or fresh water. It seemed like neglect, but I didn't say anything.

With the gate unlatched, we jumped back in the car and eased up the lane to the two-story, brick country house, with the dogs yelping and racing along beside us. Once Tony parked, he swept delightfully into the trunk as if dancing on air, gathering our overnight bags. I looked around. Save for a single outdoor light, it was pitch black out here. I knew his daughter Mary Catherine's farm was nearby, but I strained to see it—or anything, for that matter. Tony had told me his place was outside Front Royal, but I couldn't see town lights in the distance. I heard crickets chirping in the autumn stillness. It occurred to me that I had no idea where I was.

Tony unlocked the front door, motioned me inside, and set down our bags. He flipped on a dim light revealing a small kitchen, but otherwise, the house was dark and icy. It smelled dusty and stuffy, as though no one had been here in a long time. I waited for Tony to give me a tour, or at least show me where the bathroom was. Instead, he set to building a fire in the woodstove at the center of the living room. I tried to peer out a window, but it might as well have been painted black. I wondered where the phone was. Then I wondered why I was thinking that. Who did I want to call anyway? I was already with the person I trusted most on Earth. I rubbed my palms together to ward off the chill.

Soon, the fire was burning bright—the only light in the living room. Tony dashed off to the kitchen while I stood there nervously wondering what to do next. I looked around. The place was humble and simple, and the furnishings—what I could see of them anyway—were rustic, bare bones. It was nothing like his stylish, professional office.

He returned with something red and plastic in his hand. It took me a few seconds to realize what it was: a bong full of pot. He flicked a Bic lighter and took a deep hit. "Here," he coughed a little, handing it to me. "Try some. It always helps me relax on the weekends."

Reluctantly, I took the bong, then awkwardly inhaled. I started coughing wildly, and felt as if I couldn't stop. He brought me a cool glass of water. I drank.

I remembered the last time I had smoked dope. It wasn't good. I'd had a few bad experiences in high school and college, and the drug always made me feel stupid.

"Oh boy, Tony," I said, shaking my head. "I *never* do well on pot. It makes me paranoid, foggy-brained . . . really out of it."

"This cannabis is different, Carrie" he said confidently. "It's home-grown on the farm, more pure," he assured me. "It's highly unlikely to spark a bad ride. Here, have some more."

I was surprised that my psychiatrist was growing his own marijuana and now urging me to get high with him. Since I hadn't felt any effect yet, I took a bigger, longer hit, then another. I just wanted to be relaxed and act natural. Plus, didn't my doctor know what was best for me?

In a few moments, I felt my thoughts shifting into a lower gear. Where was Tony? At that moment, he emerged from the darkness with a glass of white wine for me.

"I don't drink anymore since giving up booze years ago, but here, you might enjoy this."

I watched the green glass gleam in the firelight.

I drank some wine. At least, I think I did. My head was swimming. It felt too light, as though it was a helium balloon that might float off my shoulders to the ceiling. I reached for something to steady myself. It felt like the back of the kitchen chair. If I could just sit down for a minute . . . and everything went black.

The next thing I knew, Tony was kissing me, then undressing me, while leading me to the couch. My sluggish brain couldn't think of what to say or do. My body felt like a limp rag. I was shocked and scared. Was something wrong with him? This man didn't feel like my doctor. Was there something wrong with me? His lust for me was uncontrolled and primal. I couldn't fight him here, sixty miles from home in some remote valley. I might as well surrender. Maybe Tony was right, and I had been denying my unconscious sexual appetite. My thoughts spread out as I tried to connect the dots. What was happening?

He was fascinated with my body, and the words he spoke were lewd and raw. The only time I had heard such language was when I watched a porn film once with a college boyfriend. No one had ever talked to *me* like that. Tony made his final move on me sexually, and my body responded in a way I had never experienced. It was as if it was disconnected from my emotions. I was horrified. And the drug was wearing off.

I sat up in a flash and tried to cover myself with my shirt. "What are you doing?!" I blurted out. "You're my therapist! This isn't supposed to be happening!"

"What are you talking about?" Tony's voice was cold, his eyes colder. "You were totally into it. I didn't rape you," he said indignantly.

Held Captive in the Underworld

Gone were the life and light Persephone had radiated in the world above. Coldness fell over the land. Those left behind mourned her loss, desperate to know what had become of the goddess of springtime.

~14~

I couldn't remember the rest of the weekend. I couldn't even remem- ber how I got home. Now it was another mundane Monday night at the Tansey house, and I stood at the kitchen sink peeling potatoes while my mother thawed pork chops in the microwave.

"I think we have some applesauce in the fridge. Can you grab it, Carrie?" Mom asked. "That will be yummy with the pork chops—especially if I manage to overcook them again," she giggled, poking fun at herself.

I tried to act normal as I searched the fridge, even though a vague sense of nausea permeated my entire body. Why had I smoked that pot? I didn't know what to think about what had happened with Tony and me last weekend. Did I want that? He certainly did.

I plunked a peeled potato into the pot and picked up another one. Scrape, scrape, scrape. The idea of being Tony's lover filled me with dread. Yet my body had responded to his touch in a way it never had done with other boyfriends. How could my body react as it did when my mind was repulsed? Was that the pot? The wine? Or did I really have this repressed sexual appetite he said I did? As if we were in session, I could hear Tony's voice inside my head for the umpteenth time, insisting that my uptight upbringing had really "fucked me up."

Well, I sure felt fucked up right now. I could never tell anyone about this. No one would believe me anyway. It was my fault. I had misread the cues. Tony and I could talk this through at my next appointment. Another wave of nausea washed over me.

I had no appetite for the meal Mom and I had prepared. I shuffled my way to the dining room where my dad, brother Bob, and sister Polly sat waiting. Mom followed, placing the serving dishes on the table, just as she did every night at six o'clock.

Dad sat at the head of the table, with Polly and me on either side of him. He grasped our hands in his, and the rest of the family followed suit.

"Bless us, O Lord, and these thy gifts, which we are about to receive from thy bounty, through Christ, Our Lord, Amen," he said. Dad gave my hand a big squeeze, released it, then boomed, "Hey Bob, please pass the applesauce."

Dad turned to Polly. "How was school today?" he asked, as the blue-flowered Corning Ware casserole dish floated his way.

"Good, Dad, we're studying about the signers of the Declaration of Independence, and I can't wait to start my project on Benjamin Franklin, the most intriguing of all of the signers," Polly said, her curly brown bob bouncing as she speared a pork chop, placed it on her own plate, then passed the platter to Bob.

"Well, Carrie, you're awfully quiet tonight," Dad said, giving me a penetrating look.

Crap, was it that obvious?

"Yeah Dad, I'm tired, and I have a lot of homework to do."

"Well now, don't burn the candle at both ends, Carrie. You were away all weekend, and now you're paying the price."

"I know, Dad, I know," I said, staring at my plate.

Did I know? Why couldn't I remember what had happened after Friday night? I replayed my last memory, yelling at Tony, "You're my therapist! This isn't supposed to be happening!" Another wave of nausea flowed through me, and I clenched my teeth to keep from throwing up.

"Well, Carrie, you can't expect to do well at Hood College if you're gone from home so much."

"Dad, I *know*! I want this more than any of you. Goddammit!" I yelled, dropping my fork onto my plate with a clang.

Dad lurched backward, eyes wide, as if he'd been blasted by a strong wind. Mom's mouth dropped open, but no sound emerged. Bob's head jolted up from his plate as he quickly looked to Dad for direction. Polly gasped, applesauce squirting from her mouth. I threw my napkin down on the table and ran from the room, up the stairs, and into my bedroom, slamming the door behind me.

Shit! I should have listened to my parents. Now Dad's voice echoed in my head: "What are his plans while you're there? No, honey, this is highly unusual."

They would be furious with me if they knew I'd snuck out to be with Tony. I couldn't tell anyone what had happened. This had to stay between me and Tony, or it was all over—my therapy, his career, my life.

I lay down on my bed, surrounded by my textbooks. I put my hands on them. They were real. My plans were real. I would excel. I would not become paralyzed by depression as I had been at Virginia Tech. I would finish college no matter what. No one needed to know about what happened three days ago. That was the past. My doctor was my ally, my mentor, my friend. He would get me through this.

With my feet on the floor and my hands on my books, I grounded and comforted myself. These books were my way out. My studies were my way out.

I shook my head. I felt a large, dark hole open up inside my belly as I felt myself falling, going down into a void where there was no sound, no light, nothing to hold on to. In the void, there was no God, no Tony, no family, no me. My feet on the floor and my hands on my books steadied me.

I am a good student, and I am still here.

I picked up my anthropology book and used all my will to focus my thoughts on it. I *would* succeed at this. The dark void in my belly rumbled, and my mind pushed it back, steadying me. The nausea and the pull of the abyss subsided. Carrie The Student shut out everything but the words on the paper. Into the world of cultural anthropology I dove.

As I was leafing through chapters, the used textbook suddenly flipped out of my hands onto the floor. When I picked it up, it fell open to a passage highlighted in pink by the previous owner:

"In all human societies, there have always been individuals who have acquired religious power, usually in solitude and isolation, when the 'Great Spirit,' 'the Power,' or 'the Great Mystery' was revealed to them. These persons became the recipients of certain gifts, such as healing or divination. Upon returning to society, they were frequently given another kind of religious role, that of the shaman."

I felt a flutter inside at the thought of God, or the Great Spirit, working through shamans throughout the course of human history. Was God working through me in my relationship with Tony? I remembered the night at church when he had seemed to awaken to the light of God within him. My memories of Friday night seemed to dim.

I silently prayed: "Dear God . . . Great Spirit . . ." (I liked the way "Great Spirit" sounded), "Please reveal to me what you would have me do about Tony. What am I to do about this man I love but I'm not supposed to be with? This man who just showed me a part of himself that I don't like?"

"Carrie, I need to talk to you." I jumped as Dad walked through my bedroom door. *Jeez, couldn't he knock?*

I had complained about this habit of his to Tony, and now I heard his voice in my head: "Your family seems to have poor boundaries. Maybe you can put a lock on your door. This will support your sense of being separate, your individuation."

"Is everything okay?" Dad's voice penetrated my reverie. He stood at the end of the bed staring down at me with a stern look on his face. "Goodness, I don't like that kind of language at the dinner table. I don't like that kind of language any time."

His eyes looked concerned, searching for the daughter he used to know.

"Honey, you just seem so moody lately. Is everything going okay in therapy? I know it's probably hard to be in therapy while you live at home. Please, just don't shut us out."

I looked into his teary blue eyes and thought of Tony counseling me to distance myself from my family's struggles—after all, they weren't mine—and just say "fuck it." Dad was so square, worried about me cussing when I was twenty-one years old. He was so out of touch.

Guilt welled up in my gut. I didn't want to be disrespectful to my father, but he couldn't be more different from my doctor. How could Dad possibly teach me how to function in modern life? I mean, grace at every meal? No cussing? Who did he think we were? The Waltons?

I felt myself grow cold toward Dad. My parents had never taken genuine interest in my studies. If Dad was so interested in my well-being, why wasn't he asking me what I was studying now? Because he didn't care. Right now, I just wanted him out of my room.

"It's okay, Dad. I'm sorry I said that. I'm just tired."

"Yes, it's important to get rest with the heavy course load you're carrying."

My body bristled with anger. Why was he so patronizing? Hadn't I been an honor student every quarter for the past three and a half years? He was treating me like a kid. Tony was right. My parents *were* fostering my dependency.

"Dad, I know. You don't have to tell me. Remember, I'm a great student."

"Okay, well, just remember, no profane language in our house."

I wanted to stand up on my bed and yell at the top of my lungs, "Jesus Christ, what difference does it make?" but that would only prolong the hassle. "I've got to study now," was all I said as I focused my eyes on my book.

He paused a minute before quietly saying, "Okay," and left, shutting the door behind him. I took a deep breath, relieved to be alone again with my thoughts and my books. I read until bedtime and proudly checked off all my assignments on the syllabuses.

As I switched off the beside lamp, the void beckoned me. The darkness, the emptiness—its call was almost as strong as the call to the light.

~ 15 ~

The next day, I got to my anthropology class in time to snag a choice seat up front as the tiny East Indian professor was hooking up the movie projector. I had two classes this morning, then my first session with Tony since the incident. I dreaded it. I felt the dark void's presence in my belly trying to snatch me into its nothingness. I pressed my feet more firmly into the floor. Keep it together, Carrie. Focus.

The professor led a short discussion on the importance of exploring a society's religion as part of understanding its culture, and then she asked:

"Does anyone know what the oldest religion on the planet is?" I struggled to stay present and alert. What would Tony say about my hysterical reaction last Friday? Should I blame it on the pot? I was so embarrassed.

"Shamanism is the oldest religion on the planet, various forms of it arising at the same time in different areas of the world without contact between tribes," she answered. "When you think how widespread it remains today, it's almost as if it is *the* religion of the human psyche."

She turned off the lights and flipped on the old video clip, which crackled with age before erupting into the hypnotic, all-encompassing sound of beating drums. I forgot about everything else as I was transported to a scene of indigenous people dressed in feathers, beads, and animal masks dancing around a large fire. It was if all my classmates, my teacher, the desks had suddenly receded into the background while earthy, colorful people stepped out of the screen into the room. Their voices chanted as the medicine man worked his magic by shaking rattles and waving a bundle of burning sage over the body of a young woman laid out on a blanket beside the fire. Bright eyes shone through the shaman's mask, piercing the darkness of the night, suggesting an unseen power at work as the healing ceremony went on. The colors, the textures, the sounds spoke to places deep inside me that nourished my senses and my soul. Within me, a little speck of light flickered in the midst of the dark void.

"Not everyone can become a shaman," the narrator explained. "It's a terrible experience to survive the calling, and, thus, one should not wish to be a shaman. Often, a person will become severely mentally or emotionally ill during the calling. The calling is not a request but rather a divine command."

I sat there transfixed as the documentary continued, "One may be raised in a Christian family that rejects the path of the shaman, but to ignore the call would be a fatal mistake," said the narrator. "Surviving the call is what gives the shaman the experience needed to begin healing others."

In that moment, I wondered if shamanism was a better fit for me than the Christian path. I imagined Jesus as a long-haired shaman sitting with me and the others around the fire. Was this what I had been looking for? Was I meant to use my hands to heal others just like the early Christians? Or was I more suited to journeying into the underworld as a female shaman with my rattles and drums? What was healing anyway? This path seemed more real, more complete, more accepting than what I saw in the church. The words "I am a shaman" welled up from the depths of my soul and flowed behind my eyes across the screen of my mind.

The professor stopped the video and flipped on the lights. The words of the narrator echoed in my head: "One may be raised in a Christian family that rejects the path of the shaman, but to ignore the call would be a fatal mistake."

My true path was finally revealing itself: Catholic . . . Christian . . . artist . . . psychologist . . . shaman. Good grief, my majoring in psychology was enough of a stretch for my family. How could I tell them I think I'm *a shaman*?

I could hear Dad sipping on his Manhattan and saying, "Of all the lame-brained, kooky ideas you've ever come home with, Carrie, this one takes the cake."

What *was* a shaman anyway? After class, I quietly roamed the stacks of books in the college library before finding an old dusty text on the top shelf in the anthropology section. The lights were dimmed by the large, dark cases of books, and I squinted to read *Shamanism: Archaic Techniques of Ecstasy* by Mircea Eliade. "A shaman is an intermediary or messenger between the human world and the spirit world. Shamans treat illness by mending the soul."

A shaman mends the soul . . . the soul . . . the soul. I'd never heard Tony talk about the soul, only the mind. I continued leafing through the book and taking in the photographs of the beautiful, shining faces of these mystic healers. They radiated peace and wisdom.

So many of the Christian women I had been spending time with didn't seem very comfortable with darkness, their bodies, or the Earth and all its wisdom. As lovely and sincere as they were, my Christian friends presented me with carefully selected, contained boxes and approved colors, but shamanism offered a full, exquisite palette. The artist in me sensed the truth of shamanism: the beauty, the darkness, the animals, the rattles, the drums, the Earth, the caves, and altered states of consciousness.

As I closed the book, I realized this was way too trippy to get into while I was still living at home. "I bet Christ was a shaman," I thought, knowing that if I said this out loud, I'd surely get my ass kicked out of church. Yet it all fit: He was a healer, a man of the people, he journeyed alone in the desert, then into the darkness of the tomb. He died but then re-emerged, stronger, renewed, filled with light.

With lunch and the day's classes behind me, I walked across campus to Tony's office. I thought of the night we had kissed after the Mass in Gaithersburg. Everything felt so pure then, so blessed. That was a little more than two weeks ago. How could this be the same man who had taken advantage of me Friday night? It must have been the pot that made everything so dark, so disturbing. I longed to go back to that night at the Brennan Manning service and believe once more that the divine was at work in our lives, but I didn't know how. Could we start over? Somehow, seeing the shaman at work on the video had made me think there was an even larger truth about man and God than what I had experienced through Catholicism. The concept of shamanism showed me that things could be dark, and colorful, and out of the box, and there was still hope; things could be healed. I could be healed. There had to be a way Tony and I could heal whatever had happened last weekend.

I opened the door to his building and saw him walking down the hallway, turning the corner toward the restroom. He hadn't seen me. I walked down the hall and stepped into the warm, comforting office that had become my second home, and felt myself unwind. I sat down in my usual space on the couch and felt my feet on the floor. I sensed the expanse of the void in my belly but also the energetic shift in my mind, stimulated with fresh ideas and visions from my enriching class this morning. My world was opening up, and last weekend was part of my opening. Even though I felt darker, heavier, and even a little dirty from all of it, I also felt a bit wild like the shaman in the movie. My days of being the Catholic girl praying for blessings were no longer. I was now entering a phase of being a woman in the world, and my doctor, who loved me, would be my guide.

Upon entering the office, Tony jumped at the sight of me. "Oh, I didn't see you come in! You startled me." His face immediately softened into a big, wide grin. "How are you?"

I could feel my body sigh with relief. *He is here, and all will be well again. My heart will trust him.*

"Maybe next time you come to the farm, we can go during the day, and we can be sure you get a horseback ride," he said. "I have so much to show you there."

I said nothing. I had nothing to say. I had to believe him. I was already a changed person, and my grace-saying, no-cussing family would never understand me now.

"I just saw this amazing movie on shamanism," I said. "Shamans travel through the darkness to retrieve lost souls. Did you know that?"

Tony's face glowed. "You are so amazing. You are so curious. Please, tell me more."

I launched into a description of the documentary and what I experienced while watching it, and as I did, I could feel the room open up to the world beyond, and I could see myself looking down upon us in our conversation as if I were part of the divine. Just then, everything seemed so right.

"Maybe I'm a shaman," I said, giving Tony a spontaneous wink. I surprised myself at how natural that felt.

"Ah yes, I always thought you'd make a great psychologist," he said. "And as I promised way back in the spring, my corporation will fund your education if you'll agree to work for me after graduation."

We sat there in silence for a moment, but our communication was thorough nevertheless. My training as a therapist, as a healer, perhaps as a shaman was calling to me, and he was part of it. We would not speak about that Friday night. I had classes to take and a degree to finish.

I felt the dark shame in me dissolve as he looked into my eyes. He seemed to forgive me for my intense reaction, and I forgave him for all that occurred—even the things I didn't remember. In that moment, an even deeper bond was forged between us—a bond forged by a secret that must be kept at all costs.

~ 16 ~

Tony greeted me at the door of his office building, this one in Langley Park, with a warm smile. I pulled off my mittens and shoved them in my purse. The semester was nearly over, and my finals-week schedule meant I could see him only on Thursday, the day he was always in Langley Park. So instead of meeting in Frederick as usual, I'd driven the family station wagon to this little burg on the outskirts of Washington.

Once I was inside, he swiftly opened another door to a large, light-filled room with taupe carpet and bunches of white pillows scattered on the floor. "I thought we'd meet in here today. This is our group room. Make yourself comfortable," he said, taking off his shoes.

I slipped off my shoes too and plopped down on the floor. Images of patients sitting around Tony, lotus-style, drifted through my imagination. He knew so much and had helped so many people. In that moment, I felt lucky that he gave me his undivided attention. He saw something in me that no one else did.

"I didn't know you worked with groups, Tony."

"Well, I don't so much anymore, but I used to lead a lot of groups, psychodynamic and psycho-educational, especially when I was working in the addictions field."

He sat down close to me. "Today, instead of our usual talk session, I thought I would show you a way of deeply relaxing, reducing anxiety."

I wondered who else was in the office suite. I tuned my ears toward the door, straining to hear any voices. It was quiet. I felt a twinge of anxiety shoot into my stomach, and my head became light.

"First, you lie down and make yourself comfortable," he said, demonstrating.

"See how I'm tucking my tailbone under, relaxing my pelvis and letting my toes turn outward?" Tony said with his eyes closed. I was interested but not entirely convinced. How would lying on the floor, even on this soft carpet, reduce my anxiety?

"Just grab that pillow and come lie here beside me," he urged.

I felt self-conscious but didn't want to give myself away.

"Um, I'll just observe you," I said, pulling the pillow beneath me and assuming the lotus position. "After all, you're the expert," I said with a smile.

He grinned. I was glad he hadn't pushed the lying-down part.

"Complete relaxation opens the door to altered states of consciousness," Tony went on. "I actually had the experience of floating in a Lilly isolation tank. Dr. John Lilly is a genius—pioneering the nature of consciousness, the influence of sensory deprivation, and the mind-expanding nature of psychedelic drugs. I floated there on my back, naked, in complete darkness. It was like being in the womb."

I felt flushed at the idea of Tony naked. The thought had never occurred to me before. I didn't want to think about it now.

"The silence amplified my thoughts," he went on. "I got a deep sense of knowing what conceptions of myself had been instilled by my mother, by my father, by Catholicism. I got much more clear on how I had been trained to think and feel. It was liberating. You would probably love the experience. Oh, there is so much to teach you!"

With his eyes closed, Tony continued talking. As much as I wanted to hear more about his fascinating mystical experiences, I looked at my watch. It was almost five o'clock. Lately, our sessions had been lasting as long as three hours. I knew Mom and Dad expected me home by eight. I had told them I might run some errands after my session, which wasn't true. I just wanted to make sure I had plenty of time to meet with Tony.

My stomach rumbled. Tony's ears seemed to prick up, though he stayed prone.

"Hungry? We're about done anyway," he said. "What say I take you out for Chinese after this?"

My stomach tightened with more than just hunger.

"Tony," I said gently, feeling nervous but knowing I had to get this off my chest. "I enjoy our time together so much. I love learning from you, and, well, none of my professors would be so frank with a student about the clinical uses of psychedelics and things like that . . . ."

"Yes?" he said, sitting up, his deep blue eyes penetrating mine. I felt my resolve wilting but took a deep breath and pressed on.

"I just . . . I just don't think you should be billing my parents for these extra-long sessions now that we have . . . um, another kind of relationship."

He stood and brushed the dust off his trousers. "What?" He gave me what I thought was a dismissive look—the kind he gave me when he thought I was being uptight or in denial. "I disagree. I don't have any trouble billing your parents because of all the ways I'm helping you."

He walked into his adjoining office, and I followed. Then he grabbed his sport coat from the hook by his desk and slipped it on.

He looked me and wiggled his eyebrows. "So? Chinese sound good?"

Tony always got a huge kick out of my voracious appetite for and endless curiosity about foreign cuisine, I thought to myself as we walked behind the building to his Fiat. And he knew I loved kung pao chicken.

He drove leisurely up University Boulevard, cut over East-West Highway to Connecticut Avenue, then headed into D.C. Soon, we were cruising amid the sparkling lights of DuPont Circle. Now, a rush of excitement replaced my initial apprehension. There were so many fascinating restaurants. "Wow! Indian food, Ethiopian, Thai—it looks like this part of town has everything!"

"I'm taking you to a special place I just know you'll love."

He drove a couple more blocks, turned, then parked. We entered a building with an ornate facade resembling an imperial palace. The lights were dim as we came upon a lighted pond full of shimmering orange koi, emerald-green bamboo, and pink lotus blossoms. Looking to the dining room beyond, my gaze fell on a glistening fountain topped with a porcelain sculpture of Guanyin, the Buddhist goddess of compassion. Tony giggled as he saw my eyes grow wide.

"Dr. Romano, your table is ready," said a lovely, young Chinese woman, gesturing for us to follow her through the exquisite dining room portioned off by jade and mother-of-pearl screens. "Here you are. Does this table look good to you?" she asked Tony while eyeing me.

She seemed to know him. I felt self-conscious. Did she think I was his daughter here for my birthday celebration? A tinge of nausea swept over me. What did other people think?

"You look so nervous," Tony said as he pulled out my chair for me and I sat down. "What's wrong, Carrie?"

"I guess I'm aware of how strange we must look together," I said, fiddling with the chopsticks absentmindedly. "I mean, you're thirty-one years older than I am."

"Oh, Carrie," said Tony, taking his seat. "Many men prefer younger women, especially by the time we enter mid-life. Look around the room. Who do you see?"

I peeked past the screen separating our table from the main dining area, and sure enough, I saw several other "couples" composed of well-dressed, obviously accomplished men who looked fifteen to twenty years older than the women they were dining with. The restaurant was just blocks from Embassy Row. I wondered if these men were foreign diplomats or politicians from Capitol Hill.

"Age doesn't matter, Carrie. You and I have such a special connection. When I look at you, I don't see a twenty-two-year-old woman. I see my soul mate."

His eyes misted over.

"I was reading an article in *Playboy* today about John Derek, you know, the Hollywood director who's married to the bombshell Bo Derek? He's thirty years older than she is."

My thoughts flashed to the movie *10* and Bo's beaded braids bouncing as she ran down the beach in her barely-there bathing suit. Many guys I had gone to college with had posters of her in their dorm rooms.

"Well," Tony said awestruck, "here is this famous, rich Hollywood director who admitted he would founder if he lost Bo." Tony's eyes twinkled as he told me more of the interview.

I was silent, but my mind was reeling. *Did he say he was just reading Playboy today? When would he do that if he was seeing patients all day? Did our relationship remind him of John and Bo Derek's? Would Tony founder if I left him? Was I really even with him?*

"So age doesn't make one bit of difference when two people are meant to be together," Tony said as my attention returned to the restaurant and the waiter placing our steaming entrees before us. The kung pao chicken smelled delicious. I watched the other patrons gracefully using their chopsticks while I fumbled with mine. Tony took a sip of his jasmine tea.

"Based on some things you mentioned last week, I know your dad needs to sell his second car, that Volkswagen Rabbit of his, and you're trying to find a way to buy it for yourself," he said.

It was true. I knew Dad wished he could just give me the car—and so did I—but with three kids in college, he couldn't afford to.

"Listen, you need a car. Your dad could use the money. Let me chip in and help you buy it from him."

Tony reached into his jacket pocket and produced a white envelope. "Here's $500 cash. I can give you another $500 next week. If you're going to start working for me in January, you'll need your own wheels. Besides, this will help you get away from your family sooner rather than later."

I remembered Tony's pledge to help me pay for graduate school and his recent offer for me to earn extra money by helping him with office cleaning and paperwork. He handed me the envelope. I counted . . . one, two, three, four, five crisp $100 bills. I'd never held this much money in my hand. I thought of my parents. They were sacrificing so much for me. Yes, I should have my own car, and yes, Dad needed to sell the Rabbit. He was asking $1,500 for it. Tony's generosity left me almost speechless.

"Okay, I'll tell Dad tomorrow."

"Just think, when you have your own wheels, you can come see me anytime," Tony said with a smile.

My heart warmed at the thought of being liberated from the Tansey house, from going most places on foot, from borrowing Mom's station wagon—while the void in my belly seemed to darken. Suddenly my head felt spacey, as if it could float off my neck. I put the envelope in my purse and put its strap over my shoulder, clutching it closely. We walked out of the restaurant into the chilly winter air.

Two nights later, I lay on my bed chipping away at the reading for my experimental psychology class. Twenty pages down, forty to go. I was reading about B.F. Skinner and his learning theory based on experiments with mice in operant conditioning chambers, or Skinner Boxes. Skinner believed that free will was an illusion. Creepy—fascinating but creepy. He also concluded that human actions were guided solely by the consequences, or lack thereof, of previous actions.

"Carrie, come to dinner!" Mom's voice trailed upstairs, piercing my concentration. It was 6 p.m. on the dot. I had lost track of time again.

I thought about the little white mice in the college's basement lab running on their tiny wheels, pressing levers to get food while we scientists recorded the factors that reinforced their behaviors. They seemed happy and healthy enough, but my conscience cringed with the knowledge that we humans were breeding them, toying with them so we could figure out ourselves.

"Carrie, did you hear me?" Mom's voice chimed in again, this time with a tinge of irritation.

"Shit," I muttered while putting my green velvet bookmark with the gold cross in place. Once it had marked my place in the Bible. Now I used it in my new Bibles—my psychology textbooks. I'd have to make dinner short. That would be my excuse: I have sixty pages to read tonight.

I hustled down the stairs to the dining room. I couldn't help but glare at my father sitting at the head of the table waiting for his wife to serve him. I felt pressure in my chest with the drudgery of this family routine. Always the same. I didn't belong here anymore. Scooting into my chair, I looked down at my tiered skirt and peasant blouse. Somehow I couldn't stand my old preppy painter's pants and docksiders these days. They seemed so confining.

"Lost in your books again?" Dad looked at me, his eyebrows furrowed.

I dreaded making small talk so much that I seldom left my room. Instead of responding, I heard Tony in my head: "You don't have to tell them everything. Individuation is separating from 'we' to 'I.' "

"Carrie, did you hear me?" Dad pressed. "I just asked if you got lost in your books again."

My brain jumped to attention as I fumbled with my napkin.

"Yes, Dad. I have sixty pages of experimental psychology to read tonight. I want to go to graduate school to be a psychologist, and I need excellent grades to get in," I said irritably as I quickly dug into my food.

"What's wrong with me asking my daughter a question?" he said. "We rarely see you anymore. You seldom leave your room, and when you do, you're gone for long stretches with your friends."

I fought back the warm flush that was rising up my neck to my face. If he only knew where I'd been. Before my parents could notice, Bob stumbled in, even later than me.

"Now Bob, you're ten minutes late for dinner," Dad admonished. "Say grace before eating. Serve yourself."

I felt anger rise from my belly into my head. *There goes Lieutenant Colonel Tansey again, turning our house into a military installation. What does it matter if someone is ten minutes late to dinner? This is our dining room, not a mess hall!*

A voice I barely recognized blasted out of my mouth before I could stop it: "Shit, Dad! Bob is twenty-four years old! Can't you let him choose if and when he wants to say grace?!"

I wished Tony were here. He would back me up: "Your parents are infantilizing Bob to avoid problems in their marriage." I heard him loud and clear.

I stood up and gave each of them a hard stare. "I can't believe you two."

Mom and Dad looked back at me with shocked, wounded eyes. Instantly, I felt guilty for yelling at them, but I didn't know what to do except leave the room.

My studies are my way out. My studies are my way out. My studies are my way out, I chanted silently with each step up the stairs. Reaching the top, I realized I felt dirty from it all and needed a bath. I stomped into the bathroom and began filling the tub.

"I can't wait to get out of here," I murmured as I slipped into the hot water. My heart was so heavy, my stomach sick with guilt. I looked down at my naked body floating there and barely recognized it as my own. I thought of Tony in the isolation tank and hoped this soak would let me connect with *my* unconscious and free me from the conditioning of *my* childhood.

I closed my eyes, only to see visions of lab mice in their cages, pressing levers in hopes of receiving pellets of food. Gradually, my shame dissolved in the steam and the water.

~ 17 ~

A hot summer breeze wafted through the house as Mom struggled with two bags of groceries, trying to shut the front door behind her. "Carrie, can you help me? It's so hot outside I'm worried the milk will spoil."

Hearing her urgency, I jumped up from the living room floor where I had been leafing through graduate school catalogues to help her unload the car from her bimonthly trip to the commissary for discounted groceries.

As I scrambled down the front stoop to the trunk of the car, the fragrant smell of the magnolia tree from the side yard filled my nasal passages, bringing back memories of many happy summers. For an instant, I recalled myself at sixteen hanging out on the porch with my high school boyfriend, listening to the crickets chirp and watching the lightning bugs flicker in the muggy summer air. A wave of nostalgia hit me as I thought of all the times I rode my bike home with my brothers and sisters after an early evening game of tennis, getting home just in time before the street lights came on. I could almost hear my sister Jody call out from the alley behind our house, "Olly olly oxen free," beckoning us back to home base after a dozen of us neighborhood kids had hidden ourselves behind bushes, garages, and cars in a fierce game of kick the can.

During one memorable game, I slid off the back end of the station wagon, narrowly escaping my older sister but tearing a three-inch gash down my leg in the process. I had been so proud that I didn't cry that night even though quite a bit of blood gushed out. Somehow it felt like an initiation. I was strong and tough and wouldn't show my pain or fear of blood in front of the neighborhood boys. I heard Mom tell Dad, "I think she's in shock," as they loaded me into the car to take me to the emergency room. The doctor thought he could avoid stitching it up by giving me a series of butterfly bandages. The next night, I had the rapt attention of the neighborhood kids as I shared my tale of needles, doctors, and the bright lights of the emergency room.

I still had the scar. Thinking about it, my warm pride quickly turned to cold, putrid shame when I remembered how Tony had recently discovered it and interrogated me: "How did you get this? Why in the world did the doctor give you butterfly bandages and not stitches? Don't you know that men don't like their women scarred? "

I defended myself. "I've always been proud of my scar. It's *my* scar. It brings back great family memories of summers in the alley behind my house."

A little light flickered in my belly at my defiance. Tony gave me his you're-in-denial look. His voice echoed in my mind: *Don't you know that men don't like their women scarred?* What a weird thing for him to say. No other guys had ever noticed the scar before, let alone said anything about it.

"Honey," Mom's voice brought me back into the kitchen where I found myself standing in front of the refrigerator putting groceries away. "I picked up some pictures today. I think your graduation photos must be in there. I want to start a new roll for the holiday. You'll be able to be with us on the Fourth won't you, Carrie? I hope so."

"I'm not sure, Mom. I was invited to a party in D.C., so I'll probably stay over." My heart felt heavy with the weight of another lie.

She was silent, but I swore I could hear her heart sink as I stacked the corn on the cob, hamburgers, hot dogs, and pickles in the refrigerator before joining her at the work island where she was rifling through a packet of photos.

"Heavens to Betsy, this is an old roll!" she said. "It's so fun to see pictures of times we've forgotten about! Here we are on Christmas Eve drinking eggnog around the tree. Oh and here, gosh, I'm so proud of this scarf that I knit for your dad. Look at it!"

I picked up the photo to see Dad's face beaming with gratitude as he wrapped the bright red scarf around his neck, the Christmas tree sparkling in the background.

"And look how cute Polly looks! She and her partner came so close to winning districts this year." I grabbed the picture from her hand to see Polly, looking vibrant in her tennis skirt and hat, radiating health and success as she posed with her partner on the court.

Where was I for all this? What kind of sister am I, not to even know Polly went to the district final? That was so important to me in high school! I don't remember that red scarf. Mom must have spent weeks knitting it.

"Oh, yes, and Easter." Mom giggled as she pointed to Polly sticking her tongue out at Tim as he proudly showed off his basket of hand-dyed Easter eggs that won him the hunt this year.

Wow. I'm not in any of these pictures. Where have I been? I used to love getting my picture taken. My head was reeling as I leafed through more photos of happy scenes and bright smiling faces: my niece's first birthday, Mom and Dad's anniversary, my aunt and uncle's visit from Virginia.

I thought back to another event when I didn't feel like having my picture taken. I had been at the farm with Tony. Again.

In his bedroom, I often felt as if I were an actress in a low light, sepia-toned, soundless movie.

This particular time, I was sitting on the bed naked. I couldn't remember how I'd gotten there. Downstairs, Tony had given me some pot. As usual, I couldn't remember how much I had smoked. Afterward, the evening quickly turned from long, deep talks about psychology and life to that other reality in his bedroom.

"Here, have some more Carrie. Please." I looked into his eager eyes and then at the red bong on the paper plate. I didn't want to disappoint him. He took a big hit, the water in the bong gurgling as he inhaled. As he handed it to me, he quickly flicked his blue plastic Bic and lit the bong for me. I inhaled once, twice. He had been telling me so much about sex lately and how healthy adults liked to experiment in many different ways. He had shown me illustrations in *The Joy of Sex* and talked about good sex as a route to happiness. I was desperate to feel happy.

Therapy certainly wasn't working anymore.

As we lay on his bed, he whispered in my ear while he rubbed my thigh, "You are so beautiful. So sexy … you simply take my breath away. What a seductress you are." His blue eyes seemed to glow with intensity and longing.

"Oh, Carrie, look what I bought today!" He suddenly jumped up and came back to the bed with a shiny, new Polaroid camera from the top of his dresser. "I would love to take some pictures of you. For those times you can't be with me, it would be thrilling to be able to look at you. Your gorgeous skin . . . your curves."

He ran his hand along my hip, and I tried to connect with my sexiness. *Let yourself feel his hand on your skin, Carrie. You have nothing to worry about . . . let go. . . .* I tried to get into the experience, but my brain seemed to float away as my body went numb.

"Here, let's have some more" he suggested again, putting the bong back in my hand. I took another long hit and felt the room swirl. *This will make it easier.* He gave me a huge, loving smile. He was happy.

I looked at the stack of *Playboy* magazines he had shown me on the top shelf of his open closet. *So many women my age get their pictures taken nude. Maybe this will help free me up. Tony says I'm gorgeous. Maybe if I follow his lead, I'll actually feel gorgeous.*

My skin seemed to melt like a puddle into the sheets. Then Tony appeared above me with the camera instructing me what to do: "Move your leg this way, now stretch your arms up, fan out your hair . . . no, that's not quite right, do this . . . ."

He pranced around the room taking pictures of me from various angles, directing me to pose this way, then that way.

I wish . . . I was . . . as . . . sexy . . . as . . . he . . . thinks . . . I . . . am. My thoughts spaced out as my mind floated away from my body . . . *Oh look, the grasscloth wallpaper in here looks just like the wallpaper in his office. Let's see, there are three vertical lines, then a space, then a few round balls of thread . . . wow . . . look how there are actually four different shades of beige in this pattern . . . so intricate . . . .*

"Now Carrie, take some of me."

My awareness slipped down the wall and returned to its place behind my eyes. I struggled to stand up.

I picked up the camera, squinted one eye through the viewfinder, and found him lying on the bed naked. I felt a twinge of revulsion. *Look at him posing . . . oh gosh . . . how could I ever tell him I don't think he's sexy at all?* I recalled Louie's blond beachcomber haircut and his strong, sculpted legs. I looked back at Tony and felt sorry for him, repulsed by his middle-aged body. *Well I guess it's cool* <u>*he*</u> *thinks he's sexy.* I dutifully pressed the red button on the camera, the picture slid out, and I put the camera down beside him.

He took the photo and placed it gently on the bed along with the five or six photos of me.

I was so crazy for Louie, so into him, but he turned out to be such a hateful jerk. Tony loves me, lusts after me, and wants to take care of me. Maybe this is what I have to settle for. If I just try a little harder, maybe I can learn to like all of this.

I felt dizzy and lay back down on the bed, quickly covering myself with the soft, ivory comforter. It was difficult to move my head from its position on the pillow. It felt like lead. Shifting my body the tiniest bit seemed to take enormous effort. Out of the corner of my eye, I saw Tony open up a small grasscloth-covered door in the wall next to his bed. It blended so well with the rest of the wall that I had never noticed it before, He pulled out a metal box, inserted the Polaroid images, and ceremoniously announced: "Carrie, just so you know, I will never leave these pictures around where anyone else can see them. See, I'll lock them up in here, just for me—and for you." He smiled slyly as he closed the lid, turned the key, and put the box back into its secret hideaway.

The photo session was just a warm-up. I knew what Tony wanted to do next. I tried to rally my enthusiasm while the void in my belly expanded.

Can't we get the rest of this over with? Besides, I can't imagine ever wanting to look at those photos again.

"Oh, here it is Carrie," Mom's voice yanked me out of Tony's bedroom and to the daylight, to the work island in the family kitchen.

"But oh my word, why is there only one picture?" Mom leaned over me. Startled, I jumped. She didn't seem to notice and went on, "I could have sworn we took a number of them. Well, now, honey, it's not your best photo, but at least we have one that turned out."

I gulped as I looked at the photo of me in my black satin graduation cap and gown. My eyes were sunken, my skin horribly broken out. I looked like someone desperately trying to look proud when, in fact, I was empty, vacant, carved out. My parents looked happy enough, but they seemed to be literally holding me up. There were no other relatives or friends.

I thought back to my high school graduation. Now *that* was a true celebration—loads of friends and family, parties, presents—but here, on the day I had worked so hard for, I looked like an emaciated shell of myself. I had always been so proud of getting my picture taken. People used to comment on how photogenic I was, and I loved squeezing in with all my siblings or a group of friends in front of the camera. Now, I wanted no pictures. There was nothing to celebrate.

~18~

Who can it be knocking at my door?
Go 'way, don't come 'round here no more.
Can't you see that it's late at night?
I'm very tired, and I'm not feeling right.

As I sped down the highway in my VW Rabbit, I turned up the radio. The words of "Who Can It Be Now?" by the new band Men at Work eerily channeled my own state of mind. Granted, it wasn't late at night, but I had to get up before dawn to commute to my summer internship in Baltimore. These days, it seemed as if I was tired all the time and only wanted to be alone.

During the hour-long drive, I felt transformed from child to adult. Weeks ago, I had landed a position with the Department of Behavioral Pediatrics at the Kennedy Institute, an affiliate hospital in the Johns Hopkins medical system. My pulse raced with the traffic as I sped up I-70, leaving the farmlands behind as I approached Maryland's largest city. I loved the feeling of steering the Rabbit amid the streaming cars moving faster and closer together. It felt as if we were all headed toward something important. Frederick—and Tony's farm, for that matter—felt stale and old, safe but stagnant. Baltimore felt vibrant and colorful, interesting and a bit dangerous.

I felt a tug at my heart as I passed the exit to the Inner Harbor. Part of me longed for a cinchy summer job by the water, selling souvenirs, eating snow cones on my breaks, listening to musicians while people milled about eyeing the historic ships—but Tony said it would be good to get clinical experience under my belt. The internship was anything but an easy, breezy summer job. If I played my cards right and excelled, though, perhaps I'd soon receive word that I'd been accepted to a five-year doctoral program in clinical psychology.

I sighed as I drove on, exiting at Franklin Street into a not-so-great part of town, East Baltimore. Traffic slowed, and I glided through the underbelly of the city toward the medical campus of one of the most venerated hospitals in the world. I parked in an inexpensive lot eight blocks away, then took a deep breath and steeled myself for the walk through a blighted neighborhood of row houses squished together, kids playing in the street, and old men hanging out on front stoops. When I saw how the people there lived in such difficult conditions, I felt guilty for being depressed, guilty that I even considered complaining about my life. Little Frederick had only a few blocks of people living like this, while Baltimore had mile upon square mile of neighborhoods steeped in poverty. I tried to stay focused on getting to work on time, making what was probably apologetic eye contact with my fellow humans. I looked down at my white puffy-sleeved top, neatly pressed seersucker pants, and white sandals. I looked so out of place. Was I even safe here? It had seemed so practical and smart to save money by parking here instead of in the pricier hospital garage, but now I wasn't so sure.

I reminded myself that I was fortunate for the opportunity, and had to get through any difficulties and just stick with it. I was proud to be working for Johns Hopkins. Sure, I was only an intern, but twenty doctors, scientists, and scholars with ties to Hopkins had won the Nobel Prize, including Torsten Wiesel, who had received the Medicine award just last year. The Kennedy Institute, where I worked, had been founded during the Kennedy Administration, a pet project of John F. Kennedy, who had an intellectually disabled sister. It served developmentally delayed children with services ranging from speech to occupational therapy.

Arriving at the building, I shook off the images of the tourists at the harbor and the poor folks of the inner city and opened the door to the beautiful, clean but antiseptic facility. Inside, I took the elevator to the second floor and made my way down the hall. I peered in the window of the wooden door to the ward, trying to conjure up a cheerful attitude. Immediately, my heart sank. Already, four patients in wheelchairs were waiting for help from me and the nurses. I took a deep breath and opened the door.

"Good morning, Katie" I said, sitting down with a nine-year-old girl with mousy brown hair whose head always leaned to the right as if she had no muscles on that side. "Uuuhhh," she moaned, seeming to recognize me. I grabbed a fresh, white washcloth from the table in front of us and wiped off the drool dangling from her mouth.

"Your breakfast will be here soon," I said perkily. "Are you hungry?"

"Uuuhhh," she replied. It was her only form of expression, but I had a feeling we were communicating.

The day nurse entered briskly, dressed in a crisp, white uniform and carrying Katie's breakfast. "Now, Katie, this young lady, um, what's your name? You may want to put on your name tag."

"Oh, sorry. My name is Carrie, Carrie Tansey."

"Yes, Carrie, the blank name tags are at the nurses' station. Please wear one at all times. After you do that, please feed Katie, and mark down her progress on this sheet." She placed the hospital meal tray on the table and handed me a shiny metal clipboard with a checklist on it, then spun away to her next duty.

"Oh and Carrie," she yelled over her shoulder, "we have three other patients here, as you can see, so you'll need to move fast to get to all of them in the next few minutes."

My hand shook with nervous energy, and I dropped some hot oatmeal on Katie's hand. I tried to gently shove the spoon in her mouth before she drooled again.

"Uuuhhh," Katie groaned as I took a second to record her successful eating behavior. I checked the categories "Food stayed in mouth" and "for at least thirty seconds" and scrawled my initials beside it.

"Great job, Katie! You're doing great!" I encouraged.

"Uuuhhh," Katie said, head lolling, mouth open, waiting for her next bite.

"Okay, let's do a few more spoonfuls. Then your mom will be here." Katie seemed to be getting it down. I got four spoonfuls in her with no drooling or spitting up. Hooray. I was happy to be able to report progress to her mother.

"Yaaa . . . Yaaa," another voice screeched out. I knew the sound: Annabelle. I turned to see the eleven-year-old trying to catapult her twisted body toward the oatmeal on her table.

"Hold on, Annabelle. I'm almost there."

Katie's mom came in and gave her daughter a big hug. "How is my beautiful girl?" Her mom looked at me, "Thank you so much for taking such great care of my precious daughter." Her eyes sparkled. How in the world did she stay so positive? Then I thought of my own mother and her endless patience with Bob, who at times frustrated the hell out of me. Guilt nagged at my conscience when I thought of how rough I had been on Mom lately.

"Uuuhhh!"

"See, Carrie?" said Katie's mother. "Katie says thank you!"

"Yaaa . . . Yaaa," Annabelle was getting more impatient.

Another nurse entered the ward to take over the feeding of Katie and the other two patients so I could focus on Annabelle. She had fallen face-forward into her oatmeal and was trying to push herself back into a sitting position, but her weak, uncoordinated arms were not cooperating.

"My, my, Annabelle, what are we going to do with you?" came a voice from the doorway as the head nurse returned and swiftly tightened the strap that kept Annabelle in her chair and then wiped the oatmeal off her face in one smooth motion. "The orderly forgot to tighten that this morning. Sorry about that, Annabelle."

"Yaaa . . . Yaaa . . ."

Annabelle seemed unfazed by the specks of oatmeal still clinging to her red hair, and opened her mouth wide, revealing the biggest tongue I had ever seen. *No wonder she keeps falling over. Her tongue must weigh a ton! Careful, Carrie, you're getting slaphappy.* I stifled a giggle as I put the spoon on her enormous tongue, then used my other hand to help her close her mouth and swallow. I thought back to my schoolwork. There was a name for that condition . . . what was it? Ah yes, *macroglossia*, congenital enlargement of the tongue, resulting in *dysphagia*, or difficulty swallowing.

"Yaaa . . ." Annabelle seemed happy with her breakfast and remained content as I marked off the appropriate categories on her behavioral checklist.

Things finally felt manageable when the head nurse returned. "We have a new patient who was just admitted last night. His name is Billy . . ."

Just then the bathroom door flew open, and a boy around ten years old with one leg longer than the other ran and hobbled toward us with his mouth wide open revealing huge white teeth while emitting the most enthusiastic sound of glee I had ever heard. His eyes met mine as he let out a boisterous belly laugh while proudly showing me his hands, which were dark and wet. Just then, the head psychology resident appeared, wearing a summer-gray sport coat, pressed jeans, and a striped red necktie. He carried himself as if he had just entered a classroom to deliver a lecture.

"Nurse, it seems our new admit will need some help," he remarked unflappably. "Please call the orderlies."

Hands outstretched, Billy lunged toward Annabelle and me, looking as though he would smear us both down, when suddenly I caught a whiff of something so horrid I nearly puked on the spot.

The hall came alive with giggles and sounds of "Yaaa . . . Uuuhhh . . ." The feeding patients' eyes were bright with interest. They seemed entertained by a stunt I was still trying to wrap my head around.

Holy shit! That was shit on his hands! And I was the last one to figure it out! I looked at the dollop of oatmeal on Annabelle's spoon and tried to inhale its warm, cinnamon aroma to cover up the stench. I swallowed, trying to hold down the contents of my stomach.

Billy, undeterred, ran over to the freshly painted, white concrete wall and smeared his hands back and forth, laughing hysterically. I tried not to barf.

"Yaaa . . . . Yaaa . . ." Annabelle, undistracted by my distress, tried to lunge herself back at her oatmeal. The strap held.

Two young orderlies in white flew through the door, past the nicely dressed resident, and grabbed Billy, who was now smearing the nurse's station window. They removed him from the room as he howled with laughter, and things began to settle back down in the Department of Behavioral Pediatrics.

What the hell? I thought I was here to feed people, but apparently I was responsible for dealing with substances from both ends of their bodies.

"Sorry about that, Miss Tansey," said the dapper resident. "Billy is our newest patient, here for encopresis."

Encopresis, encopresis. I knew that one . . . I rifled through the medical dictionary in my mind. Oh, yes: involuntary passage of fecal matter, or Latin for pooping one's pants. And Billy had his own creative touches to add with the result.

"Because we believe that Billy's behavior is socially reinforced, we must work hard to not give him any attention for his antics," the resident said. "Your job will be to ignore his bad behavior and praise his proper behavior. We'll talk about his case and how to handle him in more detail at this morning's staffing meeting."

I was too stunned to speak.

"Well, it looks like we have our work cut out for us," the resident continued. "Not only does he soil his pants, he is also a feces smearer."

As if I needed this post-doc to explain it to me. And where did he get off saying "*We* have our work cut out for us"? It looked to me as if the orderlies did the grunt work, not him. Wow, a feces smearer . . . right alongside people who couldn't feed themselves. Now that was diversity. This staff meeting was going to be really interesting.

After finishing the feedings, I headed downstairs to the conference room. Hesitantly, I opened the door, arriving late to join the twelve post-docs and a few nurses gathered around the table. Everyone was at least ten years older than me, and they all had tons of initials after their names. I felt like such a neophyte. What was I doing here? My new job was to positively reinforce the feces smearer. Was I in over my head?

One of the post-docs presented Billy's case and showed us the checklist for his assessment and treatment. "Nurses, please train the interns and other nurses to record Billy's behavior here," he explained. "He is never to be in the bathroom alone. Furthermore, two hours after every meal, prompt him to use the bathroom every twenty minutes."

The whole situation seemed so ridiculously clinical. *For Christ's sake, why not give Billy some fingerpaints? Maybe he's just working in the wrong medium! He has great comic timing, and he entertains the other patients with his happy antics.* But I couldn't bring myself to say such things. I was in a serious meeting with people I needed to impress. I couldn't shake it off, though: Billy was the most inspirational character I'd met in these depressing halls. He was so irreverent! He literally had no shame. Not like me. I thought of the darkness, the shame, the shit inside me, and wished I could exorcise it in such an expressive way. Graphs, charts, and checklists were being passed around the conference table. I pretended to look at them seriously.

At the end of my shift, I packed up my purse along with the books I had checked out on behavior modification for patients with developmental disabilities. As I turned to leave the ward, the head nurse called me back.

"Miss Tansey?" she said, "Are you familiar with our new policy?"

I shook my head.

"Due to a recent rash of robberies and assaults in the neighborhood, all personnel will be accompanied to their vehicles by security guards. This is for your protection."

A crusty, old guard with a thick East Baltimore accent walked with me the eight blocks to my yellow Volkswagen. I was grateful for his company. The elders and kids I had seen in the morning were gone—replaced by hordes of teens standing on the corners shrouded in hooded sweatshirts. In summer.

"Thank you for walking me to my car," I said when we reached it. "Tomorrow, I think I'll park in the hospital garage."

"That's a good idea, Miss," he said. "There's some rough stuff going on in this neighborhood. If you get scared in the parking garage, call security, and they'll come get you."

I thanked him again, got in the car, and immediately locked the door. Then I looked around at the dark, nearly vacant parking lot. This morning, I hadn't noticed that most of the nearby buildings had broken windows and were in various states of disrepair. Encopresis? Robberies? Assaults? Was it too late to work at the trinket shop at the Harbor?

I pulled out onto the street, my thoughts revving up with the engine. I felt the weight of responsibility for the patients who would never walk or talk. I felt heavy for myself and for my family's struggle to find a place in this world for Bob. My eyes grew wet. But just when I felt like my heart would break, Billy came crashing through my memory in all his gleeful, shit-smearing glory. This time, I let myself laugh out loud—a belly laugh that forced the tears from my eyes. Billy made me laugh down deep. He was a ray of light that cut through the dark void I carried, a place nothing else had penetrated in years.

What did it say about me that after a day in the ward, Billy—not a doctor or nurse—was my inspiration? The idea made me feel rebellious and hopelessly crazy at the same time.

They say all great comedy is born from great tragedy.

"Thank you, God," I said. "Thank you for Billy and his shit."

I flipped on the radio; the same song that had played this morning was playing again.

I've done no harm, I keep to myself
There's nothing wrong with my state of mental health
I like it here with my childhood friend,
Here they come, those feelings again!
Who can it be now?

I laughed and cried hysterically for the entire drive home.

~ 19 ~

Summer turned to fall. Fall turned to winter. Winter gave way to spring. Late one March evening, I peeked in on Mrs. Carty, an elderly woman I cared for in Frederick three nights a week. She was in her bedroom snoring softly in the flickering blue light of the television. Doc Severinsen and the boys had just blasted out the *Tonight Show* theme song, and I clicked the TV's off button just as Ed McMahon said, "Heeeeere's Johnny!"

Quietly, I closed the door and slipped down the gracious mahogany staircase, past the portraits of her family painted in oils, and into the front parlor. Her home was a massive, four-story Victorian, complete with a back staircase for the servants. Even though I could be considered "the help," I had status in her household, with my own bedroom across the hallway from hers. Officially, I still lived at home with my parents, but now, I was there less than ever. On nights like this, her housekeeper and cook were gone, and I was free to call Tony.

I picked up the receiver of her heavy, black phone and dialed his number—no speedy pushbuttons for Mrs. Carty. It had been a while since I called him, and the rotary dial made it seem even longer.

He answered mid-ring, "Hello?"

"Tony?" I said softly.

"Oh Carrie! I've been waiting to hear from you. I can't wait to see you again. When can you get away?"

"It will have to be at least next week," I explained. "I'm swamped with my new job at the University of Maryland Hospital, I've got an hour commute each way, plus office work at your place and Mrs. Carty to look after, and this week, I'm starting that medical terminology class with Kit."

Kit was a psychiatric nurse at the hospital as well as an instructor. I had told Tony about her, and it turned out they had worked together at a treatment facility years before. Tonight he didn't say anything about her. That was uncharacteristic of him, so I went on, "I think I'll have to let go of sitting for Mrs. Carty. It's too much to juggle."

He giggled softly. "Yes, your life is filling up. Just remember to make time for *me*."

"I know, I know, Tony, but there's another thing. Remember Rebecca and Susannah, the colleagues on the unit I told you about? Well, tomorrow is Friday, and they just invited me to a night on the town after work. Then I'll stay over at Rebecca's so I don't have to drive back late. She's been dying to show me her new apartment."

"A night on the town?" he said. His tone wasn't playful anymore. "I've never heard you talk this way, Carrie."

Immediately I felt dark inside. *What was the big deal? Shouldn't he be happy for me? Most of my therapy sessions, I complained about feeling isolated from my peers. I thought this was a breakthrough.*

"Umm . . . Rebecca knows of this great band playing Friday night in Fells Point . . ."

"Carrie, can I count on you to visit me next weekend?" he interrupted. "I *must* see you. Wait, I've got a better idea. Come to my office Wednesday night after work. I'll take you out to your favorite seafood place. Then you can stay over with me."

I felt the familiar heaviness in my stomach as he pitched me his plans. I was finally making friends with peers, and I wanted him to share in my happiness. Wasn't he my closest friend and confidant? In therapy, he said he understood, but now that it was happening, he just sounded resentful—as if he wanted me all to himself. I wanted to make him happy, he'd been so good to me, but I needed to be with people my own age. I felt torn. I couldn't think of anything else to say. From upstairs, Mrs. Carty called my name.

"I've got to go, Tony. I'll call you tomorrow. 'Night."

I hung up.

Late Friday afternoon, I walked down the halls of the ward, eager for five o'clock to arrive. I hadn't been this excited in years. How could the prospect of going out with a couple of girlfriends feel so magical?

Working at the University of Maryland Hospital in the Intensive Behavioral Management program was my first paid professional job. Just four months into my internship at Hopkins, a post-doc there had offered me a position in the new clinic he was heading up. Finally, a salary! Plus, U of M hospital was in a nicer, safer part of Baltimore, just minutes from the Inner Harbor.

Finally, Rebecca, Susannah, and I finished our charting in the med room, and it was quitting time. In the staff room where we kept our things, Rebecca swept her long, black hair to the side and placed her purse on her shoulder. I noticed how pretty her blue silk blouse was against her porcelain skin. Susannah looked effortless in her midi-skirt and white blouse, and its turned-up collar was so chic with her cocoa complexion and wedge haircut. She donned a short trench coat. I wondered how I must look compared with them. We walked down to the parking garage.

"Hey Carrie, let's leave your car here; parking will be tough down by the harbor," Rebecca said. "We'll come back for it later." She turned to Susannah. "Let's meet at The Horse You Came In On Saloon on Thames Street. We can have drinks there, then head to Bertha's for dinner and music."

Keys in hand, Susannah nodded and headed toward her car.

Rebecca called out to her: "Do you know the way? Just take Greene south to Pratt. Head east until you get to Broadway, then south to Fells Point."

Rebecca really knew her way around the city. How cool was that? I was always getting turned around in Baltimore. I'd never been good with directions and stuff like that. Getting in the car, I had butterflies in my stomach but tried to hide them, feeling kind of dorky that the other two were so nonchalant when this was such a big deal to me. If they asked about the man in my life, what would I say? I felt my stomach tighten. I didn't really feel like talking about Tony. And I didn't want to tell more lies.

For years, I'd been hearing about the nightlife in Fells Point and the neighborhood's checkered past. In colonial days, the waterfront district was known for sailors, privateers, and pirates—and the bars and brothels they patronized. During the War of 1812, pirates from Fells Point looted British vessels, making Baltimore and Fort McHenry enemy targets. Since then, prosperity in Fells Point had ebbed and flowed many times, but the place still hadn't completely shed its bawdy reputation. Now it was a tourist attraction.

We got out of the car on Thames Street along the waterfront, and the sea air enveloped me as I watched a large barge float by, likely loaded with seafood and whiskey for the many colonial-style restaurants and bars all around us. I could almost imagine pirates walking on these brick streets. I saw water taxis pulling up with bright-eyed tourists, hungry with curiosity whetted by the legends of Fells Point.

"Oh my God! I love this place!" I said, barely containing my enthusiasm.

"It's full of history," Rebecca said as we began walking. "In fact, I recently read that this is where Frederick Douglass, while still a slave, learned to read. Down by the docks, he offered poor boys bread as payment for teaching him."

And he went on to become an abolitionist, author, and newspaper editor, I thought. How inspiring. I looked down a side street and tried to imagine Douglass as a young man secretly practicing his writing with a piece of charcoal on wood. I could almost feel the spirit of rebellion oozing from the bricks below my feet.

"Here's the famous Admiral Fell Inn," Rebecca said as we walked by. I let out a laugh as we peeked in the window at the gorgeous wood floors and period furniture.

Tonight, my body felt light and buoyant. Rebecca was awesome. She should be a tour guide.

We walked a little farther west on Thames and stopped at an old brick row house turned tavern. A black and yellow sign hung over our heads: The Horse You Came In On Saloon. "Established in 1775," Rebecca said. "Locals just call it 'The Horse.' It's said to have been Edgar Allan Poe's favorite bar. Legend has it he was here drinking the night he mysteriously died. Bartenders swear his ghost still haunts the place."

I felt a bit of apprehension as Rebecca, Susannah, and I entered the dimly lit pub. It was already packed with happy-hour customers being served by bartenders slinging bottles of Jack Daniel's and mugs of frothy beer. I hadn't been in a bar in years. I wasn't sure if I knew how to hang out in one anymore. I couldn't even think of what to order.

"I'll have a Kahlua and cream please," said Rebecca.

"Me too," said Susannah.

"Oh, I guess I'll join you. I haven't had a Kahlua and cream since college, but what the heck? Sounds good!"

Just as I raised the glass to my lips, a tipsy man bumped into me, sloshing the cocktail all over my tailored wool skirt.

"Oh, shoot, is that dry clean only?" asked Susannah.

I took a big gulp of what remained of my drink and responded: "Well, that cinches it. I'm buying new clothes tomorrow. I thought I needed to dress professionally for work, but let me tell you what happened this morning that's making me rethink my wardrobe." Rebecca and Susannah drew closer, trying to tune out the noisy patrons.

"You know that new patient, Bobby?

"You mean the young, skinny schizophrenic?" Susannah said. "Yeah, I saw him get checked in last night."

"Well, he was assigned to me this morning, and it was my job to get him to collate papers," I went on. "He was supposed to organize a pile of about four hundred sheets of paper into ten-page stacks and staple them." The girls nodded with familiarity. It was a fairly typical assignment.

"Of course, the clinical director told me I was *not* to engage him with any conversation other than sticking to the script," I continued.

"Oh, no, I can just imagine where this is going," Rebecca said with doom in her voice.

Susannah's eyes lit up as she leaned in.

"Well, after I had repeated the line: 'Bobby, please collate the papers,' three times, and he asked me three times: 'What are you doing?' he became agitated and started talking feverishly to an invisible person. Then he turned back to me, and from less than ten feet away, he hurled the big, metal stapler right at my face."

Susannah gasped, hand to her mouth.

Rebecca rolled her eyes and shouted, "Oh God!" to the ceiling.

Two guys seated at the bar turned around for a second and stared, then went back to their conversation.

"Let me tell you, Bobby's got quite a pitch," I said. "He must have thrown that stapler fifty miles per hour. He would have made Jim Palmer proud."

Rebecca threw her head back, "Oh, shit! What happened next? You obviously made it out alive."

"Well, you see these pretty new pumps on my feet? As I dodged the stapler, one of them went flying off. I could literally see it spinning in the air as I dove out of the way. Then the orderlies charged in, grabbed Bobby, and put him in time-out. Poor guy."

I was laughing through tears. Then I started crying for real. I quickly sipped more of my drink and pretended to cough away my sudden sadness.

"I hate those scripts." Susannah said, more passionately than I had ever heard her speak before. She was usually quiet and unassuming.

I dried my tears with my bar napkin. "Man, I don't like how I treated him. I tried telling the clinical director I thought the task and the way the script ordered Bobby around was degrading, but he didn't agree. He said we needed to keep our procedures 'standardized,' and would reinforce on-task behavior only after collecting data during the baseline period."

The three of us were silent as we stirred our drinks with their red plastic straws.

Rebecca quietly commented, "Yeah, but the question is are *we* going to survive the baseline period?"

With that, we burst into hysterical laughter. I rushed to the bathroom feeling I could pee my underpants. As I adjusted my nylons and tweed skirt, I imagined the comfy stretch pants and flat shoes I'd be buying tomorrow, realizing now how much I was physically in the front lines.

I returned to the bar, where Susannah and Rebecca were paying the tab.

"Your drink is on us," Susannah said. "You got the biggest battle scar today."

Rebecca declared "Let's high-five you, Carrie, for your reaction time."

I announced, a little louder than I meant to, "But let's also high-five Bobby! Don't you love it when the clients who are supposedly 'delayed in development' demand respect in the most brilliant ways?"

They nodded. We high-fived all around, interspersed with hoots of "Go Bobby!"

Two guys who had not-so-subtly been checking us out used this as an excuse to interact and started high-fiving too. Then one of them leaned in too close and slurred in my ear, "Hi babe. Who the hell's Bobby?"

"Let's get out of here. The natives are getting restless," Rebecca declared. "To Bertha's we go for crab cakes and music!"

Back out on the colonial brick streets, we breathed in the sea air and walked arm and arm to Bertha's. Breaking the silence, Susannah asked, "Do you ever get the feeling the patients are the ones teaching us?"

"Hell yeah," I screamed, boosted by the effects of the Kahlua.

We giggled, slapped our legs, and wondered aloud how we could possibly sit through another clinical meeting straight-faced.

"Hey, maybe we should do an experiment on the director to see if we can reduce his coffee consumption through social reinforcement," Susannah proposed. "Of course, we won't tell him what we're doing. Let's see how disoriented *he* gets during the baseline phase!"

Rebecca grasped an imaginary pencil and clipboard then pretended to note, "Patient appears agitated."

I felt the tension leave my body with each raucous laugh. Our eyes twinkled as we walked along Broadway, fantasizing about new ways to liberate ourselves from the oppression of the behavioral management clinics.

Along with the sea air, I felt as if I was inhaling normality . . . friends . . . the smell of Maryland crab cakes . . . music . . . laughter . . .

I love Baltimore. I love these women. For one beautiful night, the void deep inside me was filled with light, and I felt like I was Carrie again.

We arrived at Bertha's just as the band finished setting up. I looked at my watch. Crap, it was already nine. I'd told Tony I'd call him.

The band started playing, and we jumped to our feet and began to boogie.

I'll call him in the morning . . . and with that thought, I felt my body sway to the music.

A few nights later, I was in Baltimore again, but this time, it was more low-key. I was at Kit's place after the medical terminology class. She had kindly offered me her guest bedroom so I wouldn't have to make the late-night drive back to Frederick, and we had quickly settled into a cozy little routine.

I loved spending time with this wise woman, and cherished our talks. We'd already established that she and Tony knew each other, and I mentioned that I worked at his office part-time. One evening, while sipping vanilla tea, I spilled the beans that I was involved with a much older man.

Without missing a beat, she asked, "Is it Tony?"

I felt my face turning red. "How did you know?"

"Well, he's the only man you ever talk about." Her eyes narrowed. "Be careful of him. He's bad news."

I felt every cell of my body shake with her admonition, and said no more about it.

That night as I lay down to sleep, I could feel a clear light in the distance beckoning me. Was it possible that I felt so terrible emotionally because of Tony? What if I wasn't as crazy as I thought? What if I didn't need him?

With this awareness, I felt the heavy cloak of depression that had shrouded me for so long slip off my shoulders. I drifted off to sleep, imagining myself dancing in the streets with Frederick Douglass and the pirates of Fells Point.

~20~

The weekend was approaching, and finally, I would have a chance to see Tony at his farm outside Front Royal. At home in my bedroom, I opened the closet door and frowned. Now that it was late autumn, I'd need warmer clothes than last time, and it would probably be even cooler in the mountains—which translated to bulkier sweaters. Guess I had better use the bigger suitcase. I laid it on the bed and opened it.

Not sure of what to pack, I left the closet door open and turned my attention to my white, Samsonite train case. I might as well start with the essentials. I placed it on the dresser, flipped open the silver latches, raised the lid, and lifted out the compartmentalized tray on top. Since I was spending alternate weekends with Tony, I'd let so much stuff accumulate in my overnight bag that I wasn't sure what was in here anymore. I picked up a shiny, dark green matchbook with gold lettering: "Boar's Head Inn." Oh yeah, that was from our weekend in Charlottesville. The inn was gorgeous, but that night, I'd felt more anxious than ever once we smoked some dope and had the kind of sex he liked. Ick. I plunked the matchbook in the nearby trashcan.

Also stashed in the tray were the pearl necklace and earrings he'd given me for graduation. I should never have tossed them in here so carelessly, I thought, putting them back in my jewelry box where they belonged. I picked up a red silk necktie, the one he had tied me up with that night. How did this wind up here? Oh, never mind. I tucked it in one of the train case's fabric side pouches. I lifted the square lid of the tray's center section, and what I saw made me cringe: the pristine pink compact that held my diaphragm. Sure, I didn't want to get pregnant. In truth, I didn't want to be fucking Tony. Only I was. Early on, I was able to use my genuine fear of pregnancy as an excuse for reining in our sexual explorations, but that didn't hold Tony back for long.

"I made arrangements for you to see Dr. Costello and get fitted for a diaphragm," he'd told me matter-of-factly one evening as he stoked the fire in his wood stove at the farmhouse. "It's Friday, the 10th, at 9 a.m. I don't like the man, but he's damn good at what he does."

His statement had left me shocked and speechless, but I went to the appointment. I didn't want to have his baby. Since then, I'd occasionally imagine leaving Tony, yet I couldn't bear to actually go through with it. He would be devastated. So here I was, going through the motions, trying to hold on to the way he used to make me feel. I stared at the little pink compact. It seemed to vibrate with foreboding, like a tiny Pandora's Box.

My mind drifted back to the first time Tony and I had used it. Afterward, as we reclined on the bed, he pressed me for details about the experience. "Well, I didn't really feel much," I said truthfully.

He looked horrified. "What?" he said, eyes squinting. "Maybe you're too stoned. Maybe . . ." his voice trailed off, and he shook his head. Then he looked at me intently, like a doctor giving orders to a patient: "You should do some Kegel exercises."

Suddenly, I felt about ten years old. "What are Kegel exercises?" I said.

"It's not normal to feel so little sensation during intercourse," Tony said. "Kegels will tighten you up, make your vagina more responsive."

I cringed, feeling protective of my most private place. It had never occurred to me that there was anything wrong with it, just as it had never occurred to me that there was anything wrong with my earlobes, or my big toe, or that scar on the back of my leg. Was Tony right? Was there something wrong with my vagina? He made it sound so cold, so clinical.

If my emotional discomfort showed on my face, Tony didn't notice. He kept staring straight ahead as he talked. He went on: "Sometimes, even young women who have not had children need to do Kegels for maximum pleasure. Of course, childbirth can pose more problems. I remember when I was a resident doing my rotation in obstetrics. After I had delivered their second child, one husband said to me, 'Doctor, can you tighten her up a bit?' "

I asked a question I didn't really want the answer to. "What did he mean, can you tighten her up a bit?"

"Well," Tony said proudly, "he meant could I make a few extra stitches when I sewed her up?"

I imagined a woman exhausted from childbirth lying spread-eagled on a gurney, baby at her breast, while her husband made his request in the shadows of the room, as if the doctor were a tailor and he was taking his wife in for alterations. I was repulsed at the way Tony and the husband had acted, as though this woman's vagina didn't belong to her but to them. My jaw clamped shut while my mind raced. *I can't believe Tony is telling me this! How gross!* I felt like throwing up ... needles and vaginas . . . Kegels and diaphragms.

I looked down at Tony's flaccid penis, and my temper simmered, then boiled. A thought exploded in my mind: *Maybe you're just too small!* I glared into his eyes but suppressed the voice that wanted to rage out of me. I reached over to the bedside table, picked up the bong, and took two more long hits. Then none of it seemed to matter.

Suitcases packed, I pointed my Volkswagen Rabbit to Front Royal and the farm. Turning up the radio, I tried to fight off the pangs of anxiety and self-doubt I felt when I remembered what had happened on the last couple of drives there. As I was steering the car, I had the sensation that I was sitting beside myself. It was difficult to describe, so I hadn't told anyone. It was as though my lower body was in the driver's seat but my upper half was in the middle of the car. I was like the magician's assistant sawed in two, only this was much scarier. If I pressed both feet firmly on the floor of the car, I could snap myself back into one piece.

Tonight, my headlights sliced through the blackness on the winding roads through the Blue Ridge Mountains. I was groggy from a hard week of work, and Casey Kasem and *American Top 40* kept me upbeat. The countdown descended from Hall & Oates' "Say It Isn't So" to Pat Benatar's "Love Is a Battlefield" to Bonnie Tyler's "Total Eclipse of the Heart," and I sang along when I knew the words.

And then I found myself on a lonesome road with a dense canopy of trees overhead. I had no idea how I had gotten here. I looked at my watch. It was 11 p.m. I should have made it to Tony's place hours ago. He would have dinner waiting for me. I looked at the gas gauge. I had burned through a quarter tank. When had *American Top 40* ended? I stopped the car. I didn't recognize any signs or landmarks. I tried not to panic. It wasn't as if I had taken a wrong turn and could just retrace my steps. A chunk of time was just . . . gone. There was a blank place in my memory almost as long and dark as the road that stretched out before me.

Turning around, I managed to stave off my panic and make my way to a gas station where I asked for directions.

"Front Royal?" said a weathered attendant in denim overalls and a red plaid flannel shirt. An old pipe was hanging from his lips. "That's about an hour west of here."

West? Hadn't I been driving west? The man said I was outside Nokesville, which meant that at some point, I had turned in the opposite direction.

I tried to act casual as I bought a pack of crackers and used the restroom. I realized that a force I couldn't contain or explain had seized me and steered me away from—not toward—Tony.

Feeling like most of me was trailing a foot behind myself, I walked to the dimly lit phone booth in the darkened corner of the gas station lot. I reached inside my jeans pocket. Damn. No quarters. Tony said to call him collect from wherever I was.

"Hello," Tony answered, his voice sounding thinner and less confident than usual.

"Collect call from Carrie," asked a sleepy-sounding operator. "Will you accept the charges?"

"Of course, of course, yes." Tony sounded urgent. "Where are you? Are you okay?"

How do I tell him I'm lost? I'm so embarrassed.

"Sorry, Tony. I got held up. I'll be there in an hour or so."

"What? Where are you?"

"I'm not exactly sure. Apparently, I'm somewhere outside of Nokesburg, no wait, Nokesville. I got turned around. I don't feel so good." I suddenly felt dizzy and wanted to go to sleep.

"Nokesville? How in the world did you get there?" he said.

"Not sure, Tony. I'm on my way," I reassured him, trying to make it sound like everything was okay now. "Goodbye."

Damn it, what was going on with me? I felt so strange. My head pounded as my thoughts swirled trying to find a place to land. Maybe I was just hungry. I imagined Tony sitting in the farmhouse waiting for me. He would have candles lit and a fire blazing by now. I bet he even drew a bath for me in the Jacuzzi. My stomach tightened while my heart sank. I was fucking up again. He was going to be so mad at me.

Tony would help me figure this out. I was sure he'd seen stuff like this in some of his patients before. A sharp pain surged through my belly as I pulled out of the gas station and headed toward Front Royal. Slowly, I drove the sixty-minute trip to the farm, being extra alert for road signs and wildlife. I didn't want to get lost again. *Pay attention, Carrie. Pay attention.*

Ninety minutes later, I arrived to find Tony anxiously pacing outside his house. He grabbed my bag from the back seat and almost pushed me through the door.

"Do you mind telling me what the hell happened?"

I hoped he would help me understand what was wrong with me, but as I tried to describe what I was feeling and the fact that I had mysteriously gotten lost, he glared at me. "Why do you insist on being sick, Carrie? I told you, when I take off my therapeutic cap to be with you, I am no longer your therapist."

I looked into his accusing eyes and tried to find the doctor who had once been so eager to cure me. All I saw was a wounded old man who was irritated by my behavior. He didn't seem the least bit curious about my strange symptoms.

"I need to go to bed," I said. "I do think I'm coming down with something."

Still in my clothes, I slipped between the sheets, and my thoughts continued to swirl as I clutched my pillow to steady myself. I pretended to be asleep while through the wall, I heard Tony draining the Jacuzzi, brushing his teeth, then coming to bed. I had gotten good at faking being asleep.

"You seem so tense, Carrie," he said, sliding between the covers. "I want you to come with me for a walk, first thing in the morning. Almost all the leaves have fallen, and you can see clear up the ridge. Being outside will do you good. We can look for some of those birds you love to watch."

Now I was truly drifting off, and I imagined us walking by the stream and felt comforted by memories of the days when he took good care of me. If I could just go back to how I was, the way we were, maybe all would be well, and I wouldn't have to leave him. I felt myself shake off that thought, but it came back with even more clarity. Did I have to leave him to be well?

"Night, Carrie," Tony said, switching off the lamp. I didn't respond, holding my breath and my tears until I heard him gently snoring.

As I lay there completely still, tear after tear silently emerged. I tried to muffle my sniffles. What was I going to do? If I weren't so fucked up, it would all be clear. I cried myself to sleep making sure I didn't wake Tony.

The next day, Tony rose early and called up to me from downstairs, "Carrie, there's fresh coffee on the stove, and I made some bacon. Let's get going."

Groggy with sleep and still fully dressed, I trudged down the stairs, past the *Playboy* centerfold tacked to the laundry room door at the bottom of the staircase.

My mind wound back to the visit a few months before when his friend Jim had noticed it.

"Wow, nice picture, Tony," he had said, cautiously looking to me as if to see whether I was cool with the image of a naked woman so blatantly displayed in Tony's house. I stayed silent.

Tony had quipped back, "Yeah, well it reminds me of Carrie. Don't you see the resemblance?"

"Well, I've never seen that much of Carrie," Jim had responded, trying to be playful as he looked nervously at me again.

Now I fought back another tear as I poured myself a cup of coffee.

"Can you eat quickly?" Tony said with uncharacteristic excitement. "I'm anxious to get going."

I gulped down my coffee, gobbled a strip of bacon, wrapped myself in one of his blankets, and walked out the door behind him.

The early November morning was gray and heavy with cloud cover. As we walked toward the mountain ridge, I was startled to see a rifle in his right hand. I had seen the gun in his house before but never in his hand. I didn't like it.

"Why do you have that?" I said, wondering why our peaceful, bird-watching stroll required a huge gun.

"Shhhh, you'll scare off the deer," he said softly. "I may not make it up to Vermont for the season this year. We may see some over by the river. I hear the deer are really moving right now."

Wait, he's taking me hunting?

Just then I heard a gunshot in the distance and turned to see Tony with a big grin and a wild look in his eyes. He picked up his pace, walking in an unusual way, like a big cat stalking its prey.

Adrenaline surged through my body. I felt hyper-alert. Wary. Ready to bolt. I tried to calm myself by taking deep breaths. The smell of musty fallen leaves filled my senses as my heart pounded more intensely with each step. We continued walking in silence for another ten minutes or so through some reeds and onto a barely used trail.

"Shhh . . . see the tracks?" Tony pointed out hoof marks in the mud by the stream, which was clogged with fallen leaves. "There's a big one in the vicinity."

It was so quiet I could hear the waterfall in the distance and remembered when he had taken me to sit by it, back when things were lighter and our days were spent talking about life and God. For a split second, I felt warm inside as I remembered feeling so protected by him. Maybe I could reconnect with that guy.

Another gun fired in the distance just as a large, black crow flew over my head. We rounded a bend and heard something large moving in the brush ahead, twigs crackling under its feet. An electrical impulse surged within me.

"Move over, and get behind me." Tony whispered as he crept past me, gun raised to his shoulder, his right eye looking through the scope. Just as he inched out a foot or so in front of me, the most gorgeous deer I had ever seen emerged from the brush and onto the path just thirty feet in front of us. He froze and looked right at me.

"It's a ten-pointer!" Tony murmured as his finger released the safety.

I felt my head spin. For a moment, everything went black. My legs turned to Jell-O and fell out from under me. I hit the ground. I opened my eyes and looked up. As I lay there, Tony stayed put, angrily whispering, "What are you doing? What are you doing?"

"I think I fainted," I whispered back. I was unable to move, yet comforted by the familiar smell of the autumn leaves cradling my head.

The buck spooked and rushed off across the stream, away from us, bounding toward the mountains. I caught a glimpse of its white tail and strong haunches as it leaped out of view to safety.

Through the stars that were swirling in my mind, and despite my throbbing head, a little voice inside me called out to the magnificent creature.

"Run, Deer. Run for your life."

~21~

I stood at my kitchen sink, warm soapsuds soothing my hands and the steamy scent of lemony detergent rising from the water, happily washing my new stoneware dishes with the tan and blue stripes. After the disturbing incidents at the farm last weekend, I was doing everything I could to ground myself in the material world and my daily routines. I reminded myself that despite my difficulties, I still had a lot to be grateful for.

In the past year, I had finished my bachelor's degree at Hood College, slogged my way through an internship at Johns Hopkins, and kept my morale up even as I dodged stapler-throwing schizophrenics at the University of Maryland Hospital, and finally my dream had come true. In May, I walked through the door of the Tansey house to find my parents bright-eyed and about to burst with joy.

"Carrie," Mom said, "Virginia Commonwealth University called today."

I held my breath.

She gushed. "You've been accepted into the doctoral program in clinical psychology!" She hugged me tight. Dad was literally jumping up and down and clapping his hands. They were both so ecstatic for me that I couldn't help but cry tears of happiness.

When I returned the call to the professor who had left the message, he told me how surprised he was by Mom and Dad's response. "You're very lucky, Carrie. In my experience, something like this barely registers with some parents," he said. "It's obvious your family supports you in your dreams."

Not that my parents didn't have their suspicions. Now, I plunged two drinking glasses into the sudsy water as I remembered my exit interview with Tony months before. He had announced that he would be ending my therapy, and had brought my parents in to ask them to support my graduate education. I didn't have a voice in this. I just let him guide the way. As the four of us sat in the therapy room, he had grilled my parents about their willingness to pay for graduate school.

Dad's eyebrows furrowed the way they did when he smelled a rat. My stomach tensed, but I kept silent as I wondered what he suspected.

"Doctor, what can you tell us about Carrie's progress in psychotherapy?"

"Well," Tony said, "she made excellent grades at Hood College, she's individuating from her family, and she's on her way to furthering her education. As you know, she is a brilliant, thoughtful young lady who will make a great therapist."

Dad's expression remained unchanged. "She was a good student before she started seeing you," he said. "Her mother and I want to know what *emotional* progress she's made over the last three years." He glanced at me with worried eyes, then turned back to Tony.

"We still see her as quite fragile and overly emotional at times," Dad continued. "There has been a lot of tension at home, causing a rift between us."

Tony plowed forward, discussing finances and how it was important to get my parents' monetary and emotional support for my goal of completing my Ph.D. by the time I was twenty-seven.

My parents looked incredulous, but then again, so was I. Tony had pledged to pay for my education if I worked for him after graduation, but now, right before my eyes, he was weaseling out of it. My body bristled at the realization that he was not going to keep his full commitment to me but was trying to strong-arm my worried parents into financing his vision! In the car on the way home, Mom let fly how offended she was. "I don't know, Carrie. It just seems like all Dr. Romano cares about is money. He said next to nothing about his treatment or your healing. Your father and I understand that much of therapy is confidential, but Dr. Romano just seemed evasive. I am not impressed."

"Goodness, Carrie," Dad said, a deep look of concern on his face. "I'm not feeling good about this plan. We have to think about it. Do you really think you're ready to enroll in such a grueling course of study?"

I said nothing. How was I going to drop the bomb that Tony had another plan in store? His son, Dave, had just graduated from a college in California and had also been accepted in the Ph.D. program at VCU. Tony said he wanted Dave and me to live together in one apartment so he could save money on our housing expenses. I liked Dave well enough, but I couldn't imagine living with him. I knew my parents would never go for that, especially if they were financing my education.

Sure enough, when I told them about Tony's idea, they refused to contribute anything financially if I went along with it. I was relieved they drew the line.

"Your parents are so old fashioned and rigid," Tony had vented, dismissing their concerns.

Now I savored the cute, little Richmond apartment I'd been able to make into my cozy sanctuary after starting grad school. The dishes drying in the rack were the first complete set I'd ever owned. I handled them as if they were rare antique porcelain from the Ming Dynasty. During my first stint at college, my roommates and I had relied on the generosity of family hand-me-downs, which amounted to the typical mismatched hodgepodge. For the first time, I had a complete, matching set, and it was all mine. It dawned on me that these dishes were an extension of who I was becoming, my first taste of real independence.

My new bright-red electric wok squatted on the corner of the kitchen counter. It still had the price tag on. It made me feel like I was planning a trip to China. I wanted to try cooking with exotic ingredients from the Chinese grocery down the street. Growing up, our family had to stretch grocery trips to the military commissary to once every two weeks, and we could only buy generic food that all eight of us liked. It didn't leave much room for experimenting. I was embracing a bigger life now.

I wanted my home to have a worldly, bohemian vibe, so I filled it with earthy wicker baskets, thick pillar candles, fragrant incense, and as many plants as I could afford. Tony was chipping in $200 a month, my parents were making an even-larger contribution, and I had taken out student loans, but my grad school budget was still tight. I hung inexpensive purple and saffron Indian quilts on the walls and picked out sunny yellow sheets for my bed.

I pulled the plug and heard the water gurgle down the drain as I dried my hands. Now, it was time to do something I had been dreading. I picked up the receiver of my almond-colored phone and dialed Tony's number.

As much as I tried to seek healing in my self-made sanctuary, I was still troubled by the events of last weekend. I had tried to research what happened on my latest drive to Front Royal, and had stumbled on a possible explanation. I might have gone into what was called a dissociative fugue, a rare condition that is a type of amnesia. Then again, I was reading about and hearing lectures on mental illnesses for at least six hours a day. In my weak moments, it seemed like I was suffering from everything. Just when I thought I couldn't trust myself, something even weirder had started happening. I needed to know what Tony thought. On his end, the phone was ringing.

"Hello?"

"Hey, Tony, it's me."

"How are you feeling? Better than last weekend, I hope."

"Well, I haven't fainted again, if that's what you mean."

"Good. The next time you come to the farm, I'll have dinner waiting, and I'll make sure you slip into the Jacuzzi tub first thing. That should help ease all the pressure you're feeling from school. I can't wait to hold you in my arms again."

I made myself comfortable on the brown tweed sofa, pulling the long phone cord behind me as I ignored what he said about being in his arms.

"Tony, there's something else that's been bothering me. I'm starting to sense knives in my mind. Big, black-handled hunting knives. Lots of them. Whirling around in my head. It's kind of like an intrusive thought, but it's more like an intrusive vision."

I struggled to keep my voice calm as I described the whirling, glistening blades that made me dizzy, made me fear that I was falling down a black hole of insanity.

"I can't find anything in my texts about it. What do you think that means?"

"Carrie, like I've told you, once my therapeutic cap is off, I'm not your therapist anymore. I suggest you discuss it with Susan."

Dr. Susan Arrington had become my therapist a few months ago. We students were required to do in-depth psychotherapy as part of our training, and I knew I had plenty to resolve. I had already revealed to her many of my deep insecurities, problems with insomnia, and struggles in my relationship with "a much older man."

I was desperate to share the intense emotions I struggled to contain but had heeded Tony's admonition not to start with another therapist until I got settled into my new life in Virginia. By the time, I got to Susan's office, a full year after Tony had brought my parents into session to "terminate" my therapy and discuss who would pay for my graduate school, I was boiling over with conflicting impulses about telling the truth of my predicament. I somehow knew that once I began to reveal my internal world to Susan, Pandora's Box would be unhinged and my life would be forever changed. I protected Tony's secret with my life, not knowing how much danger I was in.

"I will, Tony, but I'm scared. What do you think it means?"

Through the receiver, I heard air snort from his nostrils.

"I guess it means you're mad at somebody," he said dismissively.

I sighed.

"Well, thanks for giving it a think," I said, trying to sound sincere. "I will discuss it with her. She must think I'm so crazy. I keep having all these symptoms. And another thing, Tony," I cautiously broached the subject, "I really feel I must tell Susan about us."

"Us? I thought you had already told her about me, your fiance. What do you mean?" I heard panic rising in his voice.

I cringed when he said "fiance." I didn't want to hurt him, but I didn't see him as my fiance. Besides, he hadn't given me a ring—not that I wanted one. He simply began talking as though we were getting married and that it was settled. My heart agonized for him but also for me. I couldn't imagine going through with such a thing, nor could I imagine a way out. Maybe Dr. Arrington could help me.

I persisted. "No, Tony, she does know that I'm involved with an older man. What I mean is, I have to tell her that you were my therapist."

"What? I simply don't understand, Carrie."

"Tony, I'm seeing these whirling hunting knives. I'm anxious all the time. I can't sleep . . . ."

He interrupted. "I hear you, but what does that have to do with our therapeutic relationship?"

Not knowing how to answer, I stayed silent. I just knew in my gut that my symptoms were related to my doctor-patient relationship with Tony, a relationship I had never truly left.

"Fine," he said. "I'll prescribe some more tranquilizers and sleeping pills."

Prescribe pills? I guess now he's my psychiatrist again. I thought he said he'd taken his therapeutic cap off. My head felt like it was spinning around on my neck, and I tried to keep from getting even angrier.

Tony assumed a voice of authority: "I have not been your therapist for a year now. Why must you tell her about that relationship? I have permanently taken off my therapeutic cap with you. Now it's just me, Tony, a man, with you, Carrie, the woman I love."

"Well, maybe *you* took your cap off, but I was never able to do the same, remove my 'patient cap'! Look at all the symptoms I'm *still* having! I have to tell Dr. Arrington the whole truth. Isn't that what therapy is about?"

He started talking faster as his voice rose in pitch, "I'm going to ask you to wait until I have a better sense of her and see how solid she is. Some therapists might overreact and jump to conclusions."

Anger rose in my belly, up through my heart, burning my throat, and searing my mouth shut. *Isn't this my therapy? What are you afraid of, Tony?*

"I've got to go . . . . I'll talk to you later," I managed to say. "I have a lot of work to do."

"I'll see you next weekend, right?"

"Yeah, talk to you later . . . love you . . . ," I mumbled perfunctorily. I pictured him inflating at my proclamation.

He giggled, sounding relieved. "I love you too."

I hung up. I felt like puking. I had to tell Dr. Arrington, and once I did, I knew, a chain of events with no going back would begin.

I rushed to my bathroom vanity, opened it, took out an amber vial of pills that Tony had given me from his supply, and gobbled down a Xanax. I felt my nerves start to calm as I settled back on the couch and lit the vanilla-scented pillar candle on the coffee table. I opened my five-pound textbook and tried to wrap my mind around advanced statistics. Probability theory felt so remote, like a language from a distant planet. A part of my brain that I rarely used stretched and strained to understand the concepts. This was a better place to be, away from the void inside me. It felt safer, further away from the knives standing guard on the periphery of my mind.

~22~

It was mid-May, and I had just completed my first year of graduate school. Much to my surprise, I had also been awarded a prestigious behavioral medicine fellowship at the Medical College of Virginia. I wanted to feel proud of myself and liberated. Instead, I felt as burdened as ever. Even though I was succeeding in my individuation from my family, Tony and I bickered constantly, and I watched in disgust as some sort of invisible force seemed to eat away at him. The eyes that were once deep, blue pools of compassion now looked shallow and faded. His hair seemed whiter, his skin paler. Had he changed, or had I? Once again, he was suffering from trigeminal neuralgia. It seemed like Tony had a flare-up whenever I did something he didn't want me to. I should have felt compassion for him, but instead, I felt manipulated and resentful.

The dreams Tony used to weave for us now seemed as fragile as cobwebs. Sometimes he still talked about the two of us moving to California after I got my Ph.D. and opening a practice along with Dave, but I knew we'd never really do it. Dave had transferred from VCU after just one semester, deeply unhappy with the focus of the program and the conservative Southern university. He knew his father and I were in a relationship. I couldn't help but wonder how much more he knew, if he suspected how much I was suffering. I wondered if another reason Dave had returned to California was that knowing his dad had broken the ethical code held sacred by our profession was too great a burden. Even if Tony and I came out as a couple, if we stopped hiding it all, I knew Lieutenant Colonel and Mrs. Tansey would never, ever, accept their daughter's involvement with a man their age, and her former psychiatrist to boot. I still had not told Dr. Arrington my secret, knowing that once I did, everything would change. There were so many unknowns, and I feared where they might lead: how my life would change, the emotional impact, the threat to Tony's license. It felt like my relationship with him was coming apart at the seams.

Tony felt it too. His solution was for us to take a trip to Jamaica before my fellowship began in June.

"We can go away to the island for a week, and you'll feel better," he had reasoned one night at the farm. "The pressure of graduate school is causing so much strain on our relationship." I wanted to believe him. Sometimes, I knew in my heart that our future together was hopeless. Other times, self-doubt would creep in, and I would wonder if that was just my depression talking.

So here I was at Dulles International Airport, suitcase packed with swimsuits, shorts, and sarongs, boarding a plane bound for Montego Bay, hoping the sun, sand, and reggae would mend things. As Tony and I took our seats side-by-side, other passengers were filing by. I watched absentmindedly as an unnaturally muscular man in a tank top stuffed his suitcase in the compartment directly overhead, triceps flexing.

Once he'd found his seat, I remarked idly, "I've never liked that bulked-up look."

"Well," Tony smirked, "now there's a reaction formation if I've ever heard one."

I tried not to roll my eyes. Even though I had a year of graduate school in psychology, he still thought he could throw diagnostic terms at me. My temper flared as I heard his voice in my head for the umpteenth time: "When I take off my therapeutic cap, I am no longer your therapist." *Really? So why couldn't he stop being my therapist right now?* Contrary to what Tony was suggesting, my comment was not a defense mechanism to hide my true feelings. I hated it when he acted as if he knew my mind and desires better than I did.

Behind my eyes, the hunting knives, always on the periphery, began whirling.

"No, Tony," I said louder than I intended. "I just said I *don't* like that Schwarzenegger-body-builder look. It's a turnoff for me."

The knives eased up a bit.

He glared at me.

The knives sharpened each other.

We sat there in silence waiting for the plane to take off to our tropical paradise. *Just one week, Carrie. Hang in there.* The week felt like it would last forever.

Once we arrived at our hotel in the resort town of Ocho Rios, I tried my best to settle down inside. Our taxi dropped us off at the white-washed, stucco resort surrounded by palm trees. I felt myself open up and absorb the vibrant colors and aromas of the tropical Eden, and for a brief moment, felt hopeful. As we walked into the lobby, the bellhop rushed to pick up our bags. I heard a high-pitched squawk beside me and turned to see a large emerald-green parrot with a black beak sitting in a gilded cage and ruffling its feathers as if to get my attention. As I paused to strike up a conversation with the bird, I heard Tony angrily raise his voice at the reservation desk: "What do you mean we don't have our reservation starting until tomorrow night? We have traveled all the way from Washington, D.C.! I must have a room now!" I reluctantly looked away from the bird to see Tony looking like a spoiled old man barking orders at "the help." The receptionist seemed annoyed but quickly made a phone call and then gave him our room keys.

I was embarrassed to be with him but relieved when we made it to the freshly appointed blue-and-white room overlooking the ocean. My eyes were drawn by the palm trees swaying just below our balcony and the sailboats gracefully floating a few hundred feet from shore. If I could just get outside, maybe I could unwind. I quickly donned my one-piece black bathing suit, wrapped a bright blue beach towel around my waist, slipped on my flip-flops, and made a beeline for the pristine, white-sand beach.

Tony was still getting ready in the bathroom.

"I'll see you down on the beach," I called through the bathroom door, not waiting for a reply.

The luxurious aroma of Jamaican Blue Mountain Coffee seduced my olfactory senses as I hurried past the tourists dining at the outdoor pavilion overlooking the beach. There was so much beauty here. I would do what I could to enjoy myself. My heart felt so heavy, and I felt like such a bitch. I wanted nothing to do with Tony, and yet did not want to hurt him. How was I going to make it through the week? I knew this was a bad idea. I wished I had stayed at my apartment in Richmond.

Lying on the cool, white sand, all I could think of was how to get away from him. When I turned and saw him walking down the palm tree-lined path from the cafe to join me, I pretended not to notice him and jumped up to go for a swim. I floated out beyond the surf and looked back to see Tony placing his towel beside mine under a blue-and-white-striped umbrella. I cringed when I saw his skinny white body in his red swim shorts, and dreaded being intimate with him later.

My heart started to race as I wondered if I could fake sickness for a whole week while also taking in some much needed R&R. I was exhausted from the rigors of school, and boy, did I need a break. Just as I laid back to float in the warm, azure waters, a handsome guy about my age swam up to me. In that instantly recognizable Jamaican accent, he told me he was selling Jet Ski rides.

"No thanks," I giggled.

I swam away thirty feet or so. He followed.

"Pretty lady, do ya won some ganja?" he asked.

"No thanks," I said, trying to keep from smiling at this charming island lad. He swam a little closer. "I know you want a ride. I can just tell. Come on, treat yourself."

Suddenly, I felt Tony's sharpshooter eyes cutting right through me.

"Sorry, gotta go. Good luck with your business." I swam away, leaving the Jamaican looking for another customer.

I nervously returned to our spot by the umbrella. "I will see you upstairs," Tony said in the voice of one who expects obedience. He stormed off to the hotel.

I didn't follow right away. I had been in Jamaica only a short time, but I'd noticed that when tourists made their requests to hotel and restaurant staff, the Jamaicans took a little more time than necessary before responding. Their free-spirited attitude and independent streak buoyed my growing rebelliousness. Or maybe it was all those Bob Marley songs perpetually playing everywhere, stoking my desire to finally be free. Slowly, I slipped on my flip-flops, looking out at the sailboats in the distance and smiling when I saw that the Jamaican guy had roped a middle-aged couple into getting on matching Jet Skis.

I took a deep breath as I reluctantly made my way back up the beach, through the lobby, and up the elevator to our room. Walking down the hallway, I wasn't feeling so laid back. My stomach began twisting itself in knots. I knew there would be severe repercussions because I had talked to another man. I fumbled with my room key, half hoping it didn't work. I opened the door to see Tony waiting for me in the white wicker chair overlooking the ocean. As I sat down on the bed across from him, he began railing at me, "Your unconsciousness is working overtime! You are so inappropriate with men!" He was waving his hands around indignantly as if scolding a child.

"You should have seen yourself out there!" he ranted. "Every man on the beach was looking at you, then at me, obviously wondering *what* you were doing! I can no longer be involved with someone who is so unconscious!"

I held tightly to the towel wrapped around my wet bathing suit, and suddenly felt quite cold. A switch flipped on in my head. For the first time, I felt no guilt about Tony's feelings or responsibility to placate him.

"I'm not in love with you anymore," I said. "I don't know if I ever was."

The statement cut him as cleanly as a sharpened blade. A swirling mass of energy shot straight out of his body, and found its way back home—to me. It was the life force he'd stolen that day in the therapy room when I confided I was afraid I was falling in love with him, and all the days after when he coerced me into being his clandestine lover rather than processing my transference toward him. Now, Tony sat limp, like a beach ball with all the air squished out of it. He looked so small and crumpled. In that instant, I was no longer his captive. I was me again. The knives stopped whirling, and then they vanished.

After I had proclaimed my truth, the weight of the situation hung in the air like a dead body. There was absolutely no chance of resuscitating the relationship; it was over. I was relieved when Tony proposed that we leave Jamaica the next day, three days sooner than planned. We coexisted in stagnant silence as we packed our bags and flew home. I had to fight off impulses to make him feel better by taking back what I had said, but it was too late. My truth had created an impenetrable wall between us.

Back at the Front Royal farmhouse, we both knew the vacation that was supposed to resuscitate our relationship was a thing of the past, and so were we. For me, it couldn't end soon enough. I hurriedly gathered my things. I wanted to say goodbye, get it over with, and go out to my car, but Tony was dragging his feet. He ran upstairs and returned with the nude Polaroids of me. He shot me a wounded look and tossed them into the woodstove's fire. The paper crackled and spit, and black smoke slithered up. I had forgotten about those photos and was creeped out that they were even on his mind. I cringed at the thought of how many times he had looked at them, and suddenly felt slimed. I felt a lightness enter my core as they vanished into the flames.

I drove away down his rural winding road feeling sad for him and enormously relieved for myself, but also a bit shaky about how my life would unfold now. Tony had been my life raft—until he began sinking and pulling me down with him. Now I could trust no one but myself.

Mostly, I was proud of my choice. The colors of the blue sky and the luminescent green leaves of the spring trees around me looked brighter and more alive than I had remembered. Cheerful yellow dandelions and buttercups lined the road as I made my way out of the valley. Baby bunnies and squirrels scampered about as I navigated my VW past the tall oak trees that canopied the country road. Did I break Tony's heart? I never intended to; I just needed to reclaim my true self. I couldn't let myself think back to him or what he was feeling. I had to keep focused ahead . . . on my life . . . on my path.

~23~

A few weeks after the Jamaica vacation, my fellowship and the summer session had started at VCU. The pressure of school had returned, and the optimism I'd felt immediately after the breakup was a mere memory. This semester, my classmates and I would begin seeing our first patients at the counseling center. Now I sat in the classroom with nine other graduate students waiting for the clinical director to arrive for our initial briefing on policies and procedures for our practicum.

I looked out the window overlooking Franklin Street in Richmond's Fan District as pedestrians strolled by the opulent, historic buildings. Some of these folks must have just walked down Monument Avenue, lined with enormous mansions from the height of the Gilded Age, a street where Confederate war heroes such as Jefferson Davis, Robert E. Lee, and Stonewall Jackson were memorialized in bronze. I wondered where each person was going and if it was too late for me to switch places with any of them. *That woman looks like an artist. Is she going to her studio? Oh, how I'd love to be going to my studio instead of being in here, using my creativity instead of being immersed in a web of psychological theory.*

"Today's briefing is the first in a series of discussions we will be having on the essentials of good, ethical psychotherapy," the clinical director began. My eyes shifted from the sidewalk traffic back into the room.

The fifty-something woman who was speaking quickly captured my attention with her perfectly coiffed short blonde hair, lilac Chanel-style suit, rosy pink lips, and matching nail polish. She exuded confidence from her shoulder pads to her pumps, a real steel magnolia, impeccable in every sense of the word.

"Of course, I don't have to tell you of the necessity of maintaining the confidentiality of your patients," she drawled, annunciating the word "necessity" for emphasis. "Before you share any identifying information about a case with other professionals or family members, the patient must sign a release form."

Some students nodded and jotted down notes.

She went on: "Just as important as confidentiality is always being mindful of setting and maintaining professional boundaries. Can anyone share what boundaries need to be in place to create a safe environment for our patients?"

My classmate Sue raised her hand, and the director nodded in her direction. "We have to be cautious when disclosing anything about ourselves to our patients."

"Good answer, Miss Simpson. How do you decide how much of your own personal information can be disclosed?"

Greta looked up from her notes, hand raised.

"Miss Wilson?"

Greta began hesitantly. "Intellectually, I fully understand the need for detachment, but at the same time, so much of being a good therapist hinges on having empathy for our patients. It seems there could be some instances where sharing a bit about ourselves could build trust." She scowled, looking conflicted. "How much do you think it's reasonable to share?"

"Good question. A little self-disclosure is acceptable, especially when it helps our patients see a way out of their problems," said the director. "However, the therapy session should always remain focused on the patient—not the therapist."

My stomach clenched as I thought about the secret night session I had had with Tony more than three years ago. Earlier that day at my regular therapy appointment, he had asked me to come back for a second session after hours, saying he had something he wanted to discuss with me. We spent much of that time talking about his trigeminal neuralgia, the power of prayer, and his yearning for spiritual understanding. In fact, there were a lot of sessions that, in hindsight, were more about Tony's needs than mine.

"What are some other examples of establishing and maintaining healthy boundaries?"

Shelly spoke up: "It seems to me that holding to our time commitment is really important. If the session is meant to be fifty minutes, we keep it to fifty minutes."

Our mentor nodded in approval. "And why are time boundaries so essential?"

"If we regularly go overtime, we could be sending a message to the patient that suggests he or she is special, different from other patients,"

Charles chimed in. "This could feed transference feelings in a way that increases the patient's dependence on the therapist."

"Yes, great example," said the director. "Let's humanize this. We all have the need to feel special, especially if our lives are painful or we feel hopeless. So often, the patient is looking to the therapist to be the source of clarity, containment, and unconditional acceptance in his or her life. Many patients will come to you when their lives have fallen apart. If we therapists aren't consistent in holding the container of therapy"—she gestured as if holding a solid but fragile vase—"it can lead to confusion about the roles and expectations between patient and therapist."

My skin prickled, and I felt light-headed as I remembered one session when Tony had asked me why I was getting up to leave after fifty minutes, saying he had more time to talk and that I could stay. In fact, he implied there was something wrong with my getting up to leave after our allotted time together. I thought back to the special "marathon sessions" he'd scheduled whose full time he didn't charge my parents for. I flushed as I remembered how special and cared for they made me feel at the time.

"Charles brought up the concept of transference," the director went on. "We know that transference regularly happens in life when we redirect feelings and desires from childhood toward individuals in our present-day lives. Frequently, patients enter psychotherapy with unmet childhood needs. This is why we must *expect* that clients will transfer such feelings onto us," she said emphatically. "This is the fundamental reason that the therapist-patient relationship is so sacred. Therefore, therapists must always be on guard and handle transference therapeutically so our patients can grow and heal without becoming overly dependent upon us."

Jill spoke up quickly, as if she couldn't wait to share. "Well, I tell you, when I was a teen-ager, my mom brought me to a therapist when my parents were having problems and I was acting up. Because I was so eager to share my internal world, and no one else in my life seemed to listen, my therapist quickly became like the parent I craved but didn't have. He was like a god in my eyes. I would have gone to the moon for him. If he had taken advantage of me in any way or reinforced that transference rather than helping me discover how to care for myself, I can't imagine how damaging that could have been to me."

Damaging . . . The word hit me like a sucker punch to the stomach. Tony had become like a god to me. I remembered the time I told him,

"I'm afraid I'm falling in love with you." I thought of the split, out-of-body experience I had when he said he was in love with me too. Had he knowingly ignored professional boundaries? Did he know he was harming me? I was such a fool. Why had I ever trusted him? Nausea washed over me, and I felt like I could puke.

At this point, students started getting involved in one-on-one discussions, even arguing a bit among themselves, and a din began to build. The director raised her voice. "People, there are few clear-cut answers here!" she said as the noise died down. "That's why we're having this discussion. This can be a lonely profession, folks, and we're here to support each other. Psychotherapy can be an intense, highly charged field, and its effectiveness hinges on the quality of the relationships we create with our patients. When in doubt, it all comes back to the Hippocratic Oath: First, do no harm."

Her words carried a weight that rendered the room silent for a moment. Was there tension in the air, or was that just me?

"Over the course of your practicum and your training at VCU, we will be exploring ways to handle transference as an essential aspect of psychotherapy," she continued. "We will also be exploring how our own feelings toward patients, known as *countertransference*, give us important information about what is going on with our patients and with ourselves. Bottom line is, we must always work to be conscious and on top of what is happening between ourselves and our patients."

She looked around the room, slowly making eye contact with each of us. You could hear a mouse breathe as we sat still, enraptured with the discussion. "Why do you think this is so important?"

Greta answered, a little unsure of herself: "Is it because there is a huge difference in power between the therapist and the patient?"

"Yes," said the director. "It is an unequal relationship that leaves the patient quite vulnerable to harm. Patients will want to please us, to make us happy. If they stop telling us their truths because they are protecting us, we have lost control of the therapeutic situation."

Her words echoed in my mind: *Lost control of the therapeutic situation, lost control of the therapeutic situation, lost control of the therapeutic situation . . . .*

I sat frozen, feeling naked before my peers as they made notes on their handouts and asked more questions, oblivious to my relationship with the man who was my psychotherapist and our former classmate's father. Silently, I gasped a sigh of relief that Dave was no longer with us. As I felt my armpits begin to sweat and my body flush with a deep and overwhelming shame, I had a strong urge to start screaming, bolt from the room, and never come back. The only problem was that I couldn't imagine where I would go.

The director said something I didn't hear, and my classmates started shuffling their papers and grabbing their backpacks. Oh, she must have dismissed us. I went through the same motions, praying I looked normal as other students began filing out of the room. I stayed put as I felt myself split apart inside.

The director raised her voice above the shuffle. "Next class—how and when to process our own feelings that arise in the therapy of our patients. We will discuss how we always need to be working on ourselves in order to provide ethical, effective therapy to those we serve."

As I stood to leave, Greta nudged my elbow. "Hey, Carrie."

My skin prickled with fear. Did she see through me?

"Sue and I are going to Edmond's for cheeseburgers and beers. Wanna come? Ask Lori to meet us there if you want."

I was paralyzed. I felt myself sinking into the ever-present void within me as black tar rushed in, smothering me, burying me alive. How could I explain what I was experiencing to anyone without Tony's getting in trouble? Or without their thinking I was crazy? *Maybe I was crazy.*

A voice I barely recognized said, "I'd love to, but I've got this presentation on depression to research. Heading home to hit the books, you know. But thanks."

Reaching my apartment, I opened the front door feeling as if I had narrowly escaped something, though I couldn't remember what. I dumped my backpack on the sofa. It landed on an empty pizza box. Glancing around, I noticed that my plants looked as wilted as I felt. I went into the kitchen past an overflowing trash can and a sink piled with crusty, smelly dishes. I opened the fridge. It was empty save for some moldy leftover containers I couldn't bear to deal with. I shut the door. Oh well, I didn't really have an appetite.

How could I be a therapist myself when my own therapist had violated the profession's most basic ethics? But he loved me. And I wound up breaking his heart. In my mind, the whirling knives appeared, then plunged downward, lodging themselves in my heart.

Shame washed over me. Could I tell anyone what really happened with Tony? Would anyone believe me? I was trying to be a clinical psychologist, but I was really just a crazy fraud. Did psychotherapy even work? Look at me, still fucked up after almost four years of it. I stumbled to my room and collapsed on the bed. There was no future for me. And there was no going back. From the kitchen, I heard a mousetrap snap shut.

The Rescue

Persephone's parents, Zeus and Demeter, summoned a search party of gods and mortals to find their daughter. They asked the sun god, Helios, to shed light, but he could not find her. Then Hecate, pathfinder between worlds, found Persephone in Hades' lair and carried the news to her distraught father and mother, who sent Hermes, the messenger, to wrench her away from the darkness and despair of Zeus's own brother.

~24~

The lights in the windowless, locked room were jarringly bright. My hospital gown was skimpy, and I tried to keep warm under the thin sheet by folding myself into the fetal position, hugging my knees to my chest. My head pounded, and I still felt groggy from the bottle of Xanax I'd swallowed. My mouth was dry and my throat sore from the aspirating tube that had run down to my stomach.

I thought of my father's questions two weeks ago, the first time he came to see me in the psych ward at St. Mary's: "Suicide, Carrie? Why?"

"I had an affair," I answered, and my mom surprised me when she immediately asked, "Was it Dr. Romano?"

Over the seventeen days that I had been hospitalized, I felt some temporary relief as I spilled the beans, not just to my parents but also to doctors, nurses, and other patients. Everyone was horrified and shocked but so supportive of me. We all thought I would be so much better now that the secret was out, but four days after my release, I was back. I had arrived on a gurney, unconscious from a drug overdose. It had been no mere impulse; I had been so intentional this time.

I felt hammered by shame and even deeper in the emotional underground. *How could I have failed?* I looked around the white room. *Wait . . . am I already dead? Is this hell?*

A tall orderly appeared and unlocked the thick steel door. Without a word, he gestured for me to follow him down the long, white hall to the office of someone who must have been important. They said he was a specialist. I went inside to wait. He wasn't there yet. Outside, the taciturn orderly stood guarding the door until the doctor arrived. *They can't leave me alone for a second,* I realized. *I'm on suicide watch.*

A distinguished-looking man in a brown tweed jacket entered and extended his hand. I numbly shook it.

"Miss Tansey, I'm Dr. Coffin."

Seriously? I just tried to kill myself, and now I have a meeting with Dr. Coffin?

His large brown eyes framed by tortoise-shell glasses pierced through me. He seated himself, and I blankly followed his lead. Directly in front of me, his deskplate read: "Stephen Kauffman, M.D." *Oh right, Kauffman, not Coffin.*

"Miss Tansey," he said. "This is a very important conversation we're having today. Do you want to tell me about what happened?"

I was beyond numb; I was deadened . . . an empty shell. I said nothing. I half suspected I no longer had a voice.

"Four days ago on July 29, you left here with a promise to stay safe, but you were unable to keep your promise." He had a calm, unwavering voice. "You have an important decision to make, Miss Tansey. You're in danger. Grave danger. I believe you have no idea how much danger you're in. We're very concerned about the likelihood that you'll be successful if given another chance. You have a choice."

I counted the specks on the square linoleum tiles beneath my feet. The word "grave" stimulated an image of my funeral in my head. Was I already in the grave, this conversation a mere passage I had to go through before they threw the dirt on me?

"Miss Tansey, are you listening to me?" His brown eyes bored into me like lasers. A distant part of me nodded yes.

"As I was saying, you have a choice, Miss Tansey. We at St. Mary's believe you need long-term treatment in an excellent facility that's equipped to help you heal from the trauma you've experienced. My associates have researched options and discussed them with your parents.

Oh no, my parents. I had almost forgotten about them. I remembered when they left me here in the hospital when visiting hours were over, after my first suicide attempt, just a few weeks ago. *They are going to be so disappointed in me.*

"Where are my parents? Are they here?" I blankly asked Dr. Kauffman.

"No, they've been notified and are on their way from Frederick."

I imagined them rushing down the stairs of my large, brick childhood home, past the American flag that always flew out front, and jumping into the station wagon to speed to Richmond to save me again. What had they told my little sister and brother?

"Carrie has tried to kill herself again." I used to be the big sister they looked up to, but that girl was dead.

"Your choice is to go willingly," he paused to let the second part sink in. "Or else we have no choice but to commit you."

Commit me?

"We don't believe it's in your best interest to be committed, Carrie," he said more urgently. "That doesn't look good for you and your future. So we're asking you to go willingly."

My future? As if I have a future. I'm a wreck that can't be salvaged. My elan, my life force, is already gone. All I want is for the empty shell of my body to catch up with it, so I can be whole again on the other side … but what did he mean by "willingly?"

Clearly, I was locked up and wouldn't be getting out anytime soon. Someone had to stay with me at all times. What if they locked me up for good? I had no choice but to go willingly, did I? Still, the part of me that had already checked out didn't give a damn. I knew the girl who was desperate to escape this world would do whatever it took to finish the job. Dr. Kauffman's voice reeled me back in.

"Carrie, what do you want to do?"

I stared at the floor and resumed counting the specks. *One . . . two . . . three . . . Well, Doc, isn't it obvious? I want to exit this miserable life.*

"We've determined that you'll need to be cared for and watched for some time. We won't let you die, Carrie. A lot of people are very concerned for you."

His words bounced around in my skull like dozens of mirror-polished balls in a pinball machine—spinning and rolling until they finally reached the jackpot, lights flashing. My hands released the flippers, and all the balls disappeared down a black hole. The words "Game Over" blinked across the back-glass of my mind.

I haven't tried a gun yet.

I'd already made two attempts to end my life. Even I knew this was serious. My vision blurred. "I'll go willingly," I heard myself say faintly. What difference would a long-term stay make, even in the best hospital? I'd already tried treatment.

Dr. Kauffman made sure his message sank in: "You must go willingly, Carrie, or we will have to commit you."

His voice echoed in the cavity of my vacant mind. He handed me a glossy brochure about the place they'd chosen: Sheppard and Enoch Pratt Hospital (a.k.a. the Sheppard Asylum, a.k.a. Sheppard Pratt).

I knew it well. It was a nationally renowned hospital in the suburbs of Baltimore, about an hour from Frederick and only fifteen miles from the University of Maryland Hospital where I'd worked the summer before.

When I'd been growing up in Maryland, it was a place people teased each other about. After catching a peer doing something a little kooky, a friend might say: "Careful, or you'll wind up in Sheppard Pratt!" followed by laughter. Only this wasn't a joke. This psychologist-in-training was being shipped off to the asylum. I couldn't believe it—only I totally could.

"Good luck," said Dr. Kauffman, softening his face to give me an encouraging smile. The orderly returned and escorted me through the long corridors. Back in my room, I crumpled onto the bed and into the fetal position again.

A nurse entered with a dinner tray and a sleeping pill. I just want to die . . . most of me already has, but they won't let me go . . . was my last thought before I drifted off.

They kept me at St. Mary's for a few days. Whatever arrangements were being made for Sheppard Pratt were handled without me. The medical staff had told me how they saw my case. It was easy to imagine the conversations among the members with their white lab coats and clipboards: "We have a twenty-four-year-old woman here who has attempted suicide twice in less than three weeks . . . . She had a sexual relationship with her psychiatrist and is very much in denial of how damaging that was . . . . She appears to be hanging on to her belief that he was a good man who loved her and doesn't see how his actions have put her where she is now . . . . We're very concerned about leaving her alone. She is impulsive and at high risk . . . . We believe she needs to stay somewhere safe for a lengthy period while she figures out what really happened to her and, hopefully, reclaims herself."

So here I was, in a holding tank of sorts, waiting to go to Sheppard Pratt, leaving behind the education I had worked so hard for, the work I once believed would be my salvation. Once the arrangements were finalized, my parents arrived to drive me there.

"Stay with her at all times," warned the middle-aged male social worker assigned to my case as they signed me out. "Even if she goes to the bathroom, stay with her."

He turned to me. "Carrie, do you pledge to keep yourself safe while being transported to Baltimore?"

"Yes," I said. Even as I said it, I wondered what would happen if I jumped out of the car as it whizzed down the highway at sixty miles an hour. I quickly realized I didn't want to put my parents through *that.* I couldn't bear the thought of their having to see me splattered on the road. Secretly, I knew I deserved it. But they didn't.

As we raced up I-95, my father gripped the steering wheel with white knuckles, his body rigid with tension. I was in the back seat with

Mom sitting dutifully beside me, holding my arm tightly. The three of us sat in silence. Outside the car windows, it was summer in Virginia, leafy and green. As we neared the exit for Kings Dominion amusement park, the highway seemed to be buzzing with other station wagons and vans packed with kids wiggling with anticipation. I imagined them screaming, hair flying back as the roller coaster sped downward, toward oblivion, and wondered why fear makes human beings feel so alive. Kings Dominion was probably the part of summer vacation they'd be talking about weeks from now. I wondered what I'd do over my summer vacation, and turned my eyes back inside the car to see a family outing that wasn't so jovial. A ridiculous thought came to me as if it were channeled from my old self, the lighter part of me that had already crossed over and died. Just another *typical family outing. Gidget goes to the insane asylum.* I started to crack up at the absurdity of it all. *Mine is the real roller coaster ride, boys and girls!* At first, Dad looked alarmed, then quickly loosened up on the wheel, and he too started laughing.

"I'll bet those guys in the white coats will slap a straitjacket on your mother as soon as they see her red shoes," he joked. I imagined my saintly looking mom, with her perfectly round silver bun on top of her head being escorted away down a white hallway in a stiff white straitjacket, her red shoes the only color in the scene. "No, I swear, she's the patient!" Mom would say pointing at me, and the orderlies would say, "Yeah, right, lady." Then I could make a quick getaway and let my mom be committed instead. I chuckled to myself.

Well, Carrie, if you didn't want to do the presentation on depression, wasn't there an easier way to get out of it? You needed to act it out? Again, giggles erupted from deep inside me, feeding a steady stream of laughter. With each one, it felt like a little drop of blood came back into my veins, supplied by a distant, higher part of myself who had been watching, waiting. I could almost feel the color rise in my cheeks as I began returning to the land of the living. My mother held my arm tightly the whole three-hour drive to Baltimore, making sure my laughter was genuine, not demented, and that I wasn't planning on opening the car door.

Swathed in Victorian French-Gothic grandeur, Sheppard Pratt looked more like a storybook chateau than a mental institution as our station wagon made its way up the shady lane. Its stone gatehouse, old, red brick buildings with soaring six-story towers, lattice-work balconies, and large, sunlit bay windows symbolized hope and healing. It managed to reach a place deep inside me that appreciated its beauty. There was such great respect paid to the details and design. Momentarily, I felt honored as we pulled up to the entrance. I envisioned some of Sheppard Pratt's first patients rolling up to the vintage gates in their horse-drawn carriages, and speculated about some of the famous patients who had been treated here, like Judy Garland and Zelda Fitzgerald. The artist in me felt nurtured, supported, respected. Still, I dreaded the sound of the doors locking tightly behind me.

By the time we reached the main entrance, the three of us were exhausted but relaxed from nearly peeing our pants with laughter. We walked through the big wooden door, united in hope. During the intake process, we tried to relay to the staff what had been so damned funny—but you had to be there. I overheard one of the professionals murmur something about "denial and release." So what! Through our laughter, I had managed to embrace the unconditional love of my parents, who were just as scared as I was, believing that as hard as this day was, I could descend no lower. From here, I would begin fighting my way upward, out of the underworld. Slowly, one finger at a time, I was digging my way through the crust.

~25~

The admitting nurse, Bruce, unlocked a pair of thick steel doors. His stocky physique made him look more like a bodyguard than a psych nurse. As I walked alongside him with my bags, I faintly remembered the admissions people telling me to pack for at least two seasons. Bruce led me to my room, my home for God-only-knew-how-long. It was directly across the hall from the nurses' station. *Of course. I've just attempted suicide twice. They can't let me out of their sight.*

The room had a twin bed, a small closet, and an antiseptic, white bathroom in the corner with no shower, only a tub. Typical. Lots of hospitals had no showerheads or any other kinds of high fixtures patients could use to hang themselves. Two windows that were sealed shut overlooked the lush, green grounds.

Bruce asked me to open my bags and pull out all my belongings. I dutifully unlatched my white Samsonite suitcase and train case, not remembering what in the world I had thrown in. Oh yeah, here were my jeans, cardigan, favorite peasant blouses, sandals, clogs, a bathing suit . . .

"I need you to give me any items that are sharp, such as eyebrow tweezers, nail files, or electrical devices, such as your hair dryer or curling iron," he said.

"I've never tried to cut myself or hurt myself like *that*," I said, trying to reassure him.

"I'm not doing this just for you," he replied. His voice had a crusty edge, yet a compassionate center. "There are other people here who *will* use sharp objects or appliances with cords to hurt themselves. They need to be protected."

My heart tightened. I'd never been around, let alone lived with, people who might purposely cut or strangle themselves. I blushed as Bruce rifled through my bras and panties, but he didn't come up with anything other than my hairdryer.

"This will be stored at the nurses' station in a cubicle labeled with your name," he said. "You may check it out for twenty minutes at a time."

It was weird not to be trusted, but who could blame him? Safety was first.

With a quick sweep through my train case, Bruce intercepted the bottle of prescription antidepressants I'd been given at St. Mary's, passing them on to the nurses' station too.

So much for downing that when no one was watching.

"Ready for the tour?" he asked.

Bruce led me down the hall, his eyes alert and ready. Another nurse, Eric, taller than Bruce at about six-foot-one, greeted us. He had a similar sturdy, strong build. At five-foot-three, I felt tiny but protected by them both. As we walked down the hall to the high-ceilinged sitting room, I noticed cozy-looking sofas and chairs strategically arranged around coffee tables holding games of backgammon, chess, and Parcheesi. Some patients were just smoking and hanging out. A pool table sat at one end of the room near a large bay window, and a couple of people were taking shots. Getting closer, though, I could sense that the fireplaces and furniture, while beautiful and obviously expensive, were coated with years of cigarette smoke and unbearable sadness.

The doorbell to the unit rang, and Eric sauntered toward the steel entrance doors, keys jingling.

"Your doctor will meet with you soon, Carrie," Bruce said. "In the meantime, let me introduce you to some of your hallmates."

He steered me to a handsome, man who looked like a younger, taller Dustin Hoffman, only with darker hair and icy blue eyes. Michael was gazing out the sitting-room windows to the rolling, green hills beyond. As we shook hands, I sensed that he wanted to be polite but wondered if it was safe to connect with me. His wariness mirrored my own. He seemed like a normal person. Maybe I'd be normal someday too.

Just as I was telling Michael "nice to meet you," I heard feet scuffling across the carpet behind me and turned to see a fast-approaching young woman. She stopped short, standing a tad too close and smiling a bit too much.

"This is Carrie," Bruce said to her, "and Carrie, this is Monica." His voice swelled with warmth when he said her name, as if she were a child he was very proud of. Monica had a faraway gaze that reached inside me. I hoped I didn't look as unnerved by her as I felt.

"You're pretty," she said, then scooted off.

As she left, I couldn't take my eyes off her odd gait: her knees barely bent as each foot brushed over the floor. *I wonder if that's what they call the Thorazine shuffle?* I remembered reading about it, a side effect of anti-psychotic medication.

Bruce remained close by my side as other patients introduced themselves. Most retreated as quickly as they appeared.

Eric returned to us. "Dr. LeGray is here," he said, guiding me toward the sunroom at the far end of the hall. I was relieved and ready to move away from the smoke and misery.

Quiet as a mouse, Dr. LeGray sat in a brown leather chair, and I took a seat on the matching sofa across from him, moving a blue tapestry pillow behind my back to get more comfortable. The way he groomed his hair and beard made him look like Sigmund Freud. Sunlight burst through several floor-to-ceiling windows and warmed the marble floor. A large TV and two damask occasional chairs completed the room.

The television was mute but tuned to MTV, showing Michael Jackson made up like a zombie, dancing with the walking dead in his "Thriller" video. I felt Dr. LeGray stare at me while I watched the TV. I was going to make him start the conversation. It was at least a minute before he spoke.

"Welcome to Sheppard Pratt, Miss Tansey," he said flatly. I pulled my attention away from Michael Jackson, who was much more interesting. "For the next seventy-two hours," LeGray went on, "you will be under observation. The door to your room must remain open at all times, and you are not allowed to leave this hall. Your meals will be delivered to the sitting room, where you will eat with a staff member."

I didn't like his demeanor at all, so I said nothing.

"Once we determine you are no longer a risk to yourself, you can earn other privileges such as walking to groups or to the dining room without staff. Eventually, you will be able, as long as you stay safe, to walk the premises of Sheppard Pratt, and even take day passes to places in Baltimore."

So I'm a rat caged in a learning chamber. If I do the right things, I might get a treat.

A Madonna video came on. She was just a bit older than me but so free. Even with the sound off, I knew the words:

Borderline. Feels I'm going to lose my mind . . .

I wanted to dance with her. I imagined myself twirling around singing "you just keep on pushing my love, over the borderline." I refrained, however, afraid I might wind up medicated like Monica.

"You and I will meet three times a week, and the charge nurse will give you a schedule of the rest of your therapeutic activities," the doctor went on.

Three times a week? With this supercilious stick-in-the-mud? Sigmund Freud: The Sequel? Give me strength!

I felt an unfamiliar spirit of rebellion swell in my solar plexus.

"I understand that you have a lot to share and that you've driven three hours to get here today, so let's meet tomorrow morning to discuss your treatment. Any questions?"

Yeah, can I trust another male psychiatrist ever again?

*Have **you** slept with any of **your** patients?*

Do you ever smile?

"No," I lied. When he said goodbye and strolled away with a slight wiggle to his hips, it comforted me to think he might not be interested in women.

"Carrie, your dinner is here." Bruce led me back to the sitting room where a tray with a stainless steel cover awaited me. I settled into a plush, blue-velvet wingback chair. Glancing around, I noticed other patients lining up to be taken to dinner in the first-floor cafeteria. The only ones left were an unbelievably short woman named Jean and me. She looked like a child in her chair as her feet dangled above the floor. She removed the tray's cover, snuck a quick peek at me, then devoured the meal as if she hadn't eaten in months. Then she kept her eyes fixed on me as I patiently twirled my fork full of spaghetti. It was cold and pasty, but I ate all of it. Once I finished, Bruce, who had been sitting a few feet away, swept in, gathered our trays, made sure all the utensils were accounted for, and delivered everything back to the cafeteria.

Eventually, the other patients returned from dinner, and I overheard a couple of young women whispering, "Who's that?" to the nurse in charge. Then they eyed me from their corner, chatting it up with Michael. Suddenly they were headed my way. Like him, they appeared so normal and healthy I just couldn't fathom why they were here.

"I'm Debbie," said a tall, athletic blonde who could have passed for a soccer champion.

"Elizabeth," said a gorgeous but shy brunette with a Southern accent. As she extended her hand, I envisioned her on the cover of

Southern Living magazine sitting at a table draped with a pure white linen tablecloth surrounded by the finest crystal, china, and candlesticks.

"What are you in for?" Debbie asked.

The truth spilled out of me. "Depression. Suicide."

"What, you tried to kill yourself?" Debbie's eyes instantly misted with tears. "Why?"

I quickly changed the subject. "How 'bout you?"

"We're in the eating disorder program," they said in perfect unison.

I must have had a blank, stupid look on my face because Debbie added, "Eating disorder. You know: bulimia? anorexia?"

Two other skinny girls cautiously approached, and Debbie introduced them. Connie and Leanne were part of the eating disorder program too. With my new companions—two bulimics and two anorexics —we added up to five broken hearts. I felt comforted that they were all about my age, attractive, and smart. Maybe I wasn't so crazy.

"Would you like to go for a walk later tonight?" The Southern belle stretched out her vowels in a way that sounded classy.

"I can't leave," I explained. "I'm under observation." We all stood there in awkward silence.

"Well, I'm sure you'll be able to go off the unit soon enough," Debbie chimed in optimistically. Just follow the rules, and you'll be free to join us soon."

Monica shuffled up to our group, moving more like a robot than a human being. "I bet you pretty girls know how to dance." We said nothing. She left as quickly as she'd come.

"Thorazine," Debbie whispered. "Monica is schizophrenic."

I knew it. Poor dear. I wondered if Monica could dance anymore.

"Well . . . see you later," said Debbie. "Please sit with us at dinner when you can." She turned. "Bruce, can you open the door for us?"

Elizabeth and Debbie walked off the unit while Leanne and Connie went back to their room at the front of the ward.

My heart warmed at the thought of having such lovely girls already wanting to be my friends. They looked so golden and full of life. I couldn't imagine them throwing up or starving themselves. I also couldn't imagine they could see me as anything but the dark, black hole that I was. But a tiny pinpoint of light glowed inside as I thought of eventually exploring the grounds with them.

Days went by, and I got oriented to the A-1 hall, the short-term ward for the higher-functioning-though-acute cases. I lived in fear that they might transfer me to the B side: the more-chronic cases that were expected to stay much longer—as in months, even years. I heard stories of aggressive patients losing control on the B side and the staff using cold wetpacks to quell them into submission. Maybe I didn't have much will to live, but I never wanted to find myself strapped to a gurney, wrapped like a mummy in wetpacks. It was scary enough that the A-1 hall had a white, padded room, the kind you saw in the movies.

Other than that, the routine at Sheppard Pratt became kind of like high school, only instead of going to class, I was always going to groups. There were process groups, occupational therapy groups, art therapy groups, horticulture therapy groups, and, of course, my dreaded individual sessions with Dr. LeGray. Breakfast, lunch, and dinner were at the same times every day, and my new friends and I eagerly went to the cafeteria together, supervised by Bruce or Eric. I liked getting to know the other residents, but it was so heartbreaking to hear the stories of what had brought them to Sheppard Pratt. One night, Michael confessed he was admitted after becoming convinced he was Satan. Elizabeth shared that in the sixth grade, she had been raped by her uncle and hadn't been able to eat normally since. My story was sounding less tragic, even though all the patients seemed shocked to think of a doctor's hurting me in the way Tony had.

Then there was the elderly but elegant Jane who would sit idly on the couch for hours with her face totally blank—that is, until I roused her from her daydreams, and she'd unfailingly burst into a smile. She was sweet and lovely, and I was stunned to hear that she had a crush on her therapist.

"Dr. LeGray, isn't he nice?" Jane swooned as she told me of their long talks about gardening.

"Really?" I said flatly, even as I smirked inside. If there was one professional who was in no danger of losing control of the therapeutic situation, it was straight-laced, sexually ambiguous, pompous, boring Dr. LeGray. Clearly, Jane was safe—and so was I. Probably the best thing for me, really.

Jane had flawless but pasty white skin, and her genteel face was framed by a dull, white coiffure. Her eyes were usually vacant until someone came to sit with her.

"Oh, yes, dear. Please come sit with me. I just love hearing you talk," she would say time and again as she beckoned me to join her on the sunroom sofa. I loved listening to stories of her children and could see how loved she was by all the family members and friends who called on her during visiting hours.

After knowing her for a week, I finally bucked up the courage to say, "Jane, I still don't know what brought you here to Sheppard Pratt."

"Well, my dear, it isn't a happy story," she said. "You see, about four months ago, I downed a box of fertilizer. It was the second time I had done it. The first was after my husband of fifty years passed away, but this time, I almost succeeded. My gardener found me. I was in a coma for over two months before coming out of it and being transferred here."

Holy crap. There were more ways to kill yourself than I had ever imagined. For the first time, I was grateful to be locked up.

Bruce arrived, "Miss Jane, it's time for your appointment."

"Oh, you're seeing Dr. LeGray?" I offered, trying to sound positive.

"Oh, no, my dear girl, I get ECT three or four times a week. I don't know, Bruce, do you think it's working?" She reached out her hand for him to help her up.

"Yes, ma'am. You're almost as good as new," said Bruce with a wink.

"I guess so," Jane corroborated. "I couldn't talk for the first month I was here. Now I just love talking to this pretty, young woman." She leaned over and squeezed my hand. "I hope you'll have dinner with me later, dear."

"I'd be honored to."

I watched Jane slowly walk off, supported by Bruce and her cane, and felt my heart sink. What would make this beautiful, elegant lady eat a whole box of fertilizer? In the coming weeks, I watched Jane come and go from the unit, spaced out and dazed after every electroconvulsive therapy treatment, but gradually, the light returned to her eyes, the brightness to her skin, the sheen to her hair. I wondered if ECT would be my fate.

"Wow, I can't believe they still do shock therapy these days," I remarked, dropping a hint to Dr. LeGray in session one day. He merely nodded, unwilling to engage in talk about Jane or any other patients.

Whereas Dr. LeGray had firm, almost-rigid boundaries with his patients, the lack of boundaries among the patients themselves could be unsettling. One day, while walking down the hall, Ernie, a two-hundred-fifty-pound schizophrenic who regularly talked to himself about football, came running toward me, lifted me up to his shoulder, and twirled me around, laughing hysterically.

"I got her, I got her!" he proclaimed with delight as if I were an imaginary football he had intercepted for the touchdown.

I screamed, "Help!" and immediately the ward's siren rang out, and three orderlies rushed in to restrain Ernie.

Not long after that, I awoke in my bed one night to find a shadow looming over me.

"You are a lesbian," came Monica's voice. As my eyes adjusted to the darkness, I could see her peering into me. I held back the urge to say, "No, Monica, *you* are a lesbian." My eyes stayed glued to hers as my right hand fumbled for the alert button and pressed it. Swiftly, the nurses swept in and gently guided her back to her room.

For more than three years, I had been isolated from family and peers, shrouded in my secret life with Tony, I thought, staring at the ceiling. Now, I was never alone in a place where everybody's everything was out in the open.

~26~

Most of the time, I tried not to think of the outside world, but I knew that back in Richmond, fall semester was about to start at VCU. I wondered what my friends like Lori, Greta, and Sue would be doing this year. I tried not to think about how long it would be before I "graduated" from Sheppard Pratt.

One day, I had just been escorted back to the unit after my 8 a.m. breakfast when the charge nurse, Kitty, approached to tell me I would be going for my first treatment team meeting later this morning. She checked the schedule posted on my door: "You'll have to miss occupational therapy." No loss. I was more interested in hearing what the staff thought of my progress and my prognosis.

When Bruce brought me to the conference room, I was surprised to find six professionals seated in a semi-circle, all fully briefed on my story. I remembered when I used to be part of a treatment team myself, recording the behaviors of my patients. Now I was on the receiving end. Taking a seat, I felt caught off-guard by how much these people knew about me.

Dr. Robert Temple, the head of my unit and acting medical director of Sheppard Pratt, started the meeting: "Miss Tansey, we're here to discuss the course of treatment for your depression."

Everyone—the art therapist, unit nurse, my psychiatrist, social worker, a mental health worker, and Dr. Temple—asked me question after question, scrawling notes on their clipboards.

"How is your appetite? We see you've lost some weight."

"We hear you're complaining about feeling as if a tight band is wrapped around your head. Can you tell us more about that sensation?"

"How are you sleeping? Any nightmares?"

"On a scale of 1 to 10, what is your anxiety level?"

Mostly Dr. Temple listened, letting others take the lead. After ten minutes or so, he leaned forward with a grave expression. "We're quite concerned to hear what took place with your former therapist, Dr. Anthony Romano. We think that he's very dangerous and must be stopped."

My breath caught in my throat. I glanced around the circle. Other heads nodded. Until this meeting, I had gotten the impression that all the professionals who encountered my story were sympathetic to me, but suddenly I felt defensive. I felt trapped. Tony and I were being judged, and he could lose everything.

This is why I wished I had succeeded with the suicide. I had already lost everything. I meant to die with the secret. Now Tony could lose everything too. These people wanted me to incriminate him.

Oh, no, Tony . . . I knew you were going to get in trouble. I'm so sorry.

My eyes scanned the carpet, falling on its pattern of subtle red diamonds, and I found myself counting them. *One, two, three . . .* As I did so, the other people in the room blurred out of focus, and I felt momentarily centered and removed.

"You have been greatly injured by this man's actions, and will need quite a lot of treatment to get well again," said Dr. Temple. "We believe it's in your best interest, Miss Tansey, to take action against him as part of your recovery, to hold him accountable, and get financial restitution to pay for your behavioral healthcare—but we can't force you to do these things. However, if you don't take action, *we* will." There was a pause.

"Carrie, are you hearing me?" I peeled my gaze off the red diamonds and looked Dr. Temple in the eyes. The room began spinning, and I had to resist throwing up.

"On your behalf, I sought the advice of the head attorney of Sheppard Pratt's legal department," he went on. "I asked him what attorney he'd never want to face in a malpractice lawsuit. His answer was Earle Plumhoff. Here's his number."

Dr. Temple extended a sheet of paper to me, but I could barely lift my hand.

"He's probably the best personal-injury lawyer in Maryland, Carrie. We think it's important for you to consult with him. What Dr. Romano did to you was egregious, and he must be stopped. It's important that you be the one to file a complaint with the State of Maryland licensing board. We are here to support you. Do you have any questions?"

"I don't think so," I heard myself say. My head felt dizzy as I tried to process what Dr. Temple had just said about Tony.

"But I think he really loved me."

I was sitting on the sunroom sofa, where Ruthie, a nurse at Sheppard Pratt, listened to me as though it was the most important part of her day.

"I don't think it's his fault that I'm so messed up." I looked out the large windows to the rolling, green hills, searching for a way to escape what lay ahead. *Please, God, don't let this be happening.* I waited, hoping for a sense of light or guidance. I couldn't feel God anywhere. I was in this alone.

I told Ruthie how Dr. Temple and his staff had said I should take legal action against Tony, report him to the licensing board, and that Dr. Temple had made it quite clear that, "If you don't . . . *we* will."

Ruthie listened attentively, without judgment, then said, "I'm sure you'll gain clarity in time, Carrie," before heading off to take a head-count of everyone who should have returned from the afternoon horticultural therapy group by now.

I sat alone in the sunroom. I had never thought of myself as a victim before. Sure, I had wanted to end the relationship with Tony. It obviously wasn't working, but until now, I had never considered that I had been abused. That's what Dr. Temple's team was saying anyway. Still, I was having trouble convincing myself that Tony had acted in my best interest, or even that he had made an honest mistake. I couldn't deny that every time I told anyone at Sheppard Pratt about how I had lived in the shadows with my shrink—the drugs, the sex, the years of lying—they all had the same reaction: horror.

A couple of days ago, when I told Bruce that Tony regularly encouraged me to smoke pot with him, Bruce had gotten so upset that he had to walk away for a moment and get a glass of water to clear his throat. When he returned, it took him a moment to gather his words.

"To think that someone whose responsibility is to heal you, numbs you with drugs and exploits you for his own selfish needs. . . ." Bruce set the glass down and rubbed his temples. "It's absolutely horrifying to me, Carrie. I can't bear to think of it."

The evidence that Tony had indeed abused me was overwhelming. Sometimes, I wondered what it meant to be abused. Sometimes, it felt like it was all my fault.

As part of my treatment plan, I had been attending an art therapy group. On my first day, an orderly had taken me to the studio on the ground floor. As I entered the classroom along with eight other patients, my heart stopped: the colors, the paints, the paper, the clay, and the wide-open tables beckoned. I inhaled the scent of fresh pigment and paper. It was like stepping into a sacred temple. For the first time in years, I felt at home.

Our art therapist, Audrey, was a sturdy, centered, middle-aged Jewish woman with a hippie vibe, a New York accent, and a boatload of compassion mixed with moxie. She was always dressed down in jeans and sweatshirts to accommodate paint and glue, and I found her presence comforting. She showed us our materials and gave us one simple instruction: "Allow whatever you're feeling in this moment to unfold and express."

I tore into a brand-new box of chalk pastels, my hands trembling with excitement. I didn't think; I just drew until I knew it was finished. Inside me, a door opened to a room containing the part of my soul that I'd lost.

Audrey gathered our creations and hung them on a giant board. It was a moment of profound validation. Our insides, those lonely and isolated parts of us, were now on the outside on full display.

"What do you want to tell us about yours, Carrie?"

I shrugged my shoulders. "I have no idea. I just started doodling."

On the board before us, an inky-black hand emerged from a psychedelic, abstract swirl of colors. Gradually, it dawned on me that it was *my* black hand reaching out from a storm of emotions, begging to be rescued.

"You are very creative," Audrey declared, and other heads in the room bobbed in agreement. *Creative.* I knew it was just a word, but to me that one word was like a drink of water to someone parched and dying in the desert. *She thinks I'm creative.*

"Yes," Debbie chimed in. "You're very creative, Carrie. And you're so funny. You make me laugh, even when I'm down."

Something unfamiliar quivered inside me. It took me a few seconds to recognize that it was a feeling of happiness. I thought back to the zany sense of humor I'd had in my teens and how my friends and I would laugh joyously at the absurdities of life. Was it coming back?

"I can tell you're creative and very resourceful," Audrey continued.

Sitting there in our art-review session, I began to see where my creativity and resourcefulness—my strengths—had helped me survive a severe depression and a poisonous relationship with my psychiatrist. It was a damned revelation.

I sat up straighter.

That night, I lay awake in bed with the door open, listening to the night staff whisper in the halls. I couldn't stop thinking about the creative energy from another realm that had poured into me in art class. She or "it" had wanted to reach out and be part of me again. This connection to my higher self felt more real and important than the suicide attempts, psychiatric commitments, lawsuits, or despicable shrinks.

Through my bedroom window, I noticed that the moon was brighter than usual. Maybe there was hope for me. Mystic and psychiatrist Carl Jung said that the psyche speaks to us through symbols rather than words. Here, I'd verbally rehashed my ordeal a hundred times over, but never once had I given myself credit for surviving it. The drawing helped me do that. I couldn't wait to go back to the studio! If I had my way, I'd be there every day, every hour, painting away all the remnants of my madness. I wanted to go as often as possible so I could expel every last drop of angst. I wanted to be done with all the mud, monsters, ugliness, and trauma, and was eager to put them where they belonged—on paper or canvas—releasing them from my mind and heart.

After painting and sketching for weeks, I continued to unearth more and more positive aspects of myself, which I could nurture and trust. One day in art therapy, I felt extremely lighthearted and found it easier than usual to draw. I grabbed some colored chalk and made a quick, simple drawing of abstract shapes on red paper. I tacked it on the board and headed back to my seat.

"Holy shit . . ." said Richard, a wonderful gay man recovering from the heartbreak of losing his partner. He stared, transfixed.

"My God, Carrie," another voice rang out.

Others in the room gasped. Someone whispered, "Jesus, Carrie . . ."

I spun around and took in the image from a distance. I froze. I hadn't really seen it before. Dozens of jagged, penis-shaped parts were pointing inward from all directions, stabbing at a void in the center. Dark shades of red, blue, and black pulsated with pain. A wave of nausea washed over me as I realized that this drawing of mine was telling a story . . . of repeated psychic rape.

Audrey addressed the shock in the room. "Do you want to tell us about your image, Carrie?" [which can be seen on my website, www.carrieishee.com/about-the-book].

I answered in an unnatural monotone: "I guess I was abused by my shrink."

Those who were still working popped up their heads from their unfinished pieces. For a few minutes, we just sat there examining what had sprung out of me. All were quiet.

I fled the studio and practically ran back to my room, not caring that I was being followed closely by a staff member. I closed the door.

I felt as if a dam built of numbness, rationalization, and denial had been holding back my grief, but now, it had crumbled irrevocably. A flood of sorrow and betrayal surged forth, drowning me. My entire body heaved with deep, urgent sobs.

The door flew open, and a nurse reminded me that I wasn't allowed to shut it. I collapsed on the floor behind the bed in an effort to gain some privacy. The flood washed away my self-blame, my misconceptions: I had been emotionally and spiritually violated and psychically shattered . . . abused by a man I had trusted . . . a doctor my parents had paid to heal me . . . a mentor with whom I had shared my deepest spiritual yearnings and dreams of a beautiful life . . . a person whom I had believed to be a father figure, a healer, my closest friend.

I couldn't condone Tony's behavior any longer; it had almost killed me.

My body convulsed, and I cried myself to sleep.

~27~

The doorbell rang on A-1, signaling that visitors were on the other side of the twin steel doors. It was the evening of my twenty-fifth birthday, and my parents were picking me up and taking me out to dinner. They visited as often as they could, frequently bringing one of my siblings with them. Each time, I could feel them straining to stay upbeat. I had been on the ward for three months now, and had only recently been deemed safe enough to leave with my parents on a special pass. As I tied the sash on my favorite gauze dress, I realized it might be too breezy for the November weather and quickly changed into a warm, fuzzy peach cowl-neck sweater, winter-white corduroy skirt, and brown boots. I lived so much of my life indoors these days that I had almost forgotten it was fall. As I headed out of my room to the sitting area, I glanced at some of my hallmates playing pool.

"Lucky birthday girl!" Marguerite shouted, walking toward me with a cue, cigarette hanging from her mouth. She pointed at my parents, anxiously waiting for me with big smiles on their faces. "You are indeed a lucky girl. I can see how much your parents love you."

Marguerite was a thirty-something schizophrenic who shuffled like Monica and smoked like a chimney. Bloated from years of heavy meds, hair greasy from inattention, she had an unnerving optimism for someone who would be forever afflicted by mental illness. "Can I meet them? They're such a handsome couple."

"Sure, Marguerite. I know they would love to meet you." As I walked with her toward Mom and Dad, I felt like I was about to introduce them to a new but rather unpredictable friend I had met on the first day at a new school.

They gave me big hugs and then greeted Marguerite. "Well, now, who do we have here?" said Dad, genuinely happy to meet my new friend.

"Mom, Dad, this is Marguerite. Marguerite—Joanne and Bob Tansey."

Leaning on her pool cue, Marguerite quickly crushed out her cigarette in a nearby ashtray and extended her hand to them. Mom had a bit of a dazed look in her eyes, but her smile was warm.

"Marguerite, pleased to meet you. Joanne Tansey," she said.

Dad broke into a huge smile. "Well, now, Marguerite, how are you doing tonight?"

"Well, you know how it goes. My new meds make me pee all the time, but they're way better than the old ones that just killed my sex drive." Marguerite let out a boisterous laugh.

My parents' eyes got bigger and rounder as they giggled nervously. Yes, at Sheppard Pratt, everyone's everything was always right out there.

Bruce jumped up from the nurses' station to shepherd us out the door. "Okay, Marguerite, put that pool cue away; we're headed to dinner soon," he hollered over his shoulder. "Carrie," he said, meeting my eyes, "have a wonderful birthday dinner. Remember, your pass ends at 9 p.m."

I felt about two feet tall as I walked down the hall. This was not how I'd imagined celebrating my twenty-fifth birthday. Sure, I had gotten lots of cards today, and my hallmates had thrown me a party with cupcakes at lunchtime, but I felt like shit. The only thing that really gave me hope was that maybe the lawyer I'd be meeting later this week would help me hold Tony accountable and climb my way out of at least the financial pieces of this mess, as the costs of my treatment kept piling up.

In the weeks after my painful revelation in art therapy, I set myself to diligently following the treatment team's plan. I went to more art therapy. I went to group therapy. I did assignments aimed at extinguishing my negative self-talk and raising my esteem. I even confronted the hardest task they had charged me with: I called Earle Plumhoff.

My hand was shaking as I dialed the number. My stomach was in knots as the phone rang, and my throat constricted something terrible when a paralegal answered pleasantly: "Nolan, Plumhoff, and Williams." But I had done it.

Now, as Bruce walked me down the main corridor to a first-floor meeting room, I felt like I could jump out of my skin. Would the attorneys believe me? What questions would they ask? As Bruce opened the door, two men stood to greet me. J. Earle Plumhoff was over six feet tall, his taupe, three-piece suit fit like a glove, and his hair looked like it had been trimmed this morning. He looked younger than I expected, fortyish, I guessed, and had a commanding presence that was approachable and impeccable at the same time, like Gregory Peck's Atticus Finch in *To Kill a Mockingbird.*

"Miss Tansey, it's a pleasure to meet you," he said, and he sounded like he truly meant it. He gestured toward a man about my age, looking preppy in his navy blue suit as he focused on a yellow legal pad through tortoise-shell glasses. "This is my colleague, Bob Hanley."

Bob extended his hand. "Miss Tansey," he said with a courteous nod.

We all sat down in the leather wingback chairs that circled a mahogany coffee table. The rich, jewel-like draperies and matching bluish green and red pillows, along with the Oriental rug on the floor, spoke of wealth and richness. There was no heavy, foreboding vibe in this room like there was on the A-1 ward. I felt a sense of shame. I didn't deserve these beautiful surroundings or these classy lawyers. Unpleasant as it was, the dreariness of A-1 was in synch with my state of mind. In here, I felt thrown off, out of place. Plumhoff smiled at me as he opened his brown leather briefcase and shuffled through some documents.

He gathered a neat, white stack of papers, and I recalled that I had sent him a typed narrative detailing my relationship with Tony, along with a timeline of key events from late 1980 until now.

"Miss Tansey," Plumhoff began. "How are you doing today?"

He waited for me to reply. A sense of space opened up for me.

"I'm okay . . . well, it's not exactly the greatest time of my life."

Looking at the two men, I felt the weight of my lost dreams. I had wanted to be a professional like them, to dress in nice clothes, to save humanity, but now I was a pathetic woman who needed saving. Would I ever be past needing someone to rescue me?

"Yes, I hear you've been through quite an experience with one Dr. Anthony Romano," Plumhoff continued. "As attorneys, we take professional ethics very seriously. It is a tragedy that you, at the young age of twenty-four, would feel so hopeless as to try to take your life immediately after ending this damaging relationship—a relationship that should have healed you. Based on the evidence you've presented, we think you have a very good malpractice case against Dr. Romano."

My head spun as if it could pop off. *Malpractice . . . malpractice.* For months, people on the ward had been telling me I had a legitimate malpractice suit against Tony, but hearing the word come out of the mouth of this prominent attorney made me suddenly feel like I was playing out a character in a novel. I was willing to do everything my doctors recommended for my healing, but I wasn't sure how going through the emotional upheaval of a trial was going to help. And I didn't see how hurting Tony was going to help either.

"I'm not trying to protect Tony," I began cautiously, "but I don't want to hurt him either, and I don't want him to lose his license."

"For the time being, we don't want him to lose it either," agreed Plumhoff. I wasn't sure I understood.

"So if I agree to go through with this, how would it help my healing process? Because it's also conjuring up a lot of . . ."—I gestured toward my belly with clawlike hands—". . . shit," I said with finality.

Hanley flashed a compassionate smile.

"I'm happy to break this down," said Plumhoff, nodding to his colleague and the legal pad. "Based on some information I got from your father, Mr. Hanley here has been crunching some numbers. First off, your parents paid Romano more than $10,000 in psychotherapy bills."

He rifled through some more papers. "Now, according to your doctors here, you're making good progress. Nevertheless, the severity of your . . ."—the articulate man paused, searching for the right word—". . . *injuries* is such that you will likely need a five- to eight-month stay. Sheppard Pratt costs $10,000 a month."

My mind reeled. I'd had no idea. Ten thousand dollars a month? I had almost been here four months. That was $40,000! I doubted my father earned $40,000 *a year*. The bill could rise as high as $80,000. I gulped.

Plumhoff continued. "Your two stays in St. Mary's cost around $7,600. And your doctors recommend that once you are released from Sheppard Pratt, you continue outpatient psychotherapy appointments for years to come. Now you are twenty-five years old, is that correct?"

"Yes."

Plumhoff scowled at some medical forms. "I understand from speaking to your father that for the time being, you are still covered by your parents' health insurance, but that will expire within the next year." He dropped the papers on the coffee table and looked at me.

Those weren't the only debts. I thought of my unfinished degree. I had a $5,000 student loan. Mom and Dad had put thousands of dollars toward graduate school—money that was down the drain if I never finished. I felt so guilty. And they had Tim and Polly's educations to pay for too. And Bob, who could never leave the nest.

"Of course, we have to consider lost earning power," Plumhoff said. He was clearly thinking along the same lines as I was, and Hanley nodded. "Had this incident not interrupted the course of your education, you might be working soon."

Even so, I thought hopelessly, an entry-level salary at a clinic or psychiatric hospital paid about $16,000 a year. Even if I could work, it would literally take me years to pay for my months in Sheppard Pratt. Suddenly, I was covered in goosebumps. In the state I was in now, I might not ever go back to school, in which case, I'd be working at an even-lower-paying job, whatever that might be. I must have looked stunned. The mountain of debt seemed infinite, and it smothered me, pushing my spirits lower.

"How much do your legal fees cost?" I asked hesitantly.

"Your case is strong enough that I'm prepared to take it on contingency," said Plumhoff confidently. "That is to say, Mr. Hanley and I only get paid if we win."

Wow. They really believed in my case. I wanted to believe in it too—but I couldn't, not completely.

"I know this may sound silly to you," I began, looking at my feet, "and maybe it's because of the way I was raised, but two wrongs don't make a right. I can't stand the thought of Tony losing everything that's important to him—his practice, his home, his farm, his car. It would devastate him."

"Miss Tansey," Plumhoff countered gently, "doctors are required by law to have malpractice insurance. If we win this case, Dr. Romano's malpractice insurance will pay the damages." His eyes opened wide with reassurance. "It is highly unlikely his personal assets will be affected. Dr. Romano's life will go on as it always has."

For a second, I was relieved, but then the realization hit me as heavily as a blow to the head. Even if I won, Tony's life would go on as it always had—hunting at the farm, dining in upscale restaurants, zooming down the highway in his blue sports car—and my life might never be the same. It also struck me with sickening certainty just why Tony had been willing to risk everything in his affair with me.

I don't know how long I sat there, wordlessly. In that moment, the way forward became clear. I had to sue Tony. I had to do it for my parents. I had to do it for my siblings. I had to do it for me.

It was the only way I could pay for the medical care I needed. It was the only way I could heal. It was my only hope.

I took a deep breath. "Okay, then. What do I need to do?"

Earle Plumhoff's eyes crinkled at the corners, and he reached for something in his briefcase.

The Pomegranate

The Dark Lord relented, but fed his naive consort a pomegranate before her departure. Hermes then delivered Persephone to the temple of her mother, harvest goddess Demeter, who embraced her, but then asked with dread if she had eaten fruit from down below, "for if you have taken such darkness into yourself, you must go back again beneath the secret places of the earth, there to dwell for a time among the lost and the dead."

~28~

"Today is Richard's last art therapy group," Audrey announced as my hallmates and I shuffled into the art therapy room on a Friday afternoon.

"Richard, as you prepare to discharge, do you want to do an art review sharing with us the process you've gone through here?" Audrey asked. For a second, Richard looked like he didn't know where to start.

"Just pick out a few of your most meaningful images to share," Audrey reassured him.

"Sure thing, Miss Audrey," Richard proclaimed with a touch of playful sarcasm. His cigarette almost leaped out of his hand as he tried to hide it from her sight, and I could tell he briefly thought of stashing it in the pocket of his faded blue jeans. Instead, he palmed it in one hand while smoothing down his bleached blond hair with the other. I giggled to myself, realizing he had broken the rules again, walking through the halls with a lit cigarette.

It never failed to amuse me just how much my hallmates and I would regress to defiant adolescent behavior when faced with the boredom and limitations of our confinement. Something about being in a locked psych ward made almost all of us take up smoking or increase the habit. Until now, I hadn't smoked since sneaking a drag behind Martha Nicodemus's barn in eighth grade. However, after resolving to sue Tony for malpractice, I quite suddenly and drastically started smoking two packs a day. Somehow, the cigarettes made me feel tougher, like the badass I was going to have to be to survive the coming legal ordeal.

As Richard pinned his creations to the corkboard at the front of the room, I caught a whiff of smoke and wondered if it was radiating off him or me. *Hell, everything and everybody in this hell hole smells like smoke.* He mounted six pieces of his artwork and then stood back, just as I had on that fateful day many weeks ago when I had put up my own shattered image. That time, Richard had broken the ice with "holy shit" at the sight of my tormented creation. This time, it was my turn.

"Wow, Richard, the progress is incredible!"

"Yes, Richard, I do believe you have gone through quite a transformation," announced Audrey in a calm, confident voice, as though she had seen this many times before.

Transformation. Transformation. I could feel myself light up inside and expand with this word. I had always known I was at Sheppard Pratt to heal—but to transform? The word gave my work ahead a whole new spin.

Richard's six acrylic paintings mounted from left to right showed a steady progression from darkness to light, brokenness to wholeness. The images leaped off the canvasses and spoke more powerfully than any words could about Richard's healing since his voluntary commitment to Sheppard Pratt.

"Well, as you can see, I came in quite hopeless, having just tried to take my life," he said, pointing to a picture of a black figure crouched in the corner of a dismal room. "All the light went out of my life when I caught Lionel with another man. I felt so betrayed."

His eyes teared up. "But with you folks, lots of TLC, and lots of talking and painting, you can see how my images change." He gestured to the next painting. "See how my room slowly gets filled up with furnishings, drapes appear on the windows, and finally that dark little guy in the corner from my drawing at admission time is sitting in my favorite wingback chair in front of the fireplace, my silly cat Jezebel at my feet."

The room was quiet as the eight of us viewed his evolution.

"I never thought of it before," he said, scratching his head, fighting back tears, "but it's so obvious now. You see, I'm an interior designer." He took a big breath. "My time at Sheppard has been about redesigning my interior," he gestured to the center of his chest, and his voice faltered for a second, "which was shattered when my heart was broken."

My eyes welled up with tears of sadness and hope as I let Richard's images touch me. They illustrated his coming back to life. And here he was before me, a man less sad, more hopeful, more complete, and more real after just six weeks at Sheppard. *Maybe there is hope for me. Maybe I can go through a similar transformation.* I felt myself sit up straighter, as if my spine had suddenly gotten stronger.

Then my heart sank. *But I can't bear to say goodbye to Richard.*

"Does anyone else have feedback for Richard?" Audrey asked.

"Richard, I'll miss your pink shirts, your high fives, even the wiggle in your walk," I offered. "You've made me laugh like no other, but you also made me smoke more cigarettes than I would have," I said, giving him a big hug. "I'll miss you, but my lungs won't."

We all laughed. More people wished him well.

"Look out for those users out there," Marguerite chimed in. "You have a heart of gold, Richard. Be choosy. That guy didn't deserve you."

"Anything else, Richard?" Audrey said.

"Well," he said over his shoulder as he unpinned his artwork, "just make sure you all remember me and these paintings. This body of work will be known as my Sheppard Period."

Giggles swept through the air before meeting up with the raucous laughter my belly let loose.

"Just don't cut off your ear on your way out," yelled Marguerite, a bit too boisterously, nearly knocking over a jar of paint.

I thought of *Starry Night,* which Van Gogh had painted when he was in an asylum in 1889, and imagined him sitting with a bunch of wounded folks like us in a room like this somewhere in the south of France nearly a hundred years ago. I wasn't sure if I should be proud or ashamed to be part of such an exclusive, albeit tragic, crowd.

"Nope, Marguerite, my ears are staying put," Richard joked back. He looked around the room. "I'll miss you guys. Please take care of yourselves." He turned to me, "Carrie, don't let that selfish, unconscionable shrink keep you down. I still miss Lionel, but now I have myself back. I know that in time, you will too."

I jumped up to hug Richard and felt the warmth of our hearts merge in a knowing embrace.

As I watched the hallmates around me heal, it reassured me that gradually, I was healing too, even if I did backslide from time to time. I had been here long enough that I began extending myself to new patients, helping them get used to the steel doors, the cubbyholes, the rules. The second day I saw a new guy on the ward, I made a point of introducing myself.

His hair was brown and short, almost military style, and his biceps bulged out of the sleeves of his navy polo shirt. He sat on the sitting-room sofa, elbows on thighs, hands dangling, surveying everyone casually.

In the distance, tiny Jean stood at one of the pool tables using it as an altar while holding a plastic silver chalice high above her head, eyes closed with reverence. The guy tried to act like he wasn't watching her. I plopped down beside him.

"Hi, I'm Carrie."

"Hugh," he said without making eye contact.

"Hugh, you're new," I said, trying to be chipper.

He raised his eyebrows and smirked reluctantly, then swept his eyes back to the pool table. "What's she doing?"

"Jean? Conducting a Mass, I guess." I squinted for a better look. "Or maybe she's a Priestess of Avalon."

"Huh?" Hugh said.

Across the room, Jean slowly lowered the glass to her lips. I had to hand it to her—weird as she was, everyone in the room watched in silence as she conducted her ritual.

"You know, *The Mists of Avalon*?"

He looked at me blankly.

"The book? The best-seller?"

He shrugged and turned back to the scene. "Where did she get a chalice?" he said as Jean offered it to others to partake. "Are chalices even *allowed* in Sheppard Pratt?"

The way he emphasized "allowed" made me think he was still stung by the intake process. Before I could ask about it, he said, more to himself than to me, "They even took my Norelco. I mean, how do you hurt yourself with an electric razor?"

"Electrocution," I answered softly.

"Didn't think of that," he conceded.

"Don't worry, you'll get it back," I said. "Or you could try a beard."

"What do the women do? Without razors, I mean," he said as some of my hallmates gingerly began partaking of Jean's libation.

"It was scratchy at first, but once I started braiding my hairy legs, it was a lot more comfortable," I deadpanned.

He shot a look at my smooth legs peeking out from under my peasant skirt and smiled. It was the first time I'd felt an attractive man noticing my legs in months, and I found myself blushing.

I nervously laughed. "Did you believe me for a minute?"

He shook his head. "I'd believe anything in here."

I heard the sounds of Monica shuffling across the carpet before I saw her. She scooted over to a woman I didn't know with short, brown hair and round, preppy glasses. I couldn't make out what Monica said but saw the woman's eyes open wider. Then Monica shuffled off as the woman stared at her.

Hugh was watching them too. He shook his head and turned to me. "She walked up to me and asked me if I knew any lesbians."

"Monica? Probably means that she likes you."

"I used to see people like her on the street. Homeless. Better that she's in here."

There was something about the authoritative way he said "on the street" that made me think. "So are you a . . ."

"A cop? Yeah. Or at least, I was."

"What are you in for?"

Hugh let out a big sigh and gave a rueful smile. I knew it was a question he never thought he'd be asked.

"Well, when I found myself with a gun in my mouth a few nights back, I thought of my kid. Somehow, I managed to call 911, and here I am."

"I'm glad you didn't succeed, but what happened to get you to that place of wanting to end your life?" I glanced at the biceps bulging from his shirt. *How could someone so strong feel so powerless?*

"Well, seven years ago, answering a dispatch call to one of the worst neighborhoods in the city, I came upon a robbery in progress. In the chaos, I shot a young black girl because I thought she was one of the robbers."

He took a long deep breath, and a few tears seeped from his eyes. He looked down at his hands. From the corner of my eye, I could see Jean raising the chalice once again.

"The bullet shattered her kneecap, leaving her permanently disabled. It turned out she was innocent."

Now my hallmates were lining up for lunch, but I couldn't tear myself away from Hugh. He was confessing. I needed to stay.

"Is this the first time you've spoken of this?"

"No, I've seen shrinks ever since. All of them prescribed me sleeping pills and tranquilizers. I guess I got addicted because when I went cold turkey a few weeks ago, I started having these intense nightmares. It's like I relive the shooting every night. That girl . . . I ruined her life, and of course, now I've ruined mine."

The tranquilizers. The nightmares. It was almost like listening to myself talking. I remembered my own first day at Sheppard Pratt, when I felt like I could sink no lower.

Hugh was fighting to hold back the sobs. I had just met him but knew I wanted to hug him. As I did, his tears poured out. "It's my fault. It's my fault," he said into my shoulder.

"Oh, Hugh. That's so much to go through. I know about self-blame." Once he stopped crying, I told him about Tony, my suicide attempts, my upcoming court battle. "Yeah, so I know what's it's like."

Hugh's face reddened as he pounded his fist on his knee. "That douchebag doctor. You can't trust any of those shrinks."

Just then, Dr. LeGray walked into the room looking for his new admit and quickly stole a glance at me. I suddenly felt guilty for sitting so close to Hugh, and scooted toward the other end of the sofa.

"Speaking of shrinks . . . ." I rolled my eyes at Dr. LeGray as he headed away from us.

"Oh, Christ, I can't wait to see who they assign me to. I asked for a psychologist, not a psychiatrist. I don't want any more meds."

"Hey, listen, Hugh. If all goes well and you work your way up to getting a pass to roam the campus, maybe you can come to the dance next weekend. It may sound pathetic that I'm so proud, but I've just been nominated dance chairwoman."

We both giggled, feeling our kinship as reluctant members of the Pathetic Souls Club.

"Just promise me the first dance, will you?" Hugh flashed me a naughty grin. His normalcy took me back. *Maybe there is life beyond our tragic stories.*

Would it be smart to let myself have a psych-ward crush on this handsome cop? I imagined Dr. LeGray scolding me, "Miss Tansey, you were sitting awfully close to that young man."

I shook my head and thought of my meeting with my attorneys later today. They had filed malpractice charges last week and already gotten the response from Tony's lawyer. His defense was that he'd fallen madly in love with me. *The last thing I need in my life is more drama with another man.*

"I'll catch you later, Hugh. Let me know how I can help you make your way around Sheppard Pratt."

I got up from the sofa and felt his eyes on me as I walked away.

~29~

The die tumbled across the Prussian blue Trivial Pursuit board. It landed on six. Marguerite took a long drag on her cigarette and considered her options.

"So if I go that way, I land on blue, which is what? Geography?"

"Yeah," I nodded before lighting up.

"Or the other way, I get orange, Sports and Leisure. Shit. I'm fucked! The only thing I'm good at is the brown, Arts and Literature. I can't believe I let you chicks talk me into playing this stupid thing."

Courtney leaned in and lowered her voice. "If you'd rather play pool with Jean, go ahead."

"Oh, kiss off," said Marguerite with a belly laugh and a big smile that really meant, "I love you guys."

Just a few days after Christmas, red tinsel and fake greenery still festooned the ward, and Courtney and Sarah (two new eating disorder patients), Marguerite, and I had gathered in the lounge for a round with the new Trivial Pursuit game.

Looking resigned, Marguerite marched her orange token ahead six spaces to the blue square, and then rolled her eyes. "All right. Lay it on me."

Sarah drew a card from the box with flourish, concealing the answers on the back with her hand. She raised her eyebrows and assumed a sort of game show announcer voice: "Where are the Nazca lines?"

Across the room, I noticed a relatively new patient who seemed to be concentrating on playing chess with an invisible partner. He was 50-ish, with a spare tire around the middle and brown hair that looked like it had just seen the barber. There was something fierce and weird about his gaze, as if he were consumed by a distant fire.

"The what?" said Marguerite, bringing my attention back to the game.

"The Nazca lines."

A few feet behind Marguerite, Bruce pursed his lips as if he was trying not to blurt out the answer. His eyes twinkled. I could tell he knew it. I wasn't sure if it was Peru or Bolivia. The room was silent except for the smack and roll of the billiard balls.

"I'm gonna say . . . Florida."

Sarah looked at the back of the card. "Nope. Bruce, do you want to guess?"

"Peru!" he announced.

She held up the card as if it were a blue ribbon for Bruce. "Correct!"

"Peru?" said Marguerite. "How would anyone know that?"

"Read it in *National Geographic*," Bruce said. "C'mon girls, leave the game for now; it's time for dinner."

Accustomed to the routine, the four of us made our way to the steel doors so we could be escorted to the cafeteria. After ambling through the line, I sat down at the gray Formica table with my friends and looked at my tray. Stringy roast beef. A big, puffy dinner roll. A pat of margarine. Green beans with fake bacon bits. Mashed potatoes. Semi-dried-out chocolate cake. Not the best. Not the worst.

"Do you ladies mind if I sit with you?" asked the chess player.

"Knock yourself out," said Marguerite.

He seated himself next to Courtney. There was something about his jowly face and the quality of his skin. He looked like he drank a lot of wine and frequented the same kinds of restaurants Tony went to. Up close, his plain blue oxford shirt was clearly expensive—the sheen of the fabric, the stitching on the collar. I could tell it wasn't from J.C. Penney like the ones my dad and brothers wore.

"Hi, I'm Carrie. This is Sarah, Courtney, and Marguerite."

"Charles," he answered with a polite nod.

Marguerite and I started eating. Sarah and Courtney picked at their food. Charles held his fork in the air and looked down his nose at his tray, trying to decide what to approach first.

"Marguerite, do you want my cake?" I asked. "Trade ya for your roll."

"No, thanks," she said. "I'm giving up dessert for a while. New Year's resolutions and all."

"Even though New Year's isn't for a few days?" I countered. "Suit yourself. By the way, anyone got any last-minute music requests for the New Year's dance? We still haven't settled on the playlist."

Charles shook his head curtly, as if to say he didn't dance.

"What?" said Sarah. "You're not coming to the party? Careful, you're sitting at a table with the dance committee chair," she said gesturing to me with her spoon.

I put my hands on my hips and stared at him with mock indignation.

"No, no," Charles said. "It's just that I won't be here that long," he said spreading margarine on his roll. "I'm here for observation and consideration," he announced in a papery-soft voice, "for placement in the Clifton T. Perkins Home for the Criminally Insane."

I swallowed a big chunk of overcooked roast beef, and tried to appear calm as I gulped iced tea to wash it down.

"You see, I've only just begun to get my revenge."

He took a bite of bread. He looked at his roll and made a face. I figured he was accustomed to butter.

"It took me decades to amass my fortune, and I trusted my stock portfolio to a broker who came highly recommended.

"He proved to be, shall we say, unscrupulous, and bilked me out of millions. So I disguised myself in a Santa suit and crashed his company Christmas party. After he'd had a few drinks, I told him the boss wanted me to give him his Christmas bonus but not in front of the other employees. Oh, the look in his greedy little eyes as I lured him to the back stairwell."

I looked across the table at my friends, whose eyes were wide, their expressions frozen. Charles had a bizarre aura about him, as if he were taking up all the air in the room. I could barely breathe. I wondered if the others felt it too.

"I bound and gagged him with supplies I'd conveniently concealed in Santa's belly, then shoved him down the stairs, out the back exit, and into the trunk of my car," he said proudly.

Across the table from me, Charles no longer looked like a winsome, middle-aged man but a ruthless psychopath. Lots of people in Sheppard Pratt told tall tales or had lost touch with reality, but I could tell Charles was telling the truth. I wished he wasn't, though. He went on to detail how he drove the man to a remote cabin, then tortured him—wearing the Santa suit all the while. I think he described what he did, but some defense mechanism inside made me stop listening. I breathed a sigh of relief and went back to nibbling my green beans when he said he let the man go. I tried to act casual as he explained that the victim recognized his voice, and police promptly arrested Charles, something he seemed to view as a minor setback.

"I have a plan, I assure you," he said, confidently.

A shiver shot up my spine.

Saying nothing, my friends and I stood up to take our trays back to the kitchen.

Back in the lounge, we resumed the Trivial Pursuit. Sarah rolled a four and deliberated a bit before moving to a yellow space.

Marguerite drew the next card from the box.

"Okay, yellow is History." She sat up a bit straighter, puffed out her chest, and read: "What did Sir Walter Raleigh's wife carry in her bag for twenty-nine years after his execution?"

Sarah scowled and repeated the question under her breath.

I was glad it wasn't my turn because I wasn't really concentrating. I thought about Charles. Then I thought of all the people I'd met in Sheppard Pratt who, like me, were actually there because they had suffered at the hands of someone else, someone they had trusted. Elizabeth trusted her uncle. Richard trusted Lionel. I trusted Tony. For crying out loud, Charles's victim had trusted Santa Claus!

"Okay, I think I know this one." She looked up at the ceiling as if it might help her remember. "His head?"

Marguerite turned the card over. "Correct! Roll again."

The die tumbled across the board, and I was lost in my thoughts as Sarah marched her token to the next space. I wondered if the man had really swindled Charles or if that was just a psychopath's imagination. As if it mattered. I wondered where and how that man was healing now. I'd met so many victims, and like me, they all blamed themselves. So many of us were striving to overcome self-doubt and shame.

Marguerite drew the next question card. "Pink is Entertainment. Okay, what film was Marilyn Monroe fired from just before her death? C'mon, Sarah. It's for the pie!"

Absentmindedly, I fished through the little plastic bag of pies, or wedges, looking for a hot pink one, in case Sarah got the answer right.

I had read in psychology books that perpetrators often felt no guilt, but meeting Charles was nothing short of chilling. If he felt any regret at all, it only seemed to be that his plans had been derailed, that he was inconvenienced. I wondered if Tony felt any guilt for what he did.

"I know this isn't it, but . . . *Some Like it Hot*?" Sarah guessed.

"Sorry," Marguerite said, turning over the card, "*Something's Got to Give.*"

Ain't that the truth? I excused myself and went to bed.

A few days later, I entered the sitting room one morning and noticed an untouched chessboard and Charles's conspicuous absence. I asked Bruce if Charles was gone, but he kept mum.

"Oh c'mon," I prodded, then lowered my voice. "Did he get sent to Clifton T. Perkins?"

"Carrie, you know I can't tell you that," he said loudly. "All patient records are—"

"Strictly confidential," I said, finishing the sentence for him. But I didn't see Charles anywhere, and I wasn't sorry.

Anyway, it was almost time for the daily hall meeting where we shared our progress in the hope of gaining more freedom to move about the hospital—for example, to walk the halls unescorted, or even earn a pass to go off-grounds for an entire afternoon.

An orderly was giving a new female patient the usual tour. As they approached, the woman, an attractive thirty-something, confidently extended her hand. She appeared strong mentally but emotionally rattled. She looked put-together in a pleated navy skirt and white silk blouse, but I had the sense that she had come here hastily from work, or somewhere, on a moment's notice. Ann felt like someone I might have grown up with, the kind of good-hearted person who leads a normal, productive life. She took a seat next to mine.

"What are you in for?" I asked, then cringed at the standard opening "prison" line, which I despised.

Ann sucked in a deep breath. "I'm here for protection from my husband. He's disappeared . . . they're worried for my safety."

"He's an abuser?" The moment I said this, I realized I'd always assumed physical abuse was worse than emotional. Until now, I hadn't thought of Tony as an abuser, since his attacks on me weren't physical but psychological.

"Well, I thought we had the perfect marriage," Ann said softly as we watched the other patients flowing into the meeting room.

"I was the envy of my friends," she went on, her eyes flickering as some of the patients began to stare. "Everyone saw our deep love and affection. Friends often commented on how lucky I was."

Ann explained how her husband, Ralph, often offered to give her a break from their two children, ages three and five. In fact, for the past two years, Ralph had taken the kids on a special outing every Saturday. He always handed Ann plenty of money to get her hair and nails done, or perhaps grab lunch with a friend.

"I thought I had it all. But then, as the kids got older, I noticed they were starting to act up a bit whenever they came back from outings with Dad. Then last week," her voice cracked, "my five-year-old daughter mentioned something about a man asking her to touch his penis."

My stomach clenched as she went on talking.

"At first, I brushed it off, thinking she'd heard something weird in day care. When I mentioned it to my husband, he acted nervous. I just thought he was worried some kid in day care had said something inappropriate."

Days later, when Ann couldn't ignore a gut feeling urging her to rummage through her husband's belongings, his files, the boxes under their bed.

"That's when the whole thing blew up," she said, admitting that her psyche hadn't yet fully accepted the sickening facts: For two years, her devoted husband, Ralph, had been taking their children to a friend's house and filming them in sexual acts as part of a child pornography ring.

"I always wondered where all the money came from," Ann said, shaking her head as if she should have known better. "He always told me he was making a lot of sales in his business.

"The children are with my mom right now, out of state. He threatened to kill me . . . . I just barely got out of the house alive, ran to a neighbor's house, and called the police. He got away. We have no idea where he is."

I sat there stunned. The room was nearly full now, and our meeting was about to begin. Suddenly, my anxiety over my legal troubles and coming deposition faded. *Please God, let this woman be delusional,* I thought to myself. *Please, don't let this horror be true.* But in my gut, I knew it was.

Early the next morning, I made my way into the sitting room, hoping to do some journaling before the hall meeting. A newspaper headline on the coffee table caught my attention: "Child Pornography Ring Busted." There was a photo of police escorting a handcuffed man to jail. I wondered if it was Ann's husband or someone else in the ring.

The comforting thing about living in a psych ward is that survivors instinctively recognize another survivor. Ann stayed with us for thirty days, and in that time, some of the more passive, disinterested hallmates suddenly came to life, wanting to support her. Even the most self-absorbed loners paid close attention as she strengthened herself day by day and prepared to face the man she thought she knew, the man she had trusted, in court.

I had my own trial to prepare for. Somehow Ann's story gave me courage to talk more openly about mine in session and in my group therapy. I still struggled to understand *why* this had happened to me and *how.*

I observed Ann closely. I wanted to learn what a woman does when she loses everything she thought was real and good, when she finds herself duped by the one person she counted on most. I longed for the clarity she had. In group therapy trying to deal with her trauma, Ann was strong and clear about who the culprit was. Even though she blamed herself for not seeing the danger sooner, she was squarely focused on finding justice for herself and her children. I was impressed by how little time she spent chastising herself, and how quickly she jumped into action to keep her family safe—and ultimately hold *him* accountable.

I don't think Ann was ever aware of how much she influenced me as I wrestled internally with the idea of Tony as a perpetrator. After one group therapy session I had with Ann, I sat silently in my room, my head spinning with thoughts.

How many times had Ralph violated the children he professed to love?

What lies had he told them to coerce them?

Like calculating Charles, had Ralph planned this from the beginning? Had Tony? Or had Ralph turned bad at some point? Had Tony turned bad? When?

My attorneys counseled me that as my case became public, other women would likely come forward. Had Tony actually done this before? Given the chance, would he do it again?

~30~

Amazingly, someone had managed to scrounge up a disco ball, and it twirled from the community room ceiling, shedding twinkling bubbles of light on the purple-and-gold banner that read "Happy New Year 1985." The wooden floor shined with a recent wax job, and tables bedecked with gold tablecloths, sprinkled with confetti, and sporting a punchbowl and snacks lined the space. I had to admit it looked pretty good.

Doug, the DJ we'd hired, looked a little like Tom Petty only preppier, dressed in docksiders and khakis. When we had talked about the playlist before the dance, I sensed that he thought a gig at a mental hospital had a certain dark cachet, and I felt he might have been genuinely disappointed at my "normal" appearance. He had been really agreeable, though, and was now cranking everyone's favorite New Year's Eve anthem:

They say two thousand zero zero party over,
Oops out of time
So tonight I'm gonna party like it's 1999.

Just about everyone who had clearance to do so had showed up, and I surveyed the room and felt a swell of love for my Sheppard Pratt friends. Some twenty patients were already gathered, and the dance was just beginning. We might have up to fifty if people could muster the energy. Courtney and Sarah were shaking it on the dance floor while Monica shuffled around them in a circle. Near the refreshments, Hugh nursed his punch, trying not to smirk and pretending not to notice as I beckoned for him to come out and join us.

Yeah, everybody's got a bomb,
We could all die any day.
But before I'll let that happen,
I'll dance my life away.

Marguerite had cleaned up nicely. I'd never actually seen her wear a dress before, but she was twirling away in her flouncy miniskirt dragging on her cigarette, her bloated white legs keeping good time to the music. *Wow, Marguerite's funky!* Bruce swept in and deftly swiped the cigarette from her mouth with an admonishing look, then grooved away from the dance floor and surveyed the scene with polite interest. I danced over to him, lip-synching obnoxiously, music-video-style, and tried to get him to join the fun, but he laughed and dismissed me saying, "Carrie, you know I'm on duty."

My sense of absurdity kicked in, and I imagined Dr. LeGray showing up in some tight, black leather pants, and laughed to myself.

Then I felt my heart drop when I saw David, a young man suffering from schizophrenia, sitting by himself in the shadows of the back corner. When a new song started up, I went over and invited him to dance, but he declined, looking awkward and slightly pained. I imagined high school dances had been rough for him, and I was bummed out that I couldn't reach him. He was here, though. He didn't have to be. That was something.

Tonight, I felt compelled to be a hostess, a leader, even if I did feel sort of guilty for being the high school equivalent of a cheerleader. Looking across the room, watching people who would always have difficulty with social skills or would always need medication, I felt guiltier still, knowing that one day, I would move on from here. For many of my companions there, the future wasn't as clear. My heart felt torn between feelings of excitement at my renewal, and loyalty and camaraderie with my fellow journeyers of the underworld. Maybe if I could shake off my shame, they could too. Watching the dance that night, it became so obvious: We all just wanted to feel loved and connected. Maybe I could heal myself and then, one day, help others heal. Was that too far-fetched?

The next morning, patients lounged around on New Year's Day, playing board games and watching the Tournament of Roses Parade on TV, and I found myself in a deep state of ambivalence. The dance had been so much fun, the boogieing, the laughing, the socializing, being a leader again, but here I was, the morning after, still in a psych ward. I had to reconcile what all of it meant to me. Deep in my thoughts, I was ready for a bit of solitude and wandered down the basement floor hall, past the art therapy room, into the library.

I hadn't been in here that much. When I first arrived at Sheppard Pratt, I was so exhausted and spacey that I couldn't concentrate long enough to read a book. Gradually, though, my brain fog was lifting, and I was beginning to enjoy reading again. Here among the blond wood bookcases and soft carpet, it was so quiet I could hear the faint buzz of the fluorescent lights overhead. I followed my feet to the psychology section, and my eyes fell on *The Psychopathology of Everyday Life* by Sigmund Freud. *Ugh, no thank you. I've had enough of Freud—and Dr. LeGray, who seems to think he's Freud . . . .* Then, near the Freud section, a book seemed to tug at me from its place on the shelf: *Man's Search for Meaning* by Viktor Frankl. I felt my arms tingle and my heart beat faster. In graduate school, I had been fascinated by his concept of logotherapy, based on the human drive to find meaning in life. I had always meant to read this. I grabbed the book and turned it over. The words on the back cover jumped out at me:

> *"Frankl argues that we cannot avoid suffering, but we can choose how to cope with it, find meaning in it, and move forward with renewed purpose."*

I checked it out and retired to my room. Flopping on my bed, I quickly became engrossed. During World War II, Frankl was a psychologist in Vienna when he was shipped off to a concentration camp. He managed to survive the horrors of the holocaust but not without tremendous personal loss and emotional pain—the kind of cruelties that make most people go mad. ". . . everything can be taken from a man but one thing: the last of human freedoms—to choose one's attitude in any given set of circumstances, to choose one's own way."

I stayed up all night reading Frankl's book, and when I finished it, I made a promise: I will do *one thing* tomorrow to help myself get better.

The next morning, depression crept in and threatened to pull me under, but instead of sleeping late and leaving my room a mess as I usually did, I forced myself to get up. Then I did something that might seem ordinary: I made my bed. In a deliberate, thoughtful way, I made my bed. As I finished, running my hands across the blanket to smooth out the creases, it was a sacred act that declared, "I *choose* life." For so long, I hadn't cared about myself, let alone my room, but I was starting to do things that sent a different message: I could no longer wait for happier emotions to return someday. I had to fight for my life, right now, with or without them.

I realized that like Frankl, I wanted to find meaning in my own experience. *I can heal from this and become a better human being because of it.* Countless others had endured unfathomable tragedy and yet were able to not only heal themselves but also resurface stronger. I might have died that day with my head stuck in the oven in that rodent-and-cockroach-infested apartment. But I didn't. I got another chance. If it was more than a coincidence that the exterminator found me just in time, then didn't I owe life . . . God . . . humanity . . . something good in return?

I felt my body open up. The heaviness in my belly dissipated, and the room looked lighter, more embracing.

Weeks passed, and on one unusually balmy February day, it was actually warm enough to play tennis outside. Not long ago, my parents had brought me my old tennis racket, perhaps in the hope that it might help their once-athletic daughter recover some part of herself. Now, my new, athletic friend, Bernice, and I carried my boom box onto the court. She had played intercollegiate tennis and was ready to hit some balls with a rusty player like me. The nearby trees were still leafless, but the ground smelled damp and rich, as if beneath the surface, roots were reaching down, plants were waking up, and soon, new green shoots would appear. Billy Ocean blasted from the boom box, and the Caribbean pop seemed to thaw any lingering frost as we smacked balls back and forth, wiggling our hips to the music between serves. It felt so good to move in the sun after being indoors all winter. The music reverberated through my body and bones, literally shaking me back to life.

I was surprised by my strength and accuracy. I managed to send almost every ball right where I wanted it. I might have forgotten who I used to be, but my body remembered. I was the girl the high school tennis coach called Annie Oakley, the sure shot. I was the girl who could accomplish anything she set her mind to, who raced home from school every day to sew a tennis dress for an upcoming tournament, and worked three part-time jobs just to pay for the fabric.

The sun warmed my face. I continued to return the ball to my opponent. I could feel the court beneath my feet and started to imagine what it might be like to live life above ground again. *Perhaps it's time to leave hell for good,* I thought, *and walk among the bright blossoms.* While my mind still reeled with sadness after all I'd been through and all I had yet to do, my body reminded me that I was still in the game.

How had I forgotten the winner I once was? How had I ever come to believe that I was a loser? That it was all over? *Tony,* came a clear voice that rang out from deep inside. *I wound up here because of Tony.*

I imagined aiming each ball right at Tony's head. Then for good measure, I imagined aiming the balls at the head of his attorney, Jack Blunt, whom I'd be meeting with later this week. For so long, I had taken all my anger out on myself. Now I felt relief having something else to focus on. I could hit this ball as hard as I wanted, as my feelings of sadness, rage, and hurt all got channeled onto one little yellow-green sphere.

I was finally starting to feel like I had my mind to myself. Tony's voice was seldom in there, and the whirling knives were long gone. I realized that at one point, my mind and body had become such toxic places that I wanted to escape myself. Now, with Tony out of my head, I wanted to embrace myself. Sure, depression still clawed at me at times. And sure, I experienced anxiety when I thought about my future: Would I go back to school? How the heck would I get a job? Where would I live? But there was no denying, after that day on the tennis court, after reading *Man's Search for Meaning*, that the scales had tipped. My internal dialogue had changed from "*they* won't let me die" to "*I* won't let me die."

A few days after the deposition, I sat alone in a corner of the cafeteria with my journal and a big cup of coffee watching the other patients file in for breakfast. I realized how much I had come to love all these people, how much I respected their struggles, and how much I wanted to tell their stories to the world. In American culture, being confined to a psychiatric hospital is considered a terrible fate. Mental illness is viewed as a sign of weakness, shameful, something to be hidden, locked up, controlled, and contained. The truth was that I'd discovered more inspiration, humanity, and love in the halls of this psych ward than in the top medical schools I'd worked at.

As I wrote, insights kept bubbling up. For instance, at Sheppard Pratt, the most powerful healings happened between patients, since they were the ones who listened most deeply and witnessed one another's pain and transformation as peers, without the roles of patient and doctor. Over the last six months, I had observed something quite extraordinary that happens to people once they hit bottom. As the ego cracks open and spills out the truth of one's life, a gentle peace settles in, along with humility and courage. The false self withers and dies, making way for the truest self to emerge. Many of my fellow patients had expressed a remarkable sense of honest-to-god sincerity that suggested the presence of something greater than the mind. It was the soul.

As I watched the cafeteria activity and transcribed my thoughts, I noticed that I was no longer judging others' pain as separate from my own, nor was I absorbed by it. I also knew with certainty and humility that I still had plenty of work to do. The only way I could trust again was to repair the relationship with myself. I had to be a person who listened to *me,* someone who still believed in the qualities of goodness, honesty, and mercy. If I couldn't step up and be that person, then how could I ever trust others to do the same?

Once, I'd been so desperate for validation and healing that I had let Tony lead me away from my own sense of morality. I had joined him in a double life and betrayed my values. Out of my own self-doubt, I had followed an unethical doctor down the wrong, rutted path, which ultimately led me to betray my family and myself. Even though what Tony did was nefarious and grossly unprofessional, *I* was the one who unwittingly followed him—and I was the leader on the path back to me.

That morning as I sipped coffee, watching my fellow patients rub the sleepiness from their eyes and prepare for another day, with my thoughts chronicled in my journal before me, I knew I could finally leave Sheppard Pratt, and that the people I'd met here would be in my heart forever.

The Return to Light

The people rejoiced at Persephone's return. Once again, the earth bloomed with fragrant flowers of every kind, and crops grew abundant, but Demeter, knowing the Dark Lord was not completely vanquished, held a wise council of elders and gods. "Tell us, daughter, how he rapt you away to the realm of darkness and gloom," she said. "Tell us that we may bear witness to your story and protect others from such fate. Tell us, daughter, how did strong Hades beguile you?"

~31~

I sat on the porch of my tiny attic apartment in Baltimore browsing a library book about Wassily Kandinsky, the father of Abstract Expressionism. I'd been out of Sheppard Pratt for a little over four months, struggling to find my place in the world, and now, on a strict budget, found refuge in library books on my favorite artists: Miró, Kandinsky, Klee, and Chagall.

The summer evening sun fell upon the page and lit up a vibrant painting, inviting my soul to dance with hues of persimmon red, periwinkle blue, and ochre yellow. *Composition VII* was created by the master in 1913. At age thirty, Kandinsky had walked away from a promising career in law and economics to follow the call of his soul to study art. He ended up creating the world's first purely abstract paintings. I felt that *Composition VII,* like the abstract pastel I had created at Sheppard Pratt, spoke of my inner experience more powerfully than words could. Kandinsky's subjective, mystical lens on life was like a strong wind disrobing a tree of its leaves. An accomplished musician to boot, Kandinsky said that when he saw color, he often heard music too. I realized how clearly this painter, who had died nearly fifty years ago, was speaking to me through his art. I felt inspired to think that maybe there was a bigger calling for me than my initial plan of having my doctorate by age twenty-seven. Like Kandinsky, perhaps I could find a more creative, authentic way to live.

Laughter disrupted my musings, and I looked out from the balcony to see my neighbors in the yard across the street gathering for a barbecue. There were Ellen, Doug, Rachel, and Andy, all twenty-somethings getting home from work to start the weekend off with Budweisers and Maryland crab cakes on the grill. My heart hurt because I wanted to join in the fun but knew I would feel like an oddball, the girl who had just gotten out of the mental hospital. Of course, no one knew about that. Nevertheless, I felt a dark cloud hanging over me wherever I went. I was sure everyone could detect it along with the ever-present tears ready to seep out from behind my eyes at the tiniest thing. No, I'd much rather sit on my balcony with my book.

Is it possible to fall in love with the spirit of a dead person because his paintings express my inner being? Is it bizarre to think of Wassily as a soulmate, or a guide of some sort? These thoughts made me feel less alone as I saw my neighbors toasting and chatting. No one had noticed me yet. Here I could safely watch and drink in a social life from a distance.

My stomach began to rumble, and the evening air was growing cool, so I went inside and turned on the stove to warm up some leftover Chinese take-out and make a pot of tea. My Sheppard Pratt bills still loomed over my head as I puttered around the kitchen. I was working for little more than minimum wage, and my lawsuit might not be decided for months or years, so for the time being, I was taking pleasure in the small things like library books, flickering candles, and good tea. I hadn't been in the apartment long, but it was starting to feel like home, with yellow sheets on the bed, vanilla candle burning, beaded curtain dangling in the doorway, and my red wok squatting happily on the countertop.

I wondered if Gary was home from work yet. He lived downstairs and liked to play the guitar on his porch. I had started singing along with him, belting out soulful tunes by Linda Ronstadt and Carly Simon, my adolescent musical heroes. Just last night, we had jammed again under the summer moon. I felt so comfortable with Gary. He understood Kandinsky, Carole King, Viktor Frankl, and Prince.

After dinner, we sat on his second-story porch directly below my balcony, and as he strummed a few chords, I surprised myself when the melody began spilling out of me. I kept my eyes closed and felt things loosen up and shift inside. I hadn't heard the tune for years but still, the words moved through me as though singer-songwriter Karla Bonoff had written them just for me. I sang:

There's somebody waiting alone in the street
For someone to walk up and greet
Here you are all alone in the city
Where's the one that you took to your side
Lonely faces will stare through your eyes in the night

Gary looked at me, and I almost froze with self-consciousness, but it felt so good to sing. I closed my eyes and let my voice grow stronger.

The summer breeze seemed to swell and carry the song out of me into the world.

And they'll say
Woman, sweet woman,
Please come home with me
You're shining and willing and free
But your love, it's a common occurrence
Not like love that I feel in my heart

A kind of edgy rawness filled my being as I imagined myself the tragic figure in the song, aching for true love but so jaded with life she was willing to settle for crumbs, for loneliness.

As Gary stroked the guitar and I belted out the lyrics, waves of darkness moved out of my heart and body, transforming into the colors of the rainbow, pouring into the street in the sweet, hot summer night.

At the end of the song, tears flowing down my cheeks, I opened my eyes to see people standing on the street below looking up at us, applauding.

"Bravo! Bravo!"

"More, more!"

Even though I cringed at the thought of talking to any of them, I knew I had communicated my angst through song, and somehow it had become acceptable. Singing made me feel I could grow big enough to hold my pain and my hope, and just like Kandinsky, I could make room for both darkness and color—and it could be beautiful.

As the weeks passed, I realized that even though I feared their rejection, I loved my new neighbors, many of them artistic types like Gary, who seemed happy with their funky, meager apartments and loose schedules. I saw that life tended to flow organically for them, and they appeared to care little about collecting academic degrees or material possessions. I wondered where people like this had been when I was in college, but I must have been too focused on my straight and narrow career path to wander into any of them.

At first, I had been worried about how I would survive outside the hospital structure, even though I still had regular outpatient sessions with Dr. LeGray. I also worried that people might grow suspicious, wondering why I wasn't a professional yet, why at twenty-five, I was working at an unskilled job with no other apparent career plans, and if they'd deduce that I'd recently gotten out of a mental institution. But after a few months, I realized nobody cared! They were into whatever they were doing, and simply assumed I was the same.

I was working at the Loyola College bookstore, just at the top of Cold Spring Lane near where I lived in the bohemian section of Roland Park. It should have been an easy job, but it wasn't. Learning to operate the cash register confused me. I stared at it and saw the numbers swirling around. My legs felt weak. *Focus, Carrie. Focus.* My stomach was taut and my shoulders hunched.

The manager, Valerie, kept showing me how to work the thing step by step, but I would forget and need her to remind me. *What is wrong with me? I used to be in a doctoral program! Now I can't operate a cash register.* I felt slow and stupid. Shame engulfed me. I thanked Valerie for the tutorial and kept trying, praying I didn't look as insecure as I felt. The first time a customer approached me to pay for a textbook and college T-shirt, I nearly fainted. When I told Dr. LeGray about my difficulties, he explained that my muddled thoughts were the residual effects of the psychological trauma that had led me to Sheppard Pratt, that I needed to be patient, and that I was healing.

After four months at the bookstore, I decided to move toward my passion and got a job at the Baltimore Museum of Art. Even though I'd still be running a cash register, at least I'd be surrounded by some of the world's great art. Besides, being at Loyola, selling books to grad students like the ones I left behind in Richmond, triggered memories of all I'd worked so hard for and lost. Graduate school felt a million miles in the past, or, depending on how I looked at it, at least 2 million miles ahead, given where I was now. I resolved to nourish myself with colors and images, maybe even see a Kandinsky if I was lucky.

The gift shop I worked in was just down the hall from the world-famous Cone Collection gallery, which held the world's largest permanent collection of works by Henri Matisse, along with those of Cezanne, Gauguin, and Van Gogh. Etta and Claribel Cone were daughters of a wealthy textile magnate and loved surrounding themselves with lavish fabrics and exquisite art. They had bequeathed their art collection to Baltimore with the stipulation that the city do a better job of embracing modern art.

After my shift was over, I would sit for hours in the gallery, letting the paintings light up my insides. When I walked through the gallery and eyed the Matisse paintings, I could see why the sisters felt so simpatico with the master. I could almost feel the textiles and textures pop out of his works and envelop me in their warm exuberance. The paintings gave me something to reach for . . . lovely, dynamic, vibrant celebrations of life.

One September afternoon as the sky was sparkling with the fall sun, my tan rotary-dial phone rang. It was Bob Hanley: "Good news, Carrie. We've asked for a speedy trial, and here we are, less than a year after filing, and we have a Health Claims Arbitration date: Friday, November 8."

Bob and Earle Plumhoff had briefed me about this. In Maryland, it was the first step in the legal process, designed to keep unworthy malpractice suits out of court. Bob explained how the hearing would unfold.

"We will present your case before a Health Claims Panel made up of a medical person, a legal person, and a lay person. A decision will be made at the end of the proceedings, and the HCA committee will decide what the case merits in terms of financial compensation for you. The whole thing could actually end here, but there is the option for either side to appeal the decision."

"So it won't end here then," I said with resignation.

"Stay positive, Carrie," Bob replied. "Your case is very strong. And we're lucky enough to be holding the hearing in Frederick. Small towns have more conservative leanings, and Earle thinks the fact that this happened to a local girl will work in your favor. We're charging Dr. Romano with count one of malpractice—negligence, carelessness, and departure from standard care. That's basically legalese for getting involved with you sexually."

"Okay," I said, keeping my voice calm even as I winced inside.

"Count two of malpractice," he went on, "is prescribing pills even after he had terminated psychotherapy," which led me to develop dependence on them.

I kind of lost track of what Bob was saying after that, as terms like "intentional infliction of emotional distress" and "negligent infliction of emotional distress" echoed through my mind.

I tried to keep my head from spinning like it always did when Bob filled me with fact after fact. I had to concentrate to keep up with him.

"Remember, they will do their best to cast doubt on you and suggest that this whole relationship was consensual from the start," he counseled.

I felt a sinking feeling in my gut.

"They may try to ask you questions loaded with doubletalk to confuse you," he went on. "They may say inflammatory things, hoping you'll lose your emotional composure and lose credibility. All you have to do is—"

"—stick to the truth." I said.

"Exactly."

The morning of November 8, I walked past rows of leafless autumn trees into the Frederick County Courthouse, my parents on either side of me. The newly built, modern structure was filled with sunlight from its tall windows. I felt small as we walked through the vestibule, and my dad had to help me open the heavy glass door to the lobby. Last night, I had driven up from Baltimore, and had spent the night at my parents' house in my old room. Getting dressed this morning, I had been so nervous I couldn't decide what to wear, and Mom had to help me. This was the first time I would be seeing Tony since saying goodbye to him on his farm nearly eighteen months ago.

As I looked at the docket to see which room we'd be in for the hearing, my eyes were pulled up to the mezzanine where a lone figure stood staring down at me, staring through me. My heart dropped, and the hair on the back of my neck stood up. It felt like the ground opened up beneath me, and I had to hold Dad's arm to steady myself, to keep from being pulled under.

"Oh God, Dad," I said under my breath. "It's him."

~32~

Suddenly, I felt false in my neat, conservative skirt and silk blouse with the tied bow. I'd been his captive, and now I realized that my courtroom outfit gave no indication of all the pain I'd endured. By all rights, I should've had writhing snakes in my hair, cold, black lips, and a pair of red-eyed jaguars skulking silently beside me, with a cord of rattling skulls trailing behind us. I needed an owl on one shoulder and a vulture circling above my head to tell the whole truth of how he'd dragged me into hell and brought me close to death, twice.

In that moment, I felt like I dissolved into a billion cells, none of them connected to another. I was surprised that my feet were still underneath me as I gripped Dad's arm and followed Mom into the elevator to head up to the second-floor conference room.

The elevator door opened, and I could see Bob Hanley at the end of the hall waving me toward the room where the panel was already gathered. He guided my parents into an adjoining room where they would wait for their turns to testify. It had already been decided that I would only be in the room for my own testimony. My doctors and lawyers had thought it best for me to avoid the traumatic impact of hearing what others would say.

Bob escorted me to the simple, white meeting room with a long conference table. The panel sat at one end: a nurse in her 60s, a retired farmer, and a middle-aged lawyer with gray hair, Chairman Strong. Opposite them, I took my seat between Bob and Earle. The brunette stenographer sat alone on one side of the table in her brown tweed suit, looking alert and ready to begin. Tony's lawyer, Jack Blunt, sat across from her, next to an empty seat by the door. As I was scanning the room, Tony darted in and took the chair at the end of the table near Blunt, closest to the panel members.

I had been betrayed by a man who had abused his power, and now I was challenging him, in a hearing to be conducted and primarily decided by other men. Could I trust anyone here? What were my chances of winning? It was hard for me to look at anyone. I stared at the tabletop, at Bob's legal pads, a coffee cup, a midnight-blue pen. I felt nauseous and full of shame.

Chairman Strong opened the hearing, and Earle began questioning me, much as he had told me he would, asking me many basic questions that I had answered time and again. Where was I born? What was my birth order? How old was I? How did I first come to Dr. Romano? What did my parents think of him initially? Earlier, Earle had briefed me that his questions would establish the evolution of my relationship with Tony—and where it had taken a wrong turn. Eventually, we were past the basics, and I was telling the panel things I had only previously discussed with professionals at Sheppard Pratt and with my lawyers, starting with my confession to Tony that I feared I was falling in love with him. Then, I described Tony's enthusiastic reaction, how he immediately began making grand dating plans for us, while I sat there dumbstruck.

"I remember being very scared. I was tickled on the one hand, because I was really crazy about him," I explained. "On the other hand, I was like, 'Oh my God, this should not be happening. I thought I could say anything in here, and it wouldn't be acted on.' I remember feeling at that moment like all my power was sucked away," I said. "Suddenly, I was his. It was very weird."

Earle resumed his questions. "You mentioned, I think, the dependency on him that you were developing. Did he know of the fact that you were dependent on him?"

"He used to deny it," I said. "I would complain about it all the time. 'I am too dependent; I am too dependent, you know. This isn't good for me.' So I voiced that a lot, but he never seemed to acknowledge what I meant."

I remembered many long, late-night talks in which I told Tony I was worried that our relationship was a bad idea. He always countered me with such confidence: No, in most cases, a love affair between doctor and patient was very wrong, but ours was different and special. In those moments, I felt both special and strangely defiled. I couldn't wrap my mind around the possibility that he was wrong, so I would do my best to quell the darkness inside me while basking in his adoration. He used to tell me how beautiful I was, that I took his breath away.

"Did he encourage you to maintain relationships with your friends, your parents, or anyone like that?" Earle asked.

"He really reinforced me in being extremely angry at my parents."

"He would talk bad about your parents?"

"Yes."

"What did he say about them?"

Out of the corner of my eye, I saw Tony cross his arms and sit back in his chair. I did my best to stare at Bob's pen on the table. *Ugh, this is awkward.* "Well, he used to say that my father had a sexual attraction to me."

I felt nauseous as I recalled those first few months of psychotherapy, how Tony had grilled me about the first time I saw my father naked, about my family's views on sexuality. I remembered feeling like I had to come up with things to say to him. He was my doctor who needed to know everything. At the time, I thought my discomfort with his questions was an indication of my problem. I remembered telling him I felt uncomfortable once I developed breasts, and self-conscious about hugging my dad and other males in the family. Tony had been very interested in those details, as if they held a lot of importance. It always seemed like he was digging for more, more . . . . I started to wonder if maybe I was denying something that had happened to me early on, something that could explain my hopelessness and depression.

My attention returned to the conference room, and I saw everyone staring at me. I squirmed in my seat. Earle nodded for me to go on.

"I remember telling Tony about the time I was walking down the stairs dressed for church, and my dad whistled and said, 'Wow, don't you look nice?' And Tony said, 'That's sexual, Carrie! That's sexual!' And now that I see that my father does that to my brothers too, I don't know that it was necessarily so sexual."

With encouraging eyes, Earle urged me to keep talking. I noticed the panel members lean in a little, but I was too ashamed to look any of them in the eyes. I felt dirty and small, like I was eleven again and embarrassed to tell my mom I had gotten my period.

"And my mother, he mentioned something at one point that she was a schizoid personality. He used that word. That was based on my discussion of how I felt my mother was somewhat aloof at times, was not really there for me in the ways that I wanted her to be. So I really started seeing my family as so terribly messed up." There was more I felt like I needed to say.

"Also, I have an older brother, Bob, who is brain damaged, and I always felt guilty that I was smarter and more popular than he was, and after I relayed that to Tony, he insinuated that Bob was not really brain damaged but the scapegoat of a very sick family. He went on to say that mine was one of the sickest he had ever seen."

I felt the words stab me in the heart all over again. I had not wanted to believe then or ever that my family was so hopeless. But he had been so convincing. And he knew so much about people.

"That your family was one of the sickest he had ever seen?" Earle reiterated.

"Yes."

"Did statements like that tend to alienate you from your family?"

"Oh, entirely. Very much so"

I remembered the fights at the dinner table once psychotherapy had started, the way I would stomp off in a rage. My heart hurt to think of the scenes I'd caused, trying to reconcile what Tony told me about my parents, what I experienced with them, and the love I felt for them.

"I won't say I wasn't mad at them, because sometimes I was, but this just really added fuel," I said. "When I first got into therapy, my sense was that I wanted to work these things out. I felt like that was what I was supposed to be working on."

"And you were not working on that?" Earle countered.

"No, not at all."

From there, we covered a lot of ground. Earle asked me question after question about the next three years. The examination felt like it took three years too. It was exhausting. Each question felt heavier than the last. I did my best to keep sitting up straight, keep answering as honestly as I could. I wondered if the panel was seeing the pattern it had taken me so long to recognize—that the longer I was with my psychiatrist, the sicker I got. At this point in the timeline, Earle asked me about events leading up to our trip to Jamaica.

"By this time, I was having a lot of trouble with aggressive and self-destructive impulses," I said, explaining the whirling knives in my mind. "Or Tony and I would be at the farmhouse, and I would be near knives, and I would be really scared that suddenly I would get out of control and take the knife and kill him or hurt him or hurt me. And I tried to tell him about it, but all he would do was smirk and say, 'Well, I guess you're mad at somebody.'"

This is so hard to talk about. I felt like an automaton, staring at the wood grain of the table, the pen, Earle's scribbled notes while my voice sounded like it was someone else's, deadened and almost expressionless.

I could feel Tony's eyes boring into me. I was afraid if I looked at him, I would break down or throw up.

"Do you know why you were mad at him?" Earle said.

"Now I do."

"Why were you mad at him?"

"Because he had totally betrayed my trust, and he was keeping me in a place that was very hard for me to get out of. I was *so* dependent on him. I was emotionally. I was financially. I was so afraid I couldn't make it without him."

"How were you financially dependent on him?"

"Well, four or five months into therapy, before we became sexual, I said something to him one day about how I would like to be doing what he was doing, which was being a psychotherapist, and he just pounced on that. He said that his corporation, Psychiatric Services, would subsidize my education if I were to go into the profession, and then the idea would be that I would come back and work for him as an intern or a first job after graduate school."

There was no sound in the room but the stenographer's keys.

"Did he or his corporation then subsidize your education at Virginia Commonwealth University?"

"Yes."

"Do you know how much was paid to you?"

"He gave me $200 a month."

"Would it be fair to say that near the time of your trip to Jamaica, your perception was that without Dr. Romano's personal encouragement, financial support, and professional influence, your chances of finishing graduate school and getting a job would be diminished?"

"That was my thinking back then, yeah. It took a lot of resolve to break it off with him."

"Can you tell me how the breakup came about?"

I told about the time I was swimming in the ocean and the young Jamaican swam up and offered me a jet-ski ride, which I politely declined, with Tony watching from the beach all the while.

"So Tony and I went up to the hotel room, and then he starts yelling at me saying, 'You are so inappropriate with men! Your unconscious is working overtime! And you know I can't be with you when you are so inappropriate with men!' And I was like, 'What did I do?' In my mind, this had been a run-of-the-mill human interaction, especially for Jamaica where locals are constantly peddling Bob Marley T-shirts, snorkeling lessons, seashell jewelry. I mean, as a tourist, you're constantly being approached by people and, like, saying 'No thank you.' But Tony had this way of turning things around on me."

I made a circular motion with my right hand showing how he always twisted things to make me dizzy with confusion. I felt myself heave inside.

"Turning his insecurities into mine. Making me doubt myself until I didn't know what the truth was anymore."

I gasped as sorrow and shame welled up in me. Tears escaped from the corners of my eyes. I clapped my hand over my mouth, attempting to hold back a heartsick sob.

Earle turned to me and whispered, "Carrie, do you need a break? This is obviously very painful. You let us know if and when you need a break." I looked up from the tabletop to his brown eyes full of concern and compassion.

I glanced at Bob, who gently smiled. I did my best to straighten my spine. In that moment, all the mind-fucking Tony had perpetrated on me for three years sparked fury and hopelessness within me. I remembered how trapped I had felt in the prison of Tony's interpretations, where I was always the sick one who needed his help. I was always the one who was "unconscious" or "in denial." I felt my body want to throw up to purge itself of all the toxins of this abuse. I wanted to scream and tell Tony *he* was the one who was fucked up, not me, but I didn't know what would actually come out of my mouth, so I put my head down to gather myself. It felt like my brain would shatter from the pressure. *Feet on the floor, Carrie. Stay grounded. Your feet are on the floor.* I took a deep breath and stared at the pen on the tabletop. I hated having all of those eyes on me right now.

~33~

"Whenever you're ready to continue, Carrie," Earle said with calm reassurance. I took another deep breath and remembered the day on the beach in Jamaica.

"So I was confused . . ."—the sound of the stenographer's keys resumed—". . . because I didn't think I was being grossly inappropriate. I mean, I think I was just being nice to the guy."

I had to fight back an urge to stare directly at Tony and yell at him, "*You asshole, you were just jealous. There was nothing wrong with me. You were just jealous.*" I shook with rage but held back the monster inside me that wanted to pounce on him.

Earle nodded curtly, as if that portion of the inquiry was complete. "Let's go back to your days in graduate school at VCU."

"Okay."

"Did you, at this time, feel you were sick?"

"Yeah, because I was having all these weird things happen. I was having attacks of anxiety where I would be in a room and I would have to run and get air. Often, I felt like I couldn't breathe. I was throwing up a lot, and I wasn't sleeping. At the time, I was taking tranquilizers, and I was taking sleeping pills, but it was—"

"Where did you get those tranquilizers and sleeping pills?" Earle interrupted.

"From Tony."

"Did he write prescriptions for you?"

I thought back to the first time he gave me a pill. I was so torn. I didn't believe in pills, but here he was, my doctor, saying this would help me.

"Yes."

"Did he write prescriptions for you after you stopped being his patient?"

"Yes."

"Did he keep a bag of drugs on hand somehow?"

"Yes."

"Like a drug kit or something?"

"Yes."

"And he gave you access to that?"

"Yes."

"What kind of drugs?"

"Xanax, Halcion, which is a sleeping pill, and Valium."

"Did he have occasion to give those to you very often?"

"Yes, even though I hated taking pills. I hated it, and I would be like, 'I don't think I should be doing this,' but he would say, 'Well, discriminate use of pills in graduate school is appropriate or okay.' Still, he didn't make me take them. I took them."

I remembered how I would start off taking a quarter of a pill, then a half, then later I popped a whole one in my mouth, then sometimes two or three at a time. I started losing track of how many I was taking.

"Were you under stress at that time?"

"Oh, my God, yeah. I was bouncing off the walls. And I was crying a lot. Everybody knew I had dropped a lot of weight. Everybody at school knew something was wrong."

"In terms of your condition now, versus when you went into Sheppard Pratt, do you yourself perceive that you are better now?"

"Better than when I went to Sheppard?"

"Yes."

"Oh, much better, yeah."

"In terms of your own self-perception, what problems do you see at the present time that you still have?"

I wasn't sure how to answer that. I stared at my fingernails. They were all broken or chewed down. *I should have filed my nails for this.* I took a deep breath but kept looking down at my nails, the tabletop, the pen.

"I'm very distrustful of other people's motives. Even though I have been with Dr. LeGray for so long, I am still afraid, at some level, that he is sick somehow and is going to manipulate me, hurt me in some way."

"Is your relationship with Dr. LeGray different than the relationship you had with Dr. Romano?"

I stifled a cynical laugh as I thought of my emotionally remote sessions with the alien Dr. LeGray.

"Very different."

"Do you call Dr. LeGray by his first name, for example?"

"No."

"Do you know anything about his family life or his home?"

"Nothing."

"He doesn't share any of his personal life with you?"

"Not in the least."

"Do you still believe that you are in need of psychotherapy at the present time?"

"Definitely."

"Do you know how much longer it is projected that you will have to be undergoing psychotherapy?"

"It's hard to say because I'm avoiding some of the things that caused me stress in the past, like going back to school full-time and being in a serious relationship with a guy. So I don't know what will come up when that happens. Right now, when guys compliment me, instead of being flattered, I tend to want to punch them."

I thought I heard a soft chuckle in the room but couldn't tell who it came from.

"It is a weird reaction," I continued, "but it's just like, 'Don't say anything like that,' you know? I think the biggest thing is really being afraid someone is going to manipulate me again, being afraid I'm going to have poor judgment and be manipulated again."

"Do you, in retrospect, now believe that you were manipulated before?" Earle asked.

"Yes."

"How were you manipulated?"

"I don't know how much of it was intentional on his part. I think that he thought he loved me, but instead of being directed toward resolving problems with family and friends, he reinforced alienation and isolation in that way. He was very . . . I don't know . . . in other relationships with men, the sexual aspect was never as potent, but the guys before him were boys, really. I mean, they were all under twenty-one. So I think he used me in that way. And I think he might not have realized that he did. . . . I don't know."

I remembered Tony's bedroom, the bong, the *Playboy* magazines, the cabinet in the wall where he hid nude photos of me, and just how weird I felt when we played out his fantasies. I so wanted to please him and believe that this was what healthy people did. God knew I was unhealthy, so I had better follow his lead. Now, I could feel his eyes on me, and I placed one hand in my lap just to feel the wool skirt on my legs and remind myself that I had clothes on.

"In terms of the sexual relationship with Dr. Romano, are you familiar with the term 'bondage'?" Earle asked.

I felt heat rise from my collarbone to my face, and figured I was probably turning red. I had never talked to anyone about this but Dr. LeGray and my attorneys. This was a secret I had hoped would die with me. I'd known Earle was going to ask me about it, but still, I had never spoken of this publicly. I stared at my fingernails. I took a deep breath.

"Yes."

"Was there ever any bondage in the relationship?"

"Yes."

"In what sense?"

"In the sense of him tying me up. There were a couple times he asked me to tie him up, but predominantly, he tied me up."

"Tied you up to what?"

"To either the bed, or to beams or something, downstairs in his basement."

I felt a putrid green slime start to rise in my belly.

"Were there times when he took photos of you?"

"Yes."

"Engaging in sexual activities?"

"Yes."

Earle asked a few more questions about the professionals at Sheppard Pratt and their reaction to my relationship with my psychotherapist. Then we took a break. I felt Tony's eyes on me as I walked out of the room with Bob, who led me down the hall to another room where a sack lunch was waiting.

Thirty minutes later, we were back in the conference room, this time with Jack Blunt questioning me. My heart beat faster. I reminded myself that his job was to cast doubt on my version of things. The malpractice insurance company wanted to win—or to pay the smallest settlement possible.

I heard Earle's words in my head: "Just stay with the truth." I coughed and sat up straighter. The nurse on the panel was gazing at me with a gentle look on her face. Then I looked at Chairman Strong and the other man. None of them looked threatening, only very interested in what would happen next.

Blunt began. "Isn't it true that when you began seeing Dr. Romano socially, you didn't tell your parents?"

"Yes," I answered honestly.

"Not only did you keep the relationship a secret from your parents but you also went to elaborate steps to deceive them, didn't you?" Blunt continued.

"Yes," I acknowledged.

"And you would tell them that you were going to be at a friend's house when you were going to the farm?"

"Yes."

"So if your parents happened to call that friend and ask for you, the friend would say, 'Oh, she stepped out,' or 'She's not available,' and then call you at Dr. Romano's farm so you could call your parents back, as if you were at the friend's house."

"Yes, in the beginning. Later, it wasn't so necessary."

"Were you a pretty good actress?" Blunt asked.

I suddenly felt like I was in a movie. *Where's he going with this?*

"Obviously, I was to a certain extent, or they would have been more suspicious perhaps, but I got that lie down pretty solidly. Tony didn't want me to tell them either."

I flashed on how in the beginning of our relationship, Tony would ask me again and again, "What did you tell your parents?" But he stopped asking me once he knew I would protect him no matter what.

Like Earle, Blunt asked about the length of my relationship with Tony—only with an emphasis on the termination of therapy. Earle and Bob had told me the defense would do this to argue that Tony wasn't at fault for my suicide attempts because at the time, I was technically, no longer his patient. The hearing had been going on over five hours now. It couldn't last much longer. *Just tell the truth, Carrie. Just tell the truth.*

Blunt's next question interrupted my internal dialogue, and I realized he was asking about the specifics of my second suicide attempt. *Yuck.* But I'd made it this far. Between therapy and all the pre-trial work, I had probably told this story over twenty times by now. I could do it once more.

"Did you scatter some pills around so if anybody came in, they could see what you had done?"

I bristled. *Was he suggesting the pills were props or something?* "I don't . . . I never . . . I don't remember doing that," I answered as earnestly as I could.

"Where did you turn the gas on?"

Where did I turn the gas on? What? Did I miss something? "In the kitchen," I said, hoping I had understood his question.

"In the stove?" he asked.

"The stove." *Well duh.* I hoped my reply didn't sound condescending.

"How did you do that?"

I looked up at him and blinked before answering. "I blew out the pilot light and turned on the knob."

"Which pilot light did you blow out?"

Clearly, he was trying to back me into a corner, but to what end? I groped through my murky memories of the day I took all those pills, drank all that beer, and put my head in the oven. It was so vague, I could barely remember any details.

"Which pilot light?" I asked back.

"Yes." he said.

I looked up, above the panel members' heads, straining to remember through the haze of that day. I caught a glimpse of Chairman Strong taking notes then quickly looking back at me.

"In the oven."

"Now, wasn't there a second pilot light for the top of the stove, for the burners?" Blunt said.

"If there was, I didn't know it was there."

"And if you just blew out the pilot light and turned on the gas, wouldn't the flame from the top pilot light have blown you to bits?"

The room was thick with tension and the sound of the stenographer's typing.

"I have no idea."

"You didn't turn on the gas?"

"Yes, I did."

"Did you? Then how did it get turned off?"

"I don't know. I was unconscious when they found me."

My head spun trying to recall precisely what I did that day, the day that I thought was my last. I thought of how I had tried to gain strength by aligning myself with Sylvia Plath. It all seemed so dark and pathetic. I mean, come on, I was new at this killing myself thing. I wasn't sure how to do it. Maybe I made a mistake. Maybe the exterminator turned off the gas. I felt myself shaking my head as I refocused on Blunt and his questions. *What the hell? Is he trying to suggest I staged all this because I wasn't really sick?* My heart pounded, and the heat rose in my face. *Keep calm, Carrie. Keep calm.*

I looked Jack Blunt in the eyes. "I am not lying about my intent to kill myself."

Blunt's voice was piercing, "Have I suggested that you were lying?"

His eyes looked as if he were going in for the kill. "You have lied about other things, though, haven't you, Carrie?"

"I object to that," Earle said firmly. The room got even quieter as the tension kept the very air from stirring.

Emotionally, I felt like I was back in Tony's clutches, and anything I said would be turned around on me to prove I was in the wrong. My body shuddered with the injustice of it.

"Is that specific or general?" Chairman Strong asked Blunt, breaking the silence.

"Well, you lied to your parents, didn't you, Carrie?" Blunt continued.

I felt like he had hurled a stone at me, and I barely had time to dodge it. "To protect Dr. Romano," I qualified. I felt my back get straighter.

"And you lied to your therapist, Susan Arrington, to protect Dr. Romano."

Another stone. "Yes. To protect Tony." Inside my head, I screamed with rage.

"But you are not protecting him now, are you?"

Blunt turned his back toward me and faced the panel as if he was getting ready to cast the final stone at the one who was guilty. Without a breath, his voice grew cold and incisive, "Do you feel better about yourself now?"

"Objection!" said Earle, louder than before.

"Overruled," said Chairman Strong.

"She has been hurt," said Blunt, in what sounded like a contemptuous tone to me. "I want to see if she feels any better."

My nerves were so rattled that I was amazed my body wasn't shaking too. I kept my eyes on Blunt.

"I feel better than when I tried to kill myself, yes," I heard myself say calmly.

"Have you discussed with Dr. LeGray or any other of your therapists that part of the maturing process is being able to recognize and accept responsibility for your own actions?"

"Yes."

"Are you prepared to do that?"

I looked at him square in the eyes knowing that after this hearing, my next step would be to take this case to the State of Maryland Licensing Board, in the hope that Tony would no longer be allowed to practice medicine or hurt anyone in the way he had ever again.

"I am doing that, yes."

His voice rose. "Are you prepared to accept the fact that your relationship with Dr. Romano was a mutual and voluntary relationship?

"I don't think I was in a place to judge that at the time, no."

"You chose when to terminate it, didn't you?"

I looked at the panel, my hands in my lap, tightly balled into fists. "I had to terminate it," I said emphatically. "I was going crazy."

~34~

Six months later, in April 1986, we all ambled up the sidewalk of the Frederick County Courthouse under trees bursting with electric-green buds, birds chirping from their branches. The good news was that I was in better shape financially because the Health Claims Arbitration panel had awarded me $700,000 including punitive damages—a rarity, Bob and Earle assured me. The bad news, which had been expected, was that Tony's insurance company had immediately appealed. Now, I saw my reflection in the large glass doors of the building as I entered it for Round 2, a civil trial before a jury of twelve. I barely recognized myself. Gray, gaunt, and deadened, I tried to look strong. Entering the lobby, my eyes immediately floated up to the mezzanine, and I breathed a sigh of relief and expanded inside when I saw that Tony wasn't there.

I felt stronger than the last time I'd faced all this at the hearing. Indeed, it seemed like because more people knew what happened, it had broken up the toxic bond between us, and he took up much less space in my head. Bob had called last night to tell me the jury would be seven women and five men, and that the judge presiding over the trial would be Clayter W. Smith. Whoa. He was the father of a childhood classmate, Wynn. I hadn't seen the Smith family for almost twelve years, so there was no conflict of interest. I was somewhat ashamed that Wynn's dad would hear all the details of this sordid tale, but I felt more numb than afraid as Mom and I entered the small holding room where witnesses waited to testify.

Mom, who was there to keep me company, pulled out some knitting. I tried to focus on a *Redbook* magazine article about getting organized, but I couldn't concentrate. Instead, I leaned back, closed my eyes, and twiddled my thumbs while listening to the hypnotic click-clack of Mom's knitting needles as they reassured me with their comforting, almost-innocent sound.

Based on what had happened since the arbitration hearing, it seemed that the defense was crumbling. Tony's insurance company had replaced Jack Blunt with a middle-aged woman named Judith Catterton. Bob had told me it was a smart decision for the defense, since she had a more likable demeanor.

He appeared in the doorway. "Carrie, it's time," he said, and led me down the hall, through a large door. As I stepped into the bright, modern courtroom, I felt like a metal robot, stiff and cold, with sharp edges. I felt twelve pairs of eyes staring at me from the jury box. It was perfectly silent as I looked at Clayter Smith, wondering if he recognized me as the eighth-grade girl who'd had a crush on his adorable son. Oh, how I wished I could be that young girl again.

My sister, Jody, sat in the front row with Dad, and I felt a twinge of guilt that they had to hear this wretched story revealed in a public forum. *At least Mom doesn't have to hear it.* I took comfort thinking of her back in the holding room, knitting away with her soft pink angora yarn, making what looked like a sweater for Jody's youngest daughter. The spacious courtroom was nearly empty, with about twenty strangers dotted across the gallery benches. *Who could these people be? Did they read about this in the local newspaper?* The Frederick *News-Post* had been covering the case since a story last Friday about the counts and the jury-selection process. I knew the rumors had to be flying around town: Something awful happened to Bob and Joanne Tansey's daughter. I looked at the spectators again and wondered which was the newspaper reporter. A middle-aged man in the back row, head down, was taking notes.

As I climbed a small step to take the stand, a young, nondescript woman in a taupe linen suit came forward to swear me in. I raised my right hand in the air. I expected someone to offer me a Bible, but no one did.

"Do you solemnly swear to tell the truth, the whole truth, and nothing but the truth, so help you God?"

"I swear."

Apparently you didn't really swear on the Bible in this court. Maybe that was something that happened only in the movies. How bizarre that it had come to this. Hadn't everything happened because I'd wanted to make sure my doctor was a man of God and understood my search for the divine? The God of the Bible seemed very far away from this courtroom.

I settled into my chair and pressed my feet firmly on the floor.

Earle, dressed in a fine spring-weight, light-brown suit, approached me from the plaintiff's table. He silently nodded a hello to the jury as he walked toward me with a warm smile. I felt myself settle down inside.

"Miss Tansey, can you give the court your full name please?"

I heard the doors open as more people shuffled in and took seats in the gallery. I waited for the silence to return.

"Yes, Carrie Elizabeth Tansey."

"And what year were you born?"

"1959," I answered numbly.

"So that makes you twenty-six?"

Twenty-six. Twenty-six. Yes, I guess I'm twenty-six. I feel like eighty-six.

"Yes, I'm now twenty-six."

"And how old were you when you first met Dr. Anthony Romano?"

"I had just turned twenty-one."

Once again, Earle asked me question after question, detailing the unfolding of my relationship with Tony. He was sitting rather far away this time, at the defense table on the other side of the courtroom. As raw as I felt, I also felt validated by the many eyes and ears that cared enough about my story to show up and bear witness to it.

The silence seemed suffocating when Earle asked, "And Carrie, when did the relationship with Dr. Romano become more personal?"

It took more than five hours to get the tale out, and I often gazed at the back of the courtroom and let my eyes go out of focus so I couldn't make out the people, the place. Even my voice seemed out of focus, distant, not my own anymore. Finally, Earle said, "I have nothing more," and nodded to Judith Catterton.

She had brown, bobbed hair and big, brown eyes. As she approached the stand in her navy blue suit, I remembered the time Tony told me I should have worn a more form-fitting skirt for my graduate school interview to enhance my sex appeal with the interviewing doctors. As Catterton began her cross-examination, I wondered if Tony had hit on her, if he had told her what to wear. *Never mind; I don't care.*

I kept talking, kept testifying, despite the sinking feeling in my gut. I kept answering Catterton's questions, almost by rote, since Jack Blunt had asked the same things. I tried not to think about the stakes, but I couldn't help it. In many other states, this would be a criminal trial, Tony's actions would be classified as sexual assault, and he would be facing a prison sentence. However, in Maryland, he was only getting sued—and if he lost, his insurance would foot the bill. The opposition would attempt use the consensual-relationship defense to dismiss the counts of malpractice and reduce or maybe even eliminate the damages paid to me. I was up against a highly paid "expert," who had never met me and an insurance company with deep pockets. A powerful lawyer was doing everything she could to cast doubt on my credibility in front of the residents of my hometown, while a newspaper reporter sat nearby, eager to publish the lurid details of the events that had broken my heart and my spirit. I yearned to feel clean and innocent again. If I could just make it through this process, maybe one day I would.

Well, I've just had my day in court, as they say, I thought to myself as Mom drove us home in the family station wagon. As at the arbitration, I wouldn't be present for the rest of the proceedings. When we left the courthouse, more spectators had arrived, and Dr. LeGray was about to take the stand. Mom and I were silent as we passed row houses, then colonials, then reached our own neighborhood of large red-brick homes with gracious front porches and green awnings. Across the street, the trees in the park sported tiny new leaves and flowers, and I tried to let the late-afternoon sunshine lift my spirits. As Mom fiddled with her keys at the front door, I imagined myself at fourteen again, full of dreams, standing in the little echo chamber of our front vestibule, belting out Carly Simon songs. I felt comforted knowing that back in Baltimore, I'd sing on the porch with Gary again once this nightmare was over. *Would any of this legal rigmarole make a difference?*

"Honey, why don't you get comfy?" said Mom, eyes full of care and softness. "I imagine you're just exhausted. Six hours on the stand, you poor dear. I'll make us a snack and some tea."

She scampered off to the kitchen while I went upstairs to the cozy little bedroom decorated with green swag curtains and wicker blinds, the one I had stayed in when I was Tony's patient. As I slipped on a pair of gray sweatpants, a light pink velour T-shirt, and fluffy pink slippers, I thought of the times my parents had tried to talk to me in this same room after one of my dinner-table outbursts, back when I didn't know whom to believe, Tony or them. I flashed on seeing Tony in the courtroom today. *Well, I guess I now know whom to believe. My parents aren't being tried. He is.*

I slowly walked down the stairs to the kitchen where the teakettle was whistling. I felt hollowed out, empty inside as I stood at the work island while Mom sliced apples and cheese.

"Well, honey, I've got some ground beef that I've got to get thawed for dinner," she said, like this was any other day at the Tansey house. "How does spaghetti sound? You look so tired. Do you want to go to the family room and relax on the couch?" She handed me my tea.

"Sure," I said, walking into the next room, happy to sink into the soft suede folds of the camel-colored sofa. Vacantly, I flipped on the television as I sipped the tea. "General Hospital" was just ending, and the credits were rolling. Darn, I had wanted to find out if Luke and Laura were still together, remembering the days when I'd rushed home from high school to watch their tumultuous love affair. Soap operas were so simple compared with my real life. Channel surfing, I landed on a rerun of "Gilligan's Island," and I faintly heard:

"The weather started getting rough,
The tiny ship was tossed,
If not for the courage of the fearless crew . . ."

How I hoped that my family, my attorneys, the jurors, and everyone testifying for me would be my fearless crew, but I didn't have the strength to think about it anymore, and fell into a deep slumber.

I must have been asleep an hour or so when I heard low voices in the kitchen. It was Jody talking to Mom. As I stepped closer to the kitchen door, I heard her say, "I kept looking around that courtroom at the reporter, the jury, the lawyers, and that creep, Romano. I kept telling myself, 'I can't believe this is real. I can't believe this happened to my sister. I can't believe this is happening to our family.'" My heart hurt at the thought of the shame I had brought on the Tansey name.

Sheepishly, I opened the door to see Mom and Jody standing close, each holding a hand over her heart. Tears welled up in Jody's eyes as she rushed forward to give me a hug. I smelled the spaghetti sauce heating on the stove.

Just then the phone rang, and Mom rushed to answer it.

"Hello, Tansey residence, Mrs. Tansey speaking," she said pleasantly. "Oh, Bob, yes. She's right here."

I took the receiver.

"Carrie, it's Bob Hanley. How are you doing?"

"Okay, I guess."

"Well, Carrie, Earle and I are very pleased with how it's going. You did a great job today."

I did? I guess that's good.

"As we've always believed, you make a very compelling witness. The jury was listening closely to every word you said."

They were? I could feel my spine straighten up a bit, and suddenly I could feel my feet in the soft slippers.

"Dr. LeGray made a very good witness too, clearly stating that Dr. Romano's unethical behavior was entirely responsible for your suicide attempts and resulting hospitalization. Our expert witness psychiatrist, Dr. Stephen Rojcewicz, corroborated everything LeGray said. That means we're in a very strong position after just one day in court. Tomorrow, your father will go on, then your mother, and your friends from graduate school, Todd and Lori. If there's time after that, we also hope to put our economist, David Farber, on the stand to estimate your lost earnings. Do you have any questions?"

"No, I don't think so," I heard myself say weakly.

"Now you take it easy. I'll call tomorrow after court."

That night, I went to bed early after a glass of white zinfandel and a full plate of spaghetti. The next morning, I awoke to hear my parents in the front hall.

"Car-rie, we have to get going," Mom called up the stairs. "Are you awake?"

I threw on my robe and went down the steps to the landing overlooking the vestibule, where my parents looked so handsome and respectable in their courtroom attire, Mom in a linen skirt and jacket, Dad in his navy sports jacket with the brass buttons, his dress shoes polished to a class-A sheen. My stomach ached as I thought of their taking the stand today, especially Mom. I saw such sadness in their faces but also determination.

"Honey," Mom said, "there are scrambled eggs and bacon in the skillet on the stove, and some coffee in the pot. Just relax today. You can make tuna sandwiches for lunch."

I looked at Dad. He seemed like he was mustering up the will to say something. I walked down the rest of the stairs.

"Good luck, Dad," I said.

"Honey . . . ," he paused. "We left the paper on the work island. Well, I guess this is a pretty big deal in Frederick County. It made the front page. If you want to wait until we're home to read it, you can, but I left it there in case you're curious."

Mom hugged me. "We'll be back soon. If you don't want to be alone, walk over to Jody's. Even if she's not there, the babysitter will be, and you can play with your nieces. Think about getting some sun and fresh air."

Fresh air. I don't know if I'll ever know "fresh" again. I imagined my skin must have looked like white paste.

"Okay, good luck, Mom and Dad." They both gave me worried smiles and headed out the door.

I returned to the kitchen for breakfast, then stopped cold when I saw the *Frederick News-Post* laying on the counter next to a neatly placed table setting. I gasped when my eyes fell on the top headline, and felt a sharp stab in my gut as I poured myself a cup of coffee.

> **Psychiatrist Faces Jury in Lawsuit**
> By George Dorsey
> News-Post Staff

George Dorsey. . . Doesn't he work with Jody's husband? Oh God . . .

In my childhood home, everything was still. Here I was. Alone. With my dreadful tale on the front page of the little newspaper everyone read.

> A Frederick County jury of seven women and five men is being asked to determine if a psychiatrist committed medical malpractice in a love affair . . . .

I gulped my coffee and read on.

> The woman's attorney, Earle Plumhoff, accused Romano of using his psychiatry and psychological skill to sexually exploit a troubled college student. "He was a doctor by day and lover by night," Plumhoff said. "He talked her into marijuana with him at his farm, sexual contact, bondage, and pornography," Plumhoff said.

My stomach convulsed, and I ran to the sink and spit out the coffee. I took a deep breath, scooped up a forkful of eggs from the pan, and resumed reading.

> . . . Romano's attorney countered, saying the psychiatrist "fell head over heels in love with her." She said the doctor-patient relationship ended by fall of 1982 while the love affair between two consenting adults continued . . .

I put my fork down. I didn't want to purge more.

The article went on to describe my suicide attempts in detail. I felt dizzy, like my head might roll off. I wondered who else was reading this. My name wasn't in the story, but *the News-Post* had leaked it last week, before Earle and Bob had confirmed that the court documents would be sealed. Everyone in Frederick probably knew "the woman" was me, anyway.

> . . . In presenting jurors with a thumbnail sketch of his client, Plumhoff said, "She is bright, attractive, intelligent. She was a high school cheerleader and class president. She was a college biology major with a B average . . . .

Shit. I'm an A student! I just got B's that one quarter when I was so depressed. With all the dirty laundry that's being aired, they could have at least gotten my grades right! I shook my head. Now I was arguing with a newspaper.

> Catterton claimed the woman tossed Romano because of their age difference.

I didn't toss him because of the age difference; I ended the relationship because I would have died if I stayed in it! How dare she! Didn't she read the medical records? What a bunch of bullshit!

> [Plumhoff said,] "She has been damaged for the rest of her life." She trusted Romano to treat her depression, but he made it worse by "running sex and therapy together."

Damaged for the rest of her life. The words sank in as I scraped the now-cold eggs down the garbage disposal. I had no appetite.

I numbly walked into the family room and flipped on the television. I started watching "The Price Is Right" but realized I must have drifted off when I heard my parents returning and opened my eyes to see that the show was over. I changed the channel. Now, Richard Dawson was smooching a female contestant on "The Family Feud." She didn't look like she wanted to be kissing him back. I turned off the TV.

Mom went about whipping up tuna sandwiches, and I followed her into the kitchen to see Dad re-reading the newspaper. I felt them both try to perk up when they saw me, but I could see the wear and tear on their faces. They were worried.

"Well, it went pretty well," Dad said. "There were twice as many people there today, and that attorney of yours, Earle Plumhoff, is a real pro. I couldn't help but glare at Romano on and off. To think that here was this psychiatrist that we trusted, that he would do this to you, to us. I wanted to deck him."

Mom tried to sound chipper, "I just can't wait for this to all be over so you can get back to life, Carrie."

"Mom, look here," I said, looking over Dad's shoulder. "My attorney said I'm damaged for the rest of my life. It feels that way, but I don't want it to be true."

I found my consciousness sinking deep within my body to a place where I could barely hear their voices urging me to be positive.

I walked upstairs to my room and put on my forest-green jogging suit and jogging shoes.

Damaged for the rest of her life. . . She tossed him . . . bondage . . . pornography . . . I had felt so strong when I left Sheppard Pratt. Living on my own in Baltimore, I felt like I was growing and healing, but now I wasn't sure. Was I backsliding?

I returned to the kitchen, still feeling like a shell of my former self.

"I'll see you soon. I'm going for a walk."

"Carrie, you barely ate anything," Mom said, looking at my plate.

"Thanks, Mom. I'm not hungry. I'm going to get some fresh air," I said, forcing what I hoped looked like a convincing smile.

I walked down the alley behind our home and remembered the childhood games of kick the can and tag we used to play here. All those kids were grown up now, some with kids of their own. My slow walk turned into a fast one, then a run. Right now, Lori and Todd were probably testifying about my difficult last days at VCU. I tried not to think about it.

I ran through our beautiful, blooming neighborhood. I ran past the tennis courts where I had played many matches, then past the high school where I had been a focused honor student and an outgoing cheerleader, had a great boyfriend, had many friends. I ran around the duck pond and saw lovers holding hands and young mothers pushing baby strollers. Then I slowed down by the old, red covered bridge. In high school, this where the stoners played hooky and smoked pot. I never smoked much pot myself until I met up with Tony, my psychiatrist. How ironic! I ran into the bridge, my footsteps echoing in the shadows, the sunny spring scene ahead of me framed by the bridge's walls and ceiling. I used to think those kids playing hooky here were losers who couldn't get their shit together. Now I was struggling to get my own shit together. I ran on, toward the light at the end of the tunnel.

~35~

The next morning, I padded to the kitchen and paused in the doorway to watch my mother, little bun of soft gray hair on her head, wearing a soft pink cotton polo shirt, neat white pants, and tennis shoes, calmly clipping yesterday's article from the newspaper. Initially, she hadn't even wanted me to sue Tony, only to put him behind me and get on with my life, but she respected my decision, and now, here she was, noting the date in the newspaper margin, and carefully placing the clipping in an envelope with others. I had threatened to write a book about this when it was all over. I guess she thought I would want these someday.

There were pancakes warming in the skillet. My place setting was perfectly lined up on the kitchen table, a small glass of orange juice and an empty coffee cup waiting for me. *Oh Mom, I'm so sorry that you ever felt unappreciated by me.*

She startled. "Oh honey, how long have you been standing there?"

"Morning, Mom. Just a few seconds."

"Want some pancakes?"

Just then the doorbell rang, and I answered. Jody was dressed in a casual navy blue suit. "Is Dad ready?" she asked. "I'm picking him up."

"Be right down, Jody!" he called from upstairs.

Wow, someone is actually earlier than Lieutenant Colonel Tansey. I tried not to smirk.

"More people are coming to the trial each day, and I want to make sure we get seats up front where I can keep my eyes on Dr. Romano," she said.

"Are you sure you want to go again today?" I asked. I didn't want my family to go through more than they had to.

"Care, are you kidding? I want to see him sweat."

Whoa! This was an unusually aggressive response from my kind-hearted sister. I felt a sharp pain in my stomach. Here I was suing Tony for malpractice but still, I hated the thought of people hating him.

Dad trotted down the stairs, kissed Mom and me on the cheek, and headed out the door with Jody. I sauntered back into the kitchen.

"I didn't clip today's story yet, honey," Mom said, handing over the morning's edition of the *Frederick News-Post.*

Front page again. I took a deep breath and read:

> **Daughter Kept 'Dreadful Secret' for 3½ Years, Mother Testifies**
> By George Dorsey
> News–Post Staff
>
> The parents of a 26-year-old woman who is suing her former psychiatrist and lover for medical malpractice said yesterday they did not learn of the affair until their daughter attempted suicide 3½ years after her first therapy session.
>
> The father said he blamed himself for choosing Anthony J. Romano, the 57-year-old psychiatrist who is being sued for $700,000 in Frederick Circuit Court.

Oh, Dad. Don't blame yourself. You didn't make a mistake. Tony did.

"He seemed safe," the father said. "He was older, and had good local recommendations and a good background."

> . . . It wasn't until July 1984 when she attempted suicide that her parents learned of the affair . . . but Romano's role still wasn't clear, her mother said. "Listening to her tell of the affair, how she protected him, I guess I was pretty naive, listening to her then. I felt some sympathy for him. I now know what he did to her, the terrible wrong."

So Mom did understand. More than I realized. I had a lump in my throat as I looked up to see her standing by the kitchen sink, turning on the tap, and squirting lemon Joy dish soap into the water.

> Within three weeks, the woman attempted suicide [again] using a gas oven. She was found by an exterminator who happened by.

Saved by the exterminator. As long as I lived, I didn't think I'd ever get over the sheer weirdness of that.

> "She was absolutely terrorized," her father said. "Her life has been shattered, destroyed," he said, and then softly added, "She's not the daughter she was."

My own eyes welled up with tears as I imagined my father struggling to keep his composure on the stand yesterday. During Bob's call last night, he said Dad had given very moving testimony.

I had to put the paper down. I didn't want to read anymore.

I looked at my mother who was quietly washing the dishes. "Mom, I am so sorry to put you through all of this."

My apology seemed so small compared with what was needed to heal us all. I just couldn't shake the feeling that I had let everyone down—Mom, Dad, my siblings, Tony. He would be taking the stand today. I wondered what he would say. As the minutes ticked by on our grandfather clock, I almost threw up thinking about it.

Hours later, I heard the front door open and Jody and Dad's voices in the front hall—much sooner than expected.

"Such a scoundrel," Dad was saying as they entered the kitchen. "What a display." His voice boiled with quiet rage. He and Jody joined Mom and me at the work island.

"Well, honey, Dr. Romano didn't come across so great today," Dad said. "He absolutely fell apart on the stand."

I waited for them to elaborate. Jody gave Dad a quick glance. I could tell they had agreed not to tell me much.

"He just unraveled," Jody said. "At one point, the courtroom was totally silent except for his sobs."

I felt my heart stop, then split in two. I had never wanted Tony to suffer this much. Had he really loved me? If he did, how had it come to this? Would the jury have more compassion for him, or for me?

"The court recessed after that," she said. "I think Romano didn't have it in him to go back on, but I don't know. That's just my guess."

Dad's face looked both drawn and relieved. His expression softened as an idea occurred to him. "Joanne, let's mix up a batch of Manhattans!"

"Make one for me too!" Jody and I chimed in at the same moment.

We both laughed as if we were eight and eleven again, and lifted our glasses in the air when Dad led the toast.

"Okay, well now, here's to moving on with life," he said, smiling through tears and stumbling over his words. He sniffed. "Carrie, a great wrong has been done to you. May a settlement allow you to heal and have a beautiful life."

Mom sipped on her drink, then slipped four ribeye steaks under the broiler.

The chocolate-brown phone on the kitchen wall rang, and I knew who it had to be.

"Hello?" my voice caught. "Hello?"

"Carrie? Bob Hanley. Good news: Romano was *not* a compelling witness. He contradicted himself repeatedly, then fell apart emotionally on the stand. The judge called a recess so the defendant could gather himself. Having been in court for hours, Earle and I used the opportunity to visit the men's room."

Why is he telling me this? There was a long pause on the other line, as if Bob were choosing his words carefully.

"Well, before he and I had even finished," he cleared his throat, "relieving ourselves, the insurance adjuster entered the room and said they wanted to settle out of court. Right there at the urinals. Earle and I couldn't believe it. I mean, yes, the defense was crumbling, but trying to strike a deal in the men's room?" Bob laughed softly.

I tried not to visualize the scene.

"The insurance company is *highly motivated* to settle, Carrie—tonight."

The Willing Descent into Darkness

Young Persephone related her tale of deception and rape. She expressed her dread at returning to the Underworld's host, but wise Demeter reminded her daughter that her sacrifice ensured the safety of others, saying, "But come my child … and be not too angry unrelentingly with the dark-clouded son of Kronos but rather increase for the people the fruit that gives them life."

~36~

It was a sunny September day, and I told myself that despite my long to-do list, I still had a few minutes to watch the U.S. Open on TV before leaving the house. I was dying to see how the tournament was shaping up, especially after John McEnroe had lost to Andre Agassi at Wimbledon a couple of months back. Bip-bop-bip, the ball went back and forth on the screen as I remembered that I had to get groceries at Golden Temple, a Sikh-owned supermarket and health food store, sign up for the fall yoga session while I was there, meet my new psychotherapist, Leslie Krohn, at 3 p.m., and get back in time to rehearse with my friend Bob Evans, the other half of our folk-rock duo, Phoenix Rising. He and I had agreed on the Indigo Girls' "Closer to Fine," and Tracy Chapman's "Baby Can I Hold You Tonight," for our gig on Saturday but still had a lot more to flesh out before then. Oh, yeah, and I still had to arrange a meeting with Sally, a client of the interior decorating business I'd established few years earlier, because the samples of Italian marble and custom vinyl flooring she wanted had finally arrived.

The match went to a commercial, and I quickly flipped through the channels, seeing Arkansas Governor Bill Clinton shaking hands on the presidential campaign trail. Oh, well. I turned off the TV.

As I picked up my car keys from the kitchen counter, my eyes lingered on the photo of Mom and Dad standing by a thatched hut on the beach, looking relaxed and happy. Of all the things I'd been able to finance with the malpractice settlement a trip to Hawaii for my parents was the most satisfying. It hadn't been easy to convince Bob and Joanne Tansey—whose idea of decadence was taking the family out for ice cream—to spend a week in the islands, but finally, they agreed. I wished I could have bought them more.

At the Golden Temple, my new favorite hangout, I breathed in the smell of curry and cumin from its restaurant as I cruised the aisles of the adjoining natural grocery, plunking hummus, red peppers, and spelt pita bread into my cart. I was embracing a healthier diet these days after being diagnosed with candida, a systemic yeast infection, probably caused by overuse of the tetracycline I'd taken for acne for four straight years in my teens and 20s. My new, holistic physician said it likely had led to the collapse of my immune system, and possibly the spacey feelings, depression, and anxiety that first led me to Tony's door. It was hard to think that a systemic imbalance, not mental illness, might very well have been at the root of my problems then, but it didn't do to dwell on that now. I had to focus on the present, and on my future.

Bag of groceries on my hip and yoga schedule in hand, I scanned the broad Golden Temple bulletin board. At my most recent yoga class, I'd been meditating, eyes closed, to the sound of chimes, inhaling frankincense with deep breathing when I became aware of a flame burning inside me, a warm, cleansing flame. Love and light washed over me, similar to my early encounters with mystical Christianity. The flame radiated from within. I felt connected to, not separate from, the divine. When I told my therapist, Leslie Krohn, about it, she encouraged me to do more seeking within. That's what I loved about her. She didn't make pronouncements about my pathology. She didn't presume to know what I needed to do with my life. Instead, she encouraged me to ask my own questions and find my own answers, gently nudging me out of the ruts whenever I got stuck in old patterns or limiting beliefs.

Wow. There were so many opportunities.

INTRODUCTORY CHAKRA CLEARING WITH
HARPREET KAUR KHALSA

On the flyer, a Sikh woman in a snow-white turban was sitting in the lotus position, eyes closed.

Looks interesting but same time as band practice. Oh, well.

TAROT READINGS BY SYLVIA DRAGONWOOD: $50

Jung loved the tarot. I really should learn more about it, but this is a little too expensive. Maybe if Phoenix Rising does well on tips next weekend . . . .

HYPNOTHERAPY AND PAST-LIFE REGRESSION WITH JONAS

Fascinating . . . but there is no way I'm going alone to open my psyche to a man I don't know. Maybe I could get a friend to go with me and do it too.

"Hey Carrie!" hollered a familiar voice.

I turned around to see my friend Molly headed my way, her own groceries in hand.

"Did you see the hummus packs, two for $2?" she asked.

"I got one tub of plain and the other of garlic herb," I said with a smile. "Listen, want to try Past-Life Regression Therapy together?" I said, gesturing to the bulletin board.

"Carrie, when it comes to healing and wholeness, you are the most motivated person I've ever met! It's almost like you're trying to cram a lifetime's worth of experiences into a few years."

If she only knew. "Oh, really?" I said with a smile. "If you don't do it with me, I won't give you the number of that acupuncturist you wanted," I teased.

On a more serious note, I needed to get to my psychotherapy appointment on time, so Molly agreed to call me later, and we'd hash out the details of past-life regression, or maybe just go out for herbal tea instead. The afternoon whirled by, and hours later, I returned to my cottage in northern Baltimore. I'd had a good session with Leslie, and as I stashed my canned goods in the cupboard, I thought about putting my life in order. A couple weeks ago, I'd read an article in the *Baltimore Sun* about TERN, the Treatment Exploitation Recovery Network, a support group for people who had been exploited by their doctors.

It really struck a chord with me. At Sheppard Pratt, I knew one other patient in a situation like mine, but a woman cited in the article said there were many more of us—enough that the *Sun* considered it front-page news. I'd talked to Leslie about it. Most of the time, I loved my new life, I said. I had come so far. And yet, there was this void, those lost years that made it difficult to relate to my peers or have a healthy relationship with a man. I longed to feel real, authentic connection with other thirty-somethings, but while they had been enjoying college, striding down their career paths, and finding mates, I had been in a dysfunctional secret relationship with a twisted shrink. I'd lost years I could never get back. Other people didn't understand, and I didn't honestly expect them to, but the isolation I felt was difficult to overcome at times.

Leslie said visiting a TERN meeting might be a way for me to connect with others who would understand, and might also be a way for me to find meaning in the experience—that Viktor Frankl piece of the puzzle that still eluded me. What she said made sense, but I was afraid it would be like my trial all over again. I was afraid of being thrust back into that place of shame and darkness, near-hopelessness and utter exhaustion. I never wanted to feel that way again. But the newspaper article was evidence that the issue of doctor-patient abuse was much larger than my own story.

"This doesn't have to be about going back," Leslie had encouraged me in our session. "It can be about going forward, connecting with others, maybe even helping them. The personal is political, Carrie."

I'd agreed to take the baby step of calling TERN to find out more. I didn't have to do anything else right away. That made it seem more approachable, less intimidating. "The personal is political," I said under my breath as I dialed, steeling myself with the famous feminist motto. I heard the phone ring on the other end and mentally rehearsed the voicemail message I expected to leave.

"Hello, Treatment Exploitation Recovery Network. This is Sharon."

Oh crap, a real person.

"Um, hi, Sharon. My name is Carrie. I read about TERN in the *Sun*, and I'm just calling to find out a little more about your organization, when it meets, things like that."

She quickly answered my questions, then asked what had brought me to TERN. I felt my body shaking but kept my voice calm as I recounted my three-and-a-half-year descent, my re-emergence at Sheppard Pratt, and the resulting malpractice trial.

". . . And that was the last time I'd ever see my doctor," I concluded. "I have a great therapist now, and—"

"—Wait, are you talking about Dr. Anthony Romano?" Sharon interrupted.

"Yes," I replied cautiously, feeling like all the air had been sucked from my lungs.

"You know he's done it again, right?"

A hot ball of fire exploded in my belly. "What do you mean?"

Any polite formality in our conversation evaporated as Sharon began talking more rapidly and emphatically.

"A few days after that story in the *Sun*, I got a call from a woman who was concerned about remaining anonymous and would only give her first name, Jill. She asked the usual questions, then described being in a relationship with her psychiatrist who had once been sued for malpractice for the same thing. She sounded torn to me, confused, as if she wanted to leave the relationship but couldn't fathom how to actually go through with it. I tried to help her, but she got off the phone very quickly. I'd hoped she'd show up at a meeting, but so far, nothing."

I put my hand on my chest to make sure I was still breathing.

"Then, last week, a man called who could only have been her husband," Sharon said. "He saw the article too. He said his wife, Jill, was involved in an affair with her psychiatrist, Dr. Anthony Romano. He said five or six years ago, Romano had even asked Jill—his patient!—" Sharon emphasized, her voice rising, "to be a character witness for him in a malpractice suit. Am I jumping to conclusions here, or was that your case?"

My entire body prickled with goosebumps.

"That had to have been my case," I said. To my knowledge, this Jill had not actually been a character witness at the trial. More likely, it was one of Tony's tactics, painting the picture of himself as the wronged, kind-hearted doctor in order to win Jill's trust if the trial publicity raised her suspicions.

"Anyway, the husband asked me how to help his wife," Sharon said. "He said she went to a psychiatrist to address her unhappiness in her marriage, but Romano seduced her into a relationship with him instead."

The line was silent for a minute.

"Carrie, are you there?" Sharon said.

"Yes, sorry. I'm just . . . stunned." I took a deep breath. "Know what, though? I have to help this guy, or at least try to. Can you give me his number?"

"Why don't I call him and ask his permission? Or I could give him your number if you prefer."

I thanked Sharon, agreed to attend the next TERN meeting, said good-bye, and hung up, jaw still dropped.

He was doing it again. After all the hell we had been through, although he did not deny malpractice, he had learned nothing. I imagined the negative publicity had harmed his business, but apparently, he still had a license to practice medicine, even though I'd done the right thing.

I needed to calm my nerves. I put the teakettle on the stove and opened a tin of chamomile, my mind reeling back six years, to the final step in my process of holding Tony accountable.

About a month after the trial and settlement, I'd made an appointment to report Tony's transgressions to the American Psychiatric Association, which I expected to in turn file a complaint with the State

Medical Licensing Board. I wanted to do whatever was needed to keep Tony from harming another patient, and there was plenty of evidence that he was unfit to practice medicine and needed to be disciplined and supervised for a period of time, maybe even lose his license. Compared with the other legal proceedings, this seemed little more than a formality. My former doctor had already been found guilty of malpractice by the state's Health Claims Arbitration panel and had settled out of court in a malpractice trial—and I had a foot-high stack of documents to prove it. Now all I had to do, I thought, was meet with the chair of the APA ethics committee, Dr. Stephen Bartley, and hand them over.

In his suburban Baltimore office, Bartley had welcomed me to take a seat opposite him. I reached across the wide desk and handed over the mounds of evidence. At that point, I was surprised when he told me that he'd already met with Tony and heard his side of the story.

In turn, I shared mine for just a few minutes. Then he leaned toward me.

"Well, Miss Tansey, what do you think your diagnosis is?" Dr. Bartley said with a smile.

It startled me that he'd ask such a question. Nevertheless, I tried to cooperate as my mind reeled.

"Um, I think I was profoundly depressed, and um, I think I have an anxiety disorder." My voice cracked a bit, and I scrambled to recover the calm self-assurance I'd been feeling until this moment.

"Do you want to know what *I* think, Carrie?" He leaned in even closer, eyes narrowing.

This didn't feel right. I felt myself getting more nervous. To my knowledge, Bartley hadn't read any documents about the case, so it was highly inappropriate to make a pronouncement about it a few minutes into our meeting, a meeting that was supposed to be about ethics. I couldn't think of anything to say that wasn't inflammatory, so I kept mum.

"I think you have borderline personality disorder," he declared with utter authority, glasses perched atop his head.

I was dumbstruck. That was a serious mental illness, characterized by idealizing, then devaluing, others, and there was no evidence of it in any of the documentation or my medical records, nor had this "professional" examined me to make a diagnosis of his own. What he said was outrageous.

"You and Tony remind me of my wife and I."

What? This was even more outrageous.

He folded his hands across his stomach, his gaze boring into me. "I think you reached the secret garden, and you couldn't handle it."

The secret garden? Who says that? Why isn't he reviewing the evidence? Why is he so defensive? If Tony and I remind Bartley of himself and his wife, does that mean they had a doctor-patient relationship too? This is so twisted! Who is he protecting? Tony? Himself?

That day, I left his office feeling slimed, diminished, and done, just done with the medical profession—its patriarchy, its pathologizing, all of it.

The teakettle whistled, reminding me I was far from done. Tony still had a license to practice medicine, and he was abusing it again! Once, I had actually felt sorry for him, but now . . . well, I couldn't be like Dr. Bartley and assume I knew what was going on. I had to assess the evidence for myself.

A couple weeks later, I walked into a dimly lit tavern-restaurant on the harbor in old town Annapolis to meet Jill's husband, Lee. After a brief phone conversation, made possible by Sharon, he said he wanted to meet me in person. *What would the man married to Tony's newest patient-turned-lover look like?* I shook my head in disbelief. This was not a question I had ever imagined asking myself.

At the hostess station, I said I was meeting a man named Lee and was led to a booth overlooking the small harbor. Light sparkled on the water as boats bobbed up and down, making it hard for me to focus my eyes when we got to the booth where a tall, slender, rather handsome man sat, twisting his salt-and-pepper mustache.

"Lee? Lee Martin?" I asked.

He stood up to shake my hand. "Yes, Carrie. Please, sit down."

As I made myself comfortable, I could feel his agitation and took a deep breath before making eye contact again.

"Carrie, thank you so much for meeting with me," he began. "I haven't known what to do about this situation with my wife, or soon-to-be-ex-wife. Quite frankly, I'm so angry with her it's really not about helping her so much anymore. It's about protecting my son."

"You have a son?"

"Yes, and if it were just her, I would say 'good riddance,' but she regularly brings my ten-year-old son to that farm with her." He winced, then went on. "And I know that she and Tony often get high there. I don't want my son exposed to that."

My stomach churned as I listened to this man so desperate to be heard.

"How long has your wife been involved with him?"

"Well she was in therapy with him for years, during which our marriage really went downhill," Lee said. "I'm not saying we didn't have problems before, but the longer she was in therapy, the worse things got. I couldn't do anything right. She no longer wanted to work things out. It started feeling like I was always the bad guy. After a while, it seemed like she was in a trance, under a spell of some sort, acting evasive, disappearing on weekends, going to retreats on his farm in God-knows-where Virginia."

Inside, I cringed.

"Did you know anything about me?" I asked. "For example, my malpractice case would have been tried around the same time you said Jill was his patient."

"Oh, yes, Jill told me all about you," he said with a cynical snort. "Of course, she only heard Tony's version," he qualified with a bitter smile, "but she said that Tony fell madly in love with you, he paid for you to finish school, and then you dumped him and sued him for a million dollars."

I felt my body bristle and a fire rise from deep inside. Instead, I smiled.

"Well, I wish I'd been awarded a million dollars," I said pleasantly. "But the real sum was much less. It's true that Tony gave me a $200-a-month stipend when I was a graduate student."

Lee's eyes widened.

"But that hardly came close to paying my tuition and expenses," I went on. "Besides, I never finished grad school because I tried to kill myself twice and was committed to Shepard Pratt instead."

Our drinks arrived, and Lee took a big gulp.

"So most of my settlement was reimbursement for my mental hospital bills, his psychotherapy bills, and my lost income during the healing process."

I could tell Lee didn't know what to say.

"In case it isn't obvious, I'm not a doctor," I said with a soft laugh. "I'm an interior decorator and a singer, and if you'd like to change out your wallpaper or have me sing you 'Happy Birthday,' I'd be glad to."

He managed a smile. "I'm sorry. This is a lot for me to take in. I've heard so much negative stuff about you, not that I believed it all, but you just seem so . . ."

". . . normal?" I finished.

"Well, yeah."

"I've been working on my healing for a long time now," I said, browsing the appetizer menu. This was a hard day for Lee. The reality was worse than his fears—but I could already tell he trusted me.

"Lee, I am so sorry this has happened—to you, to Jill, to your son," I said, fiddling with my napkin. "I know how it feels. Tony didn't just hurt me. He alienated me from my family and caused me to hurt the people I loved." As I looked up from the table into his eyes, Lee seemed resolute and purposeful.

"Ever since my trial," I went on, "I've been rebuilding my life, hoping that Tony was out there doing the same, taking responsibility, healing, moving on, but he did this *again.* I am horrified that the system allowed it."

There was a lump in my throat, and I could tell there was one in Lee's too. I had never had such an intense conversation with a stranger in such a short span of time.

"What can we do?" he said, eyes pleading.

"I don't know yet, but we have to stop him."

~37~

It was a dark-gray Saturday in late January when I struggled to get the attic door open and find the cardboard boxes of court documents and newspaper clippings from my legal proceedings seven years before. A crack of light broke through the shadows, illuminating the box labeled Health Claims Arbitration. I figured it would be a good place to start. *Man, this is heavy stuff,* I thought, biceps taut, as I carried the boxes downstairs to my den and turned on the lamp.

Since our first meeting last autumn, Lee and I had run into nothing but roadblocks when it came to stopping Tony. I went to the licensing board to see if I could reopen my complaint against him, which had been considered "resolved" when the board disciplined him with six months of mandatory supervision. At the time, I thought its response was too light, but I was just too exhausted to push the case any further. Whether or not he had meant to do so, the creepy psychiatrist from the APA ethics committee had effectively reignited my shame and silenced me. It was only when the licensing board approached my attorneys for court documents (because of the publicity of my trial) that I opened the original complaint to look at it. Of course, if I had known for an instant that Tony was capable of repeating his sexual exploitation, I would have been emboldened to push for more-stringent discipline. Now, after finding out about his actions with Jill, I was told that Tony could not be tried again in my case.

Lee tried going to the licensing board on Jill's behalf but was erroneously told that the patient must file the complaint unless she or he is a minor, which Jill wasn't, of course. Like so many bureaucratic rules and regulations, they made sense on paper but not in reality. If I knew what Jill was going through—and I was pretty sure I did—she was totally under Tony's psychological control. Only someone who wasn't could convince her to stand up to him, could stand up for her, but that was against the rules. And she was out there somewhere, suffering.

In the meantime, a different opportunity had arisen. Dr. Michael Plaut, a psychology professor at the University of Maryland, was cooperating with Maryland State Senator Leonard Teitelbaum to propose a bill in the Maryland General Assembly that would create a twenty-four-member task force of patients, psychologists, psychiatrists, nurses, social workers, lawyers, and clergy members who would study the issue of doctor-patient exploitation and propose stiffer penalties for guilty practitioners. The task force would also create consumer awareness of what responsible, ethical behavior should be for doctors and therapists. In a few days, eight women from TERN, including me, would be testifying about our experiences and the need for this bill at a committee hearing. We were making the personal political. Today, that meant refreshing my memory about the case, so I would be able to accurately answer anything the legislators might ask.

Outside the den window, snow was falling as I snuggled into my mauve loveseat, cuddling up with the fuzzy velour blanket Mom had just given me for Christmas. This was the first time I would read the transcript and learn what was said in anyone else's testimony. I opened the first of several two-inch-thick volumes, took a deep breath, and read through it.

My cozy den melted away as I was mentally transported to the clinical, white meeting room and its long conference table in the Frederick County Courthouse. In my mind's eye, I could see the three panel members, Tony, and his attorney, Jack Blunt. Tall Earle Plumhoff would have been in his three-piece suit, towering proudly over everyone else, even seated, while bespectacled Bob Hanley organized legal documents and the stenographer typed softly. At this point in the hearing, the group had already heard my testimony, and I was probably home with Mom and Dad. Now, I was about to delve into the details everyone sought to protect me from back then. My chest tightened, and I read.

Blunt said: Dr. Romano, we have a lot of ground to cover. And I guess the only way to do it is to get into it. So why don't you tell us when you first met Carrie and under what circumstances and what transpired.

Oh, this was gonna be good . . . but wait, was I not following? Tony was just rambling, with little or no prompting from either attorney. He talked about everything from Grandma's depression to Mom teaching aerobics at the YMCA. He talked about my going through puberty.

Romano: She started developing, breast development, at age eleven, and her menarche was at age eleven and three quarters . . . .

How on earth was this relevant? Did I miss something? Maybe I wasn't concentrating hard enough and needed the pep of a cup of coffee, but no, Tony meandered on like this from Page 389 to 399. Then Jack Blunt interjected: Doctor, did there come a time when you made a diagnosis of Carrie?

Romano: Yes.

Blunt: What was your diagnosis?

Romano: I was going to come to that.

Blunt: Well, I'm trying to speed things up or we will be here forever.

Chairman Strong: We are all willing to take as much time as necessary.

If Tony perceived that the officials—including his own attorney—thought he was making a fool of himself, he showed no sign of it, not from what I could gather from the transcript anyway. How I longed to see the facial expressions of everyone in the room.

Blunt: Doctor, are you still in your history-taking process now?

Romano: Yes.

Blunt: Why don't you proceed with that? Then will you get to the diagnosis?

I read a bit further.

Romano: She recalls no preschool sexual curiosity, which is, well, a little unusual. Most kids have some sexual curiosity prior to age six.

I guess I should have been embarrassed, but I had been through too much to be embarrassed by anything at this point. Besides, Tony's testimony was nuts! But no one was stopping him. He rambled on—about my wanting to be a tomboy, then later being a Girl Scout. *True but so what?* Next, he revealed the physical details of my relationships with each of my high school boyfriends, then college boyfriends. Seriously? I wondered if it had been as clear to the others as it was to me that he was absolutely obsessed with my gender identity and sexuality. This went on from Page 399 to Page 418. I glanced at my watch. It was taking me roughly a minute to read a page, and it would take longer if I read aloud at the pace he was speaking at, so he had probably been digressing like this for more than twenty minutes.

Then, what I read next made me laugh out loud.

Plumhoff: Mr. Blunt, is this in response to some question? I don't know.

Blunt: I think there was a question a long time ago.

Jeez, Louise. Now, with little if any transition, Tony was rattling off psychological jargon.

Romano: Hypersensitivity and hypervigilance are paranoid. Defect in capacity to form deep relations, histrionic schizoid. Lively and dramatic, mostly when depression lightens and allows it, histrionic . . . feeling of entitlement, "I deserve" narcissistic.

What was this? A glossary? Because he wasn't making a case that his patient had displayed these characteristics. I guess he was just trying to make it sound as if I were a basketcase.

Blunt: How often were you seeing Carrie?

Romano: Three times a week.

Blunt: And you have indicated that there was no medication you were aware of that you thought would be helpful for her, so what sort of treatment were you giving her?

Romano: Supportive, here-and-now stuff. Dealing with issues that came up from day to day.

I wondered if the attorneys and the panel looked as incredulous as I felt right now. Tony had just stated that his patient had a laundry list of serious problems but that he was basically doing nothing in particular to treat her for them.

Blunt: This would be a good time to take a break.

No doubt, it would. I put the volume down on the loveseat and shuffled into the kitchen where I still had some carrot sticks and hummus in the fridge. I shook my head. Reading the transcript would have been hilarious if it weren't so horribly wrong. I returned to the den, slumped back on the couch with my snack, and resumed reading.

Now it was Earle's turn to ask the questions.

Plumhoff: Doctor, I think you testified that you graduated from Georgetown Medical in 1956. Is that correct?

Romano: Yes, sir.

Plumhoff: Did you, sir, at that time, have occasion to take the Hippocratic Oath?

Romano: Yes, sir.

Plumhoff: Do you remember any of the terms of that oath?

Romano: No, sir.

Plumhoff: Are you aware of the fact that it contains a specific prohibition against sexual relations with patients?

Romano: Yes, sir.

Plumhoff: And that that's been in being for some 2,500 years?

Romano: Whatever. Yes, sir.

Plumhoff: You knew, didn't you, from your training, that sexual involvement with your patients was wrong?

Romano: I knew it was unethical.

Plumhoff: And that the American Psychiatric Association specifically provided prohibition against such sexual involvement, correct?

Romano: Yes.

Tony just admitted that he had knowingly violated the Hippocratic Oath, and expressed no remorse about it. I flipped through about ten more pages and read on. Now, Tony was talking about my first visit to his farm.

Romano: Well I remember she took a bong hit and I took a bong hit.

He didn't say anything about offering me the wine—which he chose not to drink himself. That certainly seemed suspicious.

Romano: And the next thing I know, we were in each other's arms. I mean, it was just like that.

As if this was spontaneous. My ass. He planned the weekend. He took me over a hundred miles away, alone, to the middle of nowhere. He planned the whole thing.

Romano: Carrie never dressed erotically. She never dressed seductively. She never really did anything that would portray what I saw when we got her clothes off.

We?

Romano: Carrie has a beautiful body.

I nearly choked on my carrot stick. *Why on earth would he say this during a legal proceeding? He was actually bragging to the arbitration panel!* I suddenly felt vulnerable, and tightened the blanket around me. I kept paging through the bound volume. Tony was describing that night—only in his version, I was actively participating, not sluggish and disoriented.

Romano: Then she said "What am I doing here? I am not supposed to be here." And she sat up. Now I'm not going to argue about it. Call it a dissociative reaction.

Of course it was a dissociative reaction—caused by trauma! How could he act so clinical, so detached, so scientific about a situation he'd orchestrated himself?

Romano: Those things are sometimes easily precipitated if somebody has been smoking marijuana or something.

Marijuana that my doctor gave to me. Unbelievable. The transcript made clear that he seemed oblivious to the fact that he was incriminating himself. Or he believed he was beyond reproach. I couldn't tell which.

I flipped through the volume from Page 440 to Page 456. Earle was questioning Tony about the Polaroids, and more.

Plumhoff: I see you have brought with you *The Joy of Sex*. Is that with you for any particular reason, sir?

I couldn't believe my eyes. I reread the line, mouth agape. Now, Earle's and Bob's confidence in my case made a lot more sense.

Romano: Yeah, it's here in case you want a popular book that's sold 4.5 million copies that mentions things like this.

Plumhoff: Do you know whether or not bondage happens to be mentioned in the DSM-III volume?

Romano: I don't think it is.

Plumhoff: You don't think it's in there. You don't think it's referred to under sexual sadism and sexual masochism?

Romano: You are talking about pathology now. I wasn't into humiliating her, or her humiliating me, or putting her in a position where I could harm her, or her me.

Plumhoff: Doesn't bondage, tying someone to a bed, isn't that somehow psychologically humiliating?

Romano: No, it was rather exciting.

Plumhoff: For who?

I don't know how long I sat there, stunned, mouth open. Tony's behavior before the arbitration panel certainly shed new light on the count of "wanton recklessness." I wondered if the others in the room were as slackjawed then as I was now. If they were, how on earth did Tony fail to notice and rein himself in? It seemed as though he was reliving his fantasy as he spoke, that he couldn't stop talking about it, even as he incriminated himself. His behavior reminded me of my graduate school training in working with alcoholics and drug addicts. Often, they enjoy reminiscing obsessively about binges they've gone on—extreme or dangerous ones in particular. Here's a psychological term for you, Tony: *euphoric recall.*

I thought about the shame it had taken me six months in Sheppard Pratt and years of psychotherapy to overcome. He didn't feel a shred of it. And he didn't notice or care that I did. He wanted to rationalize that I had enjoyed the affair as much as he had—despite the mountains of evidence to the contrary. No wonder he was a repeat offender.

I didn't want to read the next part, but I had to. Somehow, I wanted to read my own testimony to get a sense of how I came across on that day seven years ago. I took a deep breath and plunged my mind back into the white conference room. I read the dialogue transcribed faithfully by the dutiful stenographer. It was surreal.

Of course, my feelings of shame, self-doubt, and rage weren't chronicled—just my words. And wow! Unlike Tony, I answered every question clearly. I was forthright. I was even eloquent from time to time. Reading all this—and I couldn't believe what I was thinking—I actually felt some compassion for Jack Blunt. The poor attorney was on a sinking ship, and he knew it. He was struggling to defend the indefensible, and as painful as it was, as it would always be, I now understood why he had turned so nasty in the cross-examination: His only hope of winning was intimidating me into recanting my story. Only I didn't.

Earle Plumhoff's words echoed in my mind: "Carrie, you are a very compelling witness," and I realized that for the first time, I saw myself clearly. For the first time, I truly understood what he meant.

Alone with my blanket and my carrot sticks, I was as outraged as I was inspired. After shamelessly bragging about his sexual exploits in a legal proceeding, after essentially pleading no-contest to a malpractice suit, Dr. Anthony J. Romano still had a license to practice medicine. The system had to change—and I had never felt more compelled to change it.

~38~

With my suitcase splayed out on the bed, I checked its front pocket to make sure my plane ticket was still there. I was leaving for Santa Fe in two days and had just started packing. I'd tucked in a bottle of sunscreen and put my brown, pointy-toed cowboy boots in the bottom. It felt good to be leaving behind the bold gold jewelry and shoulder pads I needed for my day job selling interior design products and pack my turquoise pendant and gauzy, bohemian skirts instead.

It would be warm in May, friends had assured me, but they said the desert gets cold at night. "Layers," Lori had explained. "Everyone there dresses in layers." So I threw in my jean jacket. And I'd need something to read on the plane, so I added the book from my bedside table, *Going Within: A Guide for Inner Transformation* by Shirley MacLaine. Oh, and the new journal I had bought for the trip, with a Laurel Burch painting of a golden goddess on the cover.

So much had happened since the committee hearing at the Maryland State House last winter, and now I felt like one part of my journey was over and a new one was beginning. A few days ago, Dr. Plaut had called TERN to say that the bill growing out of our committee hearing had passed both the Senate and the House of Delegates and just been signed into law by Governor William Donald Schaefer. The task force would be organized this summer, at the beginning of the fiscal year.

I looked back on that day of the hearing with pride and gratitude. Sure, I had been nervous, driving to Annapolis, approaching the imposing facade of the majestic building that had served as the first peace-time capitol of the United States. As the sea breeze blew in from Annapolis Harbor, a group of young midshipmen, wearing crisp, white uniforms rushed past me on their way back to the U.S. Naval Academy. My late grandfather, Admiral William E. Mullan, had gone there too. I wondered if he could see me now. I felt as though he could. I wondered if he knew I was mustering up, that I was preparing to fight a major battle but of a different sort than he ever knew. I thought he did.

Inside the state house, humility washed over me when I saw Edwin White's large painting, *Washington Resigning His Commission*, commemorating the end of the Revolutionary War as Washington left his post as commander-in-chief of the Continental Army and returned to civilian life as a farmer. The thought that Washington himself had walked through this room put my own mission in perspective. He had inspired and led a vagabond troop of desperate but determined people against a seemingly more powerful entity, seeking to achieve justice for so many. Weren't we, this small group of women survivors who were there to testify that day, also trying to throw off the shackles of authority figures who had abused their power over us? Weren't we here to reclaim not only our own freedom but also that of others?

When the hearing started, it was the first time I had talked publicly about my ordeal in seven years, but overall, I felt clearheaded and confident. A wave of sobs had threatened to wash over me as I read my notes, but I held it back, saying, "Knowing the ins and outs of my psyche, my doctor knew just what buttons to push to keep me locked in a destructive situation." I was quoted saying that in the *Baltimore Sun* the next day.

Now as I stood in my bedroom packing my suitcase, I wondered if Washington had felt the same way I did. With the battle won, I just wanted to go back to everyday life. I was proud of what I had done but didn't particularly want to be in the public eye. A few months before, I'd had a wonderful dream about something entirely different. The vision had haunted me through the latest legal process, and now I was pursuing it in earnest.

In the dream, I was entertaining guests on the second floor of what seemed to be my home, while looking out a gorgeous picture window. Its view revealed desert foothills dotted with round, green shrubs, and I could see layer after layer of higher mountains beyond that blazed coppery red in the golden, early-autumn twilight. The exterior of the home looked like it was made of dried mud. Inside, the house had lots of wooden ceiling beams. A reception of some sort was taking place, and I was an older, more mature, more accomplished version of myself. I wore a loosely flowing, light-teal silk jacket hand-painted with metallics and richly toned colors of red and blue. I was an artist and healer of some sort, self-employed, and I was married to a musician whose home studio was on the lower floor. He wasn't in the room, but it felt as if he and I had been together for a long time and he would appear momentarily. The earth, the light, the people—I had never felt so grounded and happy. I had a sense of belonging, of rightness, of having arrived.

When I awoke, I knew with my deepest sense of inner knowing that I had just been to Santa Fe, New Mexico—even though I had never actually been there. And I knew I had to go there for real. Strangely, after so many stumbling blocks, after so many uphill battles over the years, the universe seemed to be helping me do it. "You belong in Santa Fe," Lori had declared when she and her boyfriend returned from a trip there not long after I'd had my dream. Then my friend Jack, a Baltimore radiologist, bought an art gallery on Canyon Road in Santa Fe, and kept telling me how much I'd love it there. Next thing I knew, my neighbors Elaine and Lee returned from a Santa Fe visit and said they had thought of me while sipping margaritas at the famous Coyote Cafe. "Carrie needs to come here," they told me they'd said, raising their glasses. Now I was on my way for a four-day trip to scope things out, maybe even relocate. I gazed into my suitcase, frowned, and replaced a pair of jeans with my white Bermuda shorts.

The phone rang, and I answered.

"Hello, is this Carrie?" said a deep, male voice.

"Yes," I answered warily.

"Carrie, this is Marc Goldbaum with CBS "48 Hours, with Dan Rather. I understand you have a very interesting story concerning unethical behavior on the part of your psychiatrist."

Oh crap. I was thrown by his directness but tried to sound calm. "Yes, I do."

"We're doing a special broadcast on this phenomenon," he went on. "I got your name as someone who might be willing to share her story."

My mind calculated quickly. In those *Frederick News-Post* articles seven years ago, I'd merely been referred to as "the woman." In the *Baltimore Sun,* the reporter had graciously agreed to use my middle name, giving me a little privacy as Elizabeth Tansey instead of Carrie. I'd even been filmed in shadow for an interview on the local TV station, and my name wasn't used. Only my closest friends recognized my voice and silhouette. But this was CBS's "48 Hours"—with Dan Rather. This was as public as it got. Silently, I gulped. I tried to sound centered and matter-of-fact as I offered Marc a Cliff Notes version of my ordeal and where I was headed now.

"Wow," he remarked. "You sound really good, really strong."

I laughed to myself. While it had gradually gotten easier to tell my story, it was never really easy. Though I was getting over the shame of the ordeal day by day, year by year, it wasn't what I wanted to be known or remembered for. Being on national TV was definitely something I needed time to think about.

"Say, Carrie, we need to get rolling with this soon," Marc said. "Do you mind if I come see you tomorrow? I can take the train down from New York. Can you pick me up at the station in Baltimore? Then we'll have lunch somewhere downtown; you pick the place."

So much for having time to think about it. The next day, I pretended to walk confidently across the marble floor of Baltimore's beautiful old Penn Station, its stained glass ceiling soaring miles above me. A tall dark-haired man with a mustache approached me, looking exactly as he'd described himself on the phone.

"Carrie?"

"Marc?"

He had a natural yet concerned way about him. His brown eyes looked gently but directly at me, and he exuded an air of calm confidence. I could tell that he was someone who had been told many secrets.

In my car, we made small talk as I negotiated city traffic and drove past skyscrapers to the Inner Harbor on our way to Phillips Seafood House. I figured Marc might as well enjoy some Maryland blue crabs while he was here. Down at the harbor, the sky was watercolor blue, and the moist, salty sea breeze blew over us as we shouldered our way through the lunch crowd to the restaurant. Once we had a table, the small talk continued, and I had to force myself to keep from getting dizzy as opposing thoughts spun in my head. *Yes, I wanted to advocate for justice, but why was this coming up just when I thought I was putting everything behind me? How would all this affect my healing process? A traumatic story retold is also a wound reopened.* Soon, I knew, the small talk would cease and we'd get down to business.

"Carrie, you have a very important story," Marc said. "I've met with a number of women who this happened to, and they can barely speak about it, they're so traumatized or so unable to find the words."

He continued his appeal with the finesse of a fine lawyer. "You express freely what happened, and it could be enormously helpful to others for you to be their voice."

Their voice? I can't even think of what to say right now.

"Of course, it's your decision," he concluded. "I'll respect whatever you decide." He casually tossed his napkin back on the table. "Do you want to think about it for a day or so and let me know?"

A day or so!

The next morning before heading to the airport, I called Marc at CBS. I cleared my throat and told him, "Yes, you can film me."

I'll go to Santa Fe. I'll put all this aside for a while, I reasoned, calming myself. *Then I'll be strong enough to come back to Maryland and do these TV interviews.* I took a deep breath. *I can do it.*

"I have another request," Marc said. "Do you mind if we follow you to Santa Fe and film you getting on with your life?"

Whoa. What?

"Yours is a great story, and will give hope to so many victims," he said emphatically. "The crew and I can be on a plane to New Mexico day after tomorrow. So we'd actually film the ending to your story first, then once you return to Baltimore, we'd film the beginning. It sounds a little backwards, I know, but that's television."

"I just . . . I just have to think about it."

"I know it's a lot to ask since you're wanting to start a new life. How about you go to Santa Fe, see if it feels right, then give me a call?"

My plane landed in Albuquerque, and as I guided my light-blue rental car up Highway 14, taking the scenic route to Santa Fe past the tiny mining towns of Madrid and Cerrillos, I became overwhelmed by the beauty of the landscape, the expansiveness of the desert, the bigness of the sky. And there was something too about the lightness of the warm, clear air. Here, I had breathing room I had never experienced in the hubbub of the city.

I had to pull my car over, hop out, and stop to take it all in: the pure awesomeness of the juniper-dotted hills spreading out to the snow-topped Sangre de Cristo mountain range shadowing the city, and all of it under an endless sky of turquoise blue. The golden sunlight on my skin. The warm earth under the soles of my shoes. All my damp, soggy fears dried up and blown away on the breeze. I could heal here. I would heal here. There was only one way forward, and it was abundantly clear. I sank to my knees on the holy, red-brown dirt.

I will heed the call.
I will move to Santa Fe.
I will do the "48 Hours" show.

As I drove into what's known as the City Different, the community, flanked by mountains, felt sacred and safe. I loved how the adobe buildings seemed to rise up out of the land instead of dominating it like all the glass-and-metal structures in the East. I checked into a funky, Route 66-era motel on Cerrillos Road. My budget was squeaky tight, and I was starting over—again. Tomorrow, I would call CBS News and tell Marc the cameras could come.

I wrote in my new journal that night: *Okay God. Okay Universe. If this is what I'm supposed to do, please bless me. Please bless this trip, this time in my life, and please let me speak in ways that do justice to this issue, for me, for other victims, and for everyone else.*

~39~

On an October morning, I awoke in my new digs, an old adobe in the countryside north of Santa Fe, at the foot of Black Mesa. I had slept soundly last night, and in that strange twilight between asleep and awake, I thought I was in my old bed back in Baltimore until I opened my eyes to the bright, New Mexico sunlight. Now, I looked around the room to get my bearings. Was I really here? Had I really made this bold move? I flashed back on the five-day drive from Baltimore, my black Toyota Celica filled to the brim with all that I would need for my life's next chapter.

I was sharing the house with Jen, a Canadian massage student, her husband, Fred, and their five–year-old daughter, Bailey. My three-hundred-square-foot bedroom, the largest one in the house, was in the back, down a long corridor from the quaint living and dining room area with its warm wood floor and pine ceiling *vigas*. Within days of being in Santa Fe, I had graduated from my sleeping bag to an affordable futon mattress.

My easel and paints were set up in one corner, my black-and-salmon flowered kilim and black directors chairs on the other side—the only furniture I had brought from Maryland. I had let go of just about everything else in a yard sale—my white wicker coffee table and chairs, my brass bed. Gone too were my tailored jackets and skirts, my gold Monet jewelry, my pantyhose and pumps. In the corner closet, I'd hung a few gauze tunics, some oversized flannel shirts, jeans, peasant skirts, and scarves.

I hadn't thought about Baltimore that much since leaving. I was absorbed in my art therapy classes at Santa Fe's Southwestern College and my part-time marketing job for *Miracles* magazine. But today, I was thinking about the city I'd left. Tonight, via the magic of television, I would be transported back to my old life.

"Mom, do you think she's up yet?" I heard Bailey say just outside my door.

"Shhh . . . honey," Jen whispered. "Let her sleep. It's Saturday."

My heart warmed. Bailey was just the medicine I needed, and I loved that she showed such interest in getting to know me. The smell of piñon coffee brewing out in the kitchen also beckoned me to get out of bed and start my day. I stared at the beamed ceiling and threw back the covers. At 9 that night, my interview would be airing on "48 Hours."

The Toronto Blue Jays and Philadelphia Phillies were playing in the World Series, and "48 Hours" had been advertised every night during the games. As promised, Marc Goldbaum had called me about the broadcast schedule and the commercials in advance—it had been about a month ago now. I remembered his emphatic voice over the phone.

"Carrie, the network thinks this is such a big story that they're airing commercials for it during the World Series. An estimated 19 million World Series viewers will see them."

As he said it, I felt nervous anticipation. After all, I'd prayed to do justice to the issue, so I guessed this was good news. The other news wasn't as good. Marc said his crew had tried its best to interview Tony but that he wouldn't cooperate. "48 Hours" had also interviewed Lee, whose wife was still in Tony's clutches. "So your segment will mainly be you telling your account of things," Marc concluded.

It was bizarre to see my own face on the commercials, sandwiched between coverage of the World Series and advertisements for Budweiser and Coca-Cola. I was glad I didn't live in Maryland anymore, where I knew everyone would be talking about it. Here in Santa Fe, I was still relatively anonymous, and even though flashes of my face were on national TV every night for a week, if people in town noticed that the same woman was sitting in their art therapy class or standing next to them in the checkout line at Wild Oats, they didn't say anything.

Lying in bed, I remembered the Santa Fe interviews back in May. Marc and the camera crew had followed me as I went apartment hunting, applied for a new job, and strolled in the desert. I couldn't help but wonder how the footage was going to come together in the finished story. I also knew mine wasn't the only case the broadcast would deal with. I wondered what the other victims would be like, where they were from.

I also remembered that day back in Baltimore when I had looked out the bay window of my brick Cape Cod to see a large, white van pull up to the curb. My heart had begun to race.

I'd watched as the back door of the van opened slowly and out spilled a man holding a large, black camera. I saw Marc Goldbaum come around the front and point to my house, then turn to wait for a woman to get out the passenger side. I waved to them. "48 Hours" correspondent Erin Moriarty, in a lovely pink suit, looked as if she had just spent time in a dressing room. I looked down at my own pink jacket, fluffed up my hair, and put on a fresh coat of lipstick. I swallowed and took a deep breath. Then I answered the door.

"Welcome, please come in."

"Hi Carrie. I'm Erin. Pleased to meet you. And this is Dennis, our cameraman, and of course, you know Marc."

I shook Erin's hand and looked into her eyes. I saw her respect for me, her professionalism, her warmth. I felt myself relax.

"Marc, hello again," I said. "Dennis, hi, welcome."

Erin looked around the room. She sat on my salmon-colored sofa and motioned for me to join her.

"What do you think, Dennis? Over here a good place to film?"

He took light readings, squinted at us a bit, then unpacked more equipment. Soon Erin and I were chatting away as the camera rolled.

She had such a great way of putting me at ease. I found myself answering question after question as if I were talking to a friend from high school. I got emotional on more than one occasion but for the most part managed to keep my composure. We also paged through my old photo albums a bit. And before I knew it, the filming was over.

"Well, Carrie, thank you so much."

"You did a great job," Marc said, shaking my hand. "You're very courageous. Your segment will inspire so many people."

"Carrie, I really respect what you're doing for other survivors," Erin said. "You are very brave."

The two men packed their bags and started to walk out the door, but Erin hung back.

"Do you know who you remind me of?" she asked as she stuffed her notepads and pens in her briefcase. "Donna Rice," she said, looking up at me again. "We did a story on her as well."

I remembered Donna Rice. Back in 1988, her face had been plastered all over the media when she was photographed at a yacht party in Miami wearing a miniskirt and sitting on the lap of then-presidential candidate Gary Hart, who was sporting a T-shirt that read "Monkey Business Crew." *Monkey Business* was the name of the yacht. Hart's presumed extra-marital affair had ended his campaign, but as I remembered the events, just as much, if not more, speculation and shaming had landed on Rice's shoulders—even though he was the one who was married.

"She was devastated by the ordeal and the publicity," Erin said. "She is a brilliant, caring young woman who didn't deserve the negative attention she got. Her story has inspired others, and so will yours."

As I closed the door and watched the journalists walk to the curb, I knew it was out of my hands now. I had to trust that "48 Hours" wouldn't make a fool out of me and would do justice to the issue. Even if it did, though, there was no telling how the public would react. Would I be demeaned and criticized like Donna Rice? There was nothing I could do but trust.

It was dark, and Bailey was already in bed. I thought it was going to be weird to explain to my new housemates that years ago, I had had a sexual relationship with my psychiatrist that almost cost me my life, and now I was going to talk about it on national television, but they accepted the information with grace and respect. Now, with the lights out, we planted ourselves in the living room. I grasped the remote and turned on the TV. "Dr. Quinn, Medicine Woman" was almost over. I turned on the VCR and made sure there was a blank tape inside.

"Tonight on '48 Hours,'" came Dan Rather's authoritative voice.

And wow, there I was on the screen, in my pink jacket with the big shoulder pads saying, "I started freaking out and saying 'What are we doing here? You're my therapist. You're not supposed to be doing this.'" Then my hand flew to my mouth as the Carrie-on-the-screen tried not to cry.

Sitting on the living room sofa, I hugged my knees.

The camera cut to a sign outside an office building that read "Anthony J. Romano M.D., P.A. Psychiatry" while Rather's voice said gravely, "Some doctors are practicing more than medicine."

My heart beat a little faster.

Now, a red-haired man I didn't know was standing in what looked like a legal library saying, "He got involved romantically, physically, sexually with a patient."

Then Erin Moriarty was crossing a parking lot, approaching a man in the distance, notepad in hand saying, "Dr. Romano? Can I talk with you for a minute?"

Then the camera cut to a black-and-white photo of Tony's eyes. It chilled me, and I hugged my knees tighter. Now, the voiceover was my own, "He was like a father figure, he was like a mother figure, he was like a guru, he was like a god." Then the screen changed to me in the pink jacket again,

The pink jacket. Ha, I don't even have that outfit anymore.

Next, there was a close-up of papers from my case file, and the camera zoomed in on the words *acute suicide attempt, chronic depression* while Rather's voiceover said, "Carrie says psychotherapy nearly cost her her life."

I looked at Jen and Fred, their faces still as stone in the flickering blue light of the television.

My own voice brought my attention back to the screen. "I didn't know who Carrie was anymore at all," said the pink-jacketed Carrie on the salmon-pink sofa. She gestured to her head. "It was like I was gone." And that Carrie was crying.

This Carrie felt okay, though.

The scene changed to a man at a baseball game, standing behind home plate as if he were a coach of some kind.

Next, a man I didn't recognize, wearing a blue suit, was saying, "He had taken over my family, my wife, my life."

Cut to footage of a naked toddler jumping into a blonde woman's arms.

Now the same woman was alone, sitting by some trees in what looked like a park, saying, "It was falling in love with someone who happened to be your doctor."

". . . and doctors are facing the consequences" came Rather's voice.

Now a clip of another man, walking past a razor-wire fence saying, "They put me in prison for doing my job as a doctor."

And suddenly Dan Rather was on the screen, his deep, brown eyes serious and penetrating. "Trusting your doctor," his voice rang out. "And feeling betrayed."

The screen morphed to an image of a silver video camera against a black background while red digital numbers counted down dramatically. Trumpets blared the program's theme song, and the episode's news correspondents flashed across the screen one by one. Then, the screen read:

CBS News: 48 Hours
"Betrayed"

"Betrayed?" That's the name of our story? Well, I guess that's fitting.

And there was Dan Rather again, staring straight at me and what felt like all of America, with his neat, dark brown hair and blue suit. He sat at a modern glass-and-aluminum desk. A montage of black-and-white photos from the week's broadcast was in the background. Most prominent among them was my own face—or at least, that's how it seemed to me.

"When you visit the doctor, you put your life in his or her hands," Rather said. "But for some patients, that act of trust turns into a shocking act of betrayal. By one estimate, nearly one out of ten doctors admits having sexual contact with patients. It may be even more widespread, with offenses ranging from inappropriate touching to long-term sexual affairs. But if you think doctors are always strictly punished for it, think again. Tonight, we bring you a revealing look at a relationship that can move from the examining room to the bedroom—sometimes with devastating results."

I got goosebumps. I braced myself.

But the first segment wasn't about me. It was about a physician who had an affair with a married patient—the blonde woman from the introduction. They even had a child together, which she initially tried to pass off as her husband's.

"The state of Maryland has suspended Hullender's medical license on charges that he had sexual relations with three of his patients, smoked marijuana with patients, and seduced them with a cult-like influence," came Rather's voice.

Gee, that sounds familiar.

The screen changed to a gray-haired man wearing a white dress shirt and suspenders. "As far as we're concerned, sex with a patient is never justified," he said.

"Dr. Israel Weiner is chairman of the Maryland State Board of Physician Quality Assurance," said the narrator's voice.

His name is pronounced weiner, like a hot dog, like an . . . um weiner? Seriously? I'm watching someone named Dr. Weiner talk about sexual misconduct? Actually, I had heard of Weiner before, as he and his board were the ones who had reviewed my complaint about Tony, but I had never seen or met him. And I guess I had assumed his name was pronounced "wine-er."

"We take our responsibility very seriously," Weiner was saying. "A doctor's license is his life."

What about the patient's life? Who was the Maryland Medical Board here to protect anyway? Doctors or patients? I felt heat rise in my blood.

"True love is no excuse," Dr. Weiner went on. "There is no medical condition which is improved by the patient seeing the genitals of the doctor."

Well, he was right about that, but something about the way he said "genitals" made me cringe. It was so clinical, so gross. Would this experience ever stop feeling gross?

Then the show went to a commercial.

~40~

I sat still, rigid with anticipation as a silver Acura zoomed up a mountain road, Candace Bergen urged America to switch our long-distance service to Sprint, a woman in a tool belt extolled the virtues of 2,000 Flushes Blue toilet bowl cleaner, and Angela Lansbury snooped around a velveted parlor in a promotion for an upcoming episode of *Murder, She Wrote.*

And then we were back. The screen read:

PHYSICAL THERAPY:
ERIN MORIARTY

Oh God. This is me.

And there I was, in that cute little batik blouse and pants set, padding across the patio of an adobe apartment compound, talking to a broomstick-skirted real estate agent.

Erin's voiceover said, "At thirty-three years of age, Carrie Tansey is starting over."

"My ultimate dream would be to have a little adobe out in the country someplace," said the "48 Hours"-me to the agent.

I actually haven't done too bad then, huh? I looked over to see Fred and Jen smiling softly.

"She's in New Mexico," came Erin's voice again as the TV Carrie peered around the compound. "Looking for a place to live, searching for a job . . ."

The TV me entered a business office for a job interview.

"Meeting new friends,"

Cut to TV Carrie in the desert near Camel Rock, wearing white Bermuda shorts and sneakers, hair in a ponytail, hiking with her new friend, Greg.

Funny, I haven't called him since I moved here. Oh well . . .

"What Carrie is leaving far behind," resumed Erin's voice, "is the stuff nightmares are made of: two suicide attempts and six months in a psychiatric hospital. The result, she says, of a love affair with the wrong man: her psychiatrist."

The screen cut to footage of a pallid, greasy-looking Tony. I leaned back, startled, and my mouth dropped open. I hadn't seen him in almost eight years. His clothes hung loosely on his body. His hair had gone completely white.

I felt a lump in my gut.

Now, Erin was in my old house in Baltimore, paging through photo albums and scrapbooks with my TV self.

"You look happy in all these pictures," she said.

"Oh yeah, I was happy," I answered.

"The affair began while Carrie was in college," came Erin's voiceover. "During her senior year, she became severely depressed after breaking up with a boyfriend."

The camera zoomed in on a photo of me and Louie at a college party. *Louie. I'd forgotten how cute he was . . . . What a waste of great dimples and a beachcomber haircut.* I laughed softly to myself.

A black-and-white portrait of Tony came on the screen. Erin's voiceover said: "When counseling at school failed, that's when she went to see a psychiatrist in her hometown of Frederick, Maryland: Dr. Anthony Romano. She was twenty-one at the time. He was fifty-one. Carrie started seeing Dr. Romano three times a week. Less than a year later, he was also her lover."

Ugh. I wish she hadn't used the word "lover." It implied consent.

Cut to TV Carrie talking on the pink sofa with Erin: "The first time that we were together, I started freaking out and saying, 'What are we doing here? You're my therapist. You're not supposed to be doing this.' "

Oh gosh, this was so hard. TV Carrie's face contorted as she tried not to cry and sniffed back her tears. I wanted to reach out and hug that woman, to comfort her. On the screen, she paused and touched her mouth, then took a deep breath.

"And he said to me, 'What do you mean? I didn't rape you. You were totally into it.' "

It wasn't exactly fun to watch myself on television, relating one of the most painful experiences of my life. I waited for the shame to wash over me, for the nausea to well up in my stomach as it usually did when I talked about this stuff. Only it didn't. Instead, I felt a steely resolve inside. The scene changed. Now Erin was interviewing Dr. Weiner in what looked like his office.

"What kind of psychiatrist sleeps with one of the patients he or she is treating?" she said.

"A bad psychiatrist," he answered definitively, "bad morally and bad professionally.

I felt gratified to hear a professional be so clear-cut about this. I felt myself grow a little calmer. I had worried that someone on the show was going to act like that creep Dr. Bartley all those years ago and blame me or other victims.

On screen, Erin tilted her head, listening as her voiceover said, "This is the kind of case that most concerns Dr. Israel Weiner and the medical board in Maryland. When the doctor is a therapist, the risk of harm to the patient is the greatest. According to Weiner, it's common for patients like Carrie to develop strong emotional ties to their doctors, a process called transference."

Dr. Weiner was talking again. "And this may vary from a strong emotional attachment to love, to even obsessive love," he explained.

Now the TV me was back on camera: "Out of my mouth came something I had never really conceived of before, but I said, 'I think I'm falling in love with you.' And after I said that, I was like, you know . . . Where did that come from?" The TV me shook her head and rolled her eyes.

Weiner was on-screen again. "This is expected to occur during the course of psychotherapy, and psychiatrists are supposed to understand it *and know how to manage it,*" he emphasized.

"Is it too strong to say that it's comparable to an incestuous relationship?" Erin asked.

"It borders on it," he answered. "Furthermore, when the relationship ends, then there's a rejection by a father figure. And we've had numerous cases where the woman patient either attempted suicide or successfully committed suicide."

The scene shifted to me and Erin again, in my home on the pink sofa. "How soon after you broke up with the doctor did you start thinking about suicide?" she asked.

"Within a couple months," I said.

Now, the red-brick edifice I had come to know so well and the sign "Sheppard and Enoch Pratt Hospital" was on the screen.

"Carrie tried twice to kill herself after the four-year relationship ended," said Erin's voiceover. "After the second attempt, she was admitted to a psychiatric hospital in Baltimore."

The camera panned my empty room and the empty halls of the ward, then the scene returned to me. ". . . They were encouraging me to talk about this, and they said, you know, if you don't take action, we're going to report him. Something needs to be done."

"What Carrie did was sue Dr. Romano for malpractice," said Erin's voiceover, and the camera panned across legal documents. "In court, Dr. Romano did admit to the affair but argued that it was consensual and not the cause of Carrie's breakdown. Still, on the fifth day of trial, he agreed to pay Carrie more than half a million dollars in settlement of the case."

The scene reverted to an image of Erin, crossing the parking lot and saying, "Dr. Romano? Can I talk with you for a minute?" It was the same clip from the opening montage.

"We wanted to talk to Dr. Romano," Erin's voice said. "He would only speak to us through his attorney. And what did we want to talk to him about? Well, ironically, Dr. Romano is now engaged to a former patient."

So he and Jill are engaged? Wow.

On the TV, an aged, deflated-looking Tony was looking away from Erin and muttering something. Then, he got into a silver BMW and simply drove away.

I sat there, knowing this particular image would be forever etched in my mind.

As his car glided out of the parking lot, Erin's voiceover said, "But this time, he says he didn't become romantically involved with her until three years after she ended therapy."

That's not what Lee said. Wow, Tony lied to CBS "48 Hours."

Erin continued: "He also says there's nothing unethical about a psychiatrist getting involved with a former patient after a certain amount of time."

Really? Then why avoid the interview, Tony? And it occurred to me why the Tony onscreen appeared so gray, so weak, so slackened: He was awash in shame. I also realized that of all the people I had seen Tony lie to—my parents, attorneys, a jury, journalists, me—he lied to himself the most.

"But that's not what the American Psychiatric Association nor other experts believe," said Erin, reeling me back into the show.

She was in Dr. Weiner's office again. "More-conservative theorists say if you've treated a patient in psychiatric treatment, in psychiatric therapy, you should never, ever have a relationship with that patient," Weiner said.

"The risks to the patient are that severe?" Erin asked.

"Yep," he said with a nod. "It's thought so by a group of psychiatric thinkers."

The scene changed to Santa Fe. Greg and I were hiking near Camel Rock. My purple T-shirt popped against the green piñon and juniper trees in the background.

"Carrie now is trying to put the past behind her," said Erin's voiceover. "Gone, but not forgotten."

The camera zoomed in for my close-up. "I really lost my whole 20s to this trauma, but I feel like I know how to take care of myself now," I said with calm self-assurance. "And it has taken a long time. It's taken a long time."

The camera zoomed out and revealed me standing at the top of a hill.

And the show went to commercial.

I stood outside under the sparkling New Mexico stars, wrapped my arms around myself, and pulled my jean jacket tighter. The night air was cool, and I was glad I had grabbed my scarf. The heady, woody, incens-y smoke of the neighbor's piñon fire warmed my heart, and I wished it would warm my fingertips too. Faintly, I could hear the opening credits of Albuquerque's KRQE News 13 at 10 coming from inside the house.

My segment of "48 Hours" had lasted just under twenty minutes. I couldn't have asked for better treatment from Erin, Marc, and their team. Of course, I knew my own story forward and backward. In terms of understanding the part of this phenomenon that was bigger than myself, the other people interviewed in the show had been enlightening—in good ways and bad.

There had been four other cases besides mine. Three involved physicians, the other a psychiatrist. All the doctors were male. All the patients were female. All the doctors were in their 50s. Three cases occurred in Maryland, one in Minnesota, and the location of one was undisclosed.

The final segment affected me the most. "48 Hours" had titled it "Fatal Attraction." In this case, a woman named Kim Meadows also had an affair with her therapist. On her third suicide attempt, she succeeded. Her husband and her ex-husband had joined together in suing her doctor for wrongful death. Like Tony, Meadows's doctor countered that the relationship was consensual. Dr. Michael Plaut, had testified as an expert witness and also stated matter-of-factly in an interview that, "By virtue of the dependency of the patient and the power of the doctor, the patient cannot truly give consent."

Thank you, Michael.

On the other hand, Meadows's sisters, Barbara and Sherry, insisted when interviewed by "48 Hours" that Kim's first two suicide attempts had been staged pleas for attention. I was incredulous. *But she killed herself!* I felt like screaming. *How can you say she just wanted attention?* Clearly, there was still more work that victims like me could do to educate the public.

I watched, enrapt, as Meadows's ex-husband and school-age son stood at her grave. It was easy to imagine my parents standing there instead, with my name on the headstone. Nine years ago, I had intended for this story to die with me. Now, I had given voice to it in a way I never could have imagined. I felt gratitude. I felt humility—but I didn't feel shame.

At the end of the broadcast, Dan Rather had concluded: "Several states have recently toughened laws against doctors that engage in sexual misconduct. In Maryland . . . a task force is now considering penalties that would make such actions a crime."

You're damned right it is, I thought, my heart swelling with pride as my eyes steamed with tears.

"I'm Dan Rather, and that's '48 Hours.'" His words rang in my ears.

Out here in the clear New Mexico night air, I kind of felt like smoking a cigarette, but I had given that up when I left Sheppard Pratt. Instead, I watched my breath rise in the chill as I exhaled. There was not a cloud in the silky, black sky, and the moon shone bright. I felt no darkness inside me, only illumination.

Yeah, in a way, Tony had "gotten away with it," so to speak, but he couldn't get away from himself. His shadow had overtaken him, and as long and harrowing as my journey had been, I was in a better place, a healthier place, than he was. I wondered if he appeared like a ghost of his former self because of the toll the ordeal had taken on him, or because he had never been the dashing, robust mentor and savior I had once believed him to be. Either way, I felt free of him in a way I didn't think I could ever explain.

I was just as content to turn off this episode of my life as I had been to turn off the VCR when the show was over—recorded, never to be forgotten, but finished just the same. Fade to black.

~41~

The sun shone on my shoulders as I sauntered down the drive-way to the mailbox at the edge of our dusty country road. Lucky, the shaggy shepherd-mix stray who had adopted Fred, Jen, Bailey, and me, trotted by my side along with a ragtag pack of contented yellow dogs that no one in our neighborhood claimed but everyone secretly fed. Ears pricked up, tails wagging, their sense of happy anticipation rubbed off on me.

The tin mailbox squeaked as I opened it. I took out a handful of brightly colored envelopes and sifted through them on my way back to the house. For days now, people had been sending cards and notes of congratulations. In my room, I opened this new batch. Oh, my gosh, this was from my new boyfriend's mother. What a sweetheart. I placed it in a shoebox with the others. I couldn't identify the return address on a yellow envelope . . . oh wow, it was from Fran, my old tennis partner in Baltimore.

"You were really brave, and my mother and I thought you looked so pretty on television," she wrote. I laughed to myself. *Oh yes, that was my top priority, looking pretty on television*, I thought sarcastically, but it was a kind compliment all the same.

Michael Plaut had a better understanding of my experience than most, so it had been validating to get a note from him too.

"The task force is moving ahead successfully," he wrote. "Thanks again for your efforts to bring attention to this matter. You did a great job on the broadcast."

I'd gotten my share of phone calls as well. A day or so after the show aired, Lee called to tell me Tony and Jill's relationship had "exploded," most likely as a result of the tale CBS had told. That was the word he used. I wondered what it really meant. I knew how good Tony had been at reeling me back in when I had my doubts about him. Even if the breakup was final, it probably meant psychologically that Jill would be vulnerable to suicidal thoughts. I hoped she would reach out to a source like TERN and get the help and healing she needed.

My parents, my siblings, and college and high school friends all shared words of encouragement. Even with their support, I felt remarkably alone, but somehow it all seemed right, like something larger was unfolding, something beyond my own vision. Somehow I was being cradled and nurtured by this foreign land where I knew practically no one but could begin again.

I had the day off today, and feeling raw and exposed from sharing my story with the nation, I was embracing solitude. I took comfort in walking a couple of miles to San Ildefonso Pueblo, this seemingly mysterious adobe village whose Native American inhabitants had lived there for over seven hundred years. One of the first few nights I was in my new home just a stone's throw from the Rio Grande, the hypnotic beat of the pueblo's drums had lulled me to sleep. Vividly, I had dreamed that hundreds of Pueblo people were dying atop Black Mesa while Spanish conquistadors surrounded it below. I had sensed that these conquerors were brutal and vicious. The pain and anguish of the innocent victims had flooded my body. When I awoke, I knew I had to remember this dream. I had fumbled for my pen and journal on the nightstand, then scrawled it down.

Days later, I had visited the Santa Fe Public Library to learn more about the history of San Ildefonso. What I discovered made me sick: In a 1694 attempt to control the pueblo's grain supplies, Spanish soldiers forced San Ildefonso's men, women, and children who had taken refuge on the mesa to either surrender or starve—just as I had dreamed—a tactic that achieved their goal.

When I came to New Mexico, I knew I was moving to a place where people believed they could connect more deeply to their dream states and what Jung called the "collective unconscious." Until now, I hadn't realized that also meant psychically connecting to some of the ugliest pain and tragedy of our nation's past.

Nevertheless, the Pueblo people had endured. They were still here, still practicing their traditions, and I was eager to find out what I might learn from them. At San Ildefonso, I went into an adobe shop and was greeted by a diminutive Native woman with leathered brown skin and jet-black hair shaped into a bowl cut. She was covered in bright turquoise jewelry, her clear, brown eyes welcoming me into her modest earthen building that felt like it was part of the land rather than on top of it.

"Welcome," she said. "Let me know if you'd like a tour."

I smiled at her, and whispered back, "Thanks."

I was on sacred land and wanted to drink in its timelessness as I leafed through albums of black-and-white archival photographs that told the tale of the pueblo over the past hundred-some years. My soul lit up with reverence for a people who had endured abuse, who had transcended oppression.

After about five minutes, I said, "I heard the drums beating my first night here, just last month, and I knew I was in a special place."

Her brown eyes twinkled, "You heard our drums?" She paused and gazed deeply into me. Something inside me twinkled back, and for an instant, I felt our hearts connect. "Ah yes," she said, "we celebrate the Corn Dance in September."

Corn Dance? I knew Native Americans often kept the details of their sacred ceremonies private, so out of respect, I refrained from asking questions. This was not a day for words. It was hard for me to pull my eyes from hers, but suddenly, they were drawn to the right of where she stood, to elegant black ceramic vessels displayed on shelves, behind glass.

"Oh, how exquisite," I heard myself say softly.

Underneath the pots was a photo of a lovely, dark-haired Native woman who looked much like my host. She was standing before an adobe home, a gorgeous black pot in her hands. Under the photo, a placard read: Maria Martinez, c. 1945.

"Yes, our most famous resident," the little lady said. Her eyes twinkled again, and I could feel myself pulled into connection with her, as if I were ascending into the nighttime sky.

I had to consciously press my feet to the ground to counteract the sensation of bursting open, something I had also experienced after dreaming of the captives on the mesa. It felt as if the veils between different time periods, different planes of existence, were much thinner in this land of ancient people.

That day in the library, I had learned that the San Ildefonso community was changed forever by the tourism that followed when potters Maria and her husband Julian Martinez drew international attention for revitalizing the ancient technique of making the black-on-black pottery displayed before me. These were glossy black vessels with subtle matte-black designs, the signature pottery style of San Ildefonso. Collectors came from across the country and around the world to buy it from the artisans here, along with jewelry and other traditional Pueblo arts and crafts. Before tourism, the pueblo had subsisted primarily on its agricultural traditions.

"Yes, I am interested in a tour, if possible," I said.

"Okay, I'll be with you in a moment." The little woman closed up and locked a jewelry case she had been cleaning and grabbed her shop key off a hook on the wall. She walked me outside, and my eyes were almost blinded by the bright New Mexican sun.

"Here's a map of the pueblo. These artists shops are open," she said, gesturing to the buildings ahead, "as is this section of the pueblo." In silence, the two of us walked to the plaza, or village center, Black Mesa towering in the distance. She must have noticed me gazing longingly at the massive, circular kiva, its tall, thin ladder descending through the flat roof into the unseen, underground pit below.

"The private homes and the kiva are off limits," she said gently.

My heart sank. Ever since I had gone into the reconstructed kiva at Bandelier National Monument, the cliff dwellings about twenty miles from here that were home to the ancestors of the San Ildefonso people, I had longed to enter a real, working kiva.

My guide seemed to read my mind as I gazed at the circular structure. "I'm sorry, dear, the kiva is only for tribal members for ceremonial purposes. You may tour the church if you like."

Disappointed as I was, I respected their integrity. Those who lived in the village in the traditional way were of *very* modest means, some hauling water and heating their homes with wood. They probably could have done a land-office business charging curious gringos plenty of much-needed greenbacks to step into their kiva—but they didn't. There was so much for all of us to learn from the first Americans.

"Okay," I said, but I had no genuine interest in the church. Centuries ago, the Spanish had forced the Native people to convert to Catholicism, building churches on their pueblos and punishing them if they reverted to the old ways. As part of that effort, they had renamed this village, called *Powhoge* in Tewa, meaning "where the water runs through," after San Ildefonso, a saint commonly associated with Spanish missions. Today, the Pueblo people could practice their first religion if they chose, and many practiced both—but I had not come here to visit a church, not even a Native one.

Something about going down into a sacred chamber that symbolized another world or another dimension called to me. I imagined myself huddled in the round chamber, smelling the ritual fire, as I and other Natives communed with the voices of ancestors who had lived on the same piece of earth for many generations. I hungered to find wisdom in the darkness of the void, then climb the ladder, and re-emerge through the square opening in the top into the light.

I remembered the documentary on shamanism I had watched all those years ago as a college senior. "One may be raised in a Christian family that rejects the path of the shaman," the narrator had said, "but to ignore the call would be a fatal mistake. Surviving the call is what gives the shaman the experience needed to begin healing others . . . . Shamans travel through the darkness to mend the soul. The soul. The soul." The words still echoed in my mind.

With the warm sun beating on my skin, my heart lifted and opened as I said a prayer and cast it in the direction of the ceremonial kiva.

"Please, Creator, continue to inspire my journey. Let me contribute in ways that will bring good to the world."

October turned to November. My art therapy class at Southwestern College was coming to an end along with the rest of the fall semester. I had no interest in psychology as a profession, but being at the college introduced me to many students who did—and what a path it was. Talking to some new friends, I realized that the curriculum and philosophy here were as far from my old days at VCU as Santa Fe, New Mexico, was from Richmond, Virginia. At Southwestern, the therapists-in-training learned to always be engaged in their own personal development, and that while boundaries were critical, there should be no sense of superiority or judgment between therapists and patients.

Right after finals, some new friends invited me to come along to the dinner party for graduates. Everyone was going to Rancho de Chimayó, the gracious hacienda-turned-restaurant in the village of Chimayó, about twenty-five miles north of Santa Fe. I felt a little out of place, but I had heard of Chimayó and was tempted to visit. It was known for its red chile peppers, traditional woolen weavings, and, most notably, the Santuario de Chimayó, a little adobe church also known as the Lourdes of the Americas thanks to its pit of holy dirt, said to bring miraculous healing. (Fascinated by the Pueblo religion as I was, I hadn't completely lost interest in Christian mysticism!) I probably wouldn't have time to explore all that on this trip, but it lured me to Chimayó nonetheless.

When we drove up to the restaurant's rambling old adobe home, I was enchanted with the pitched red tin roof hung with luscious red chile ristras. As I approached the front door in the twilight, the bits of straw in the traditional mud-and-straw adobe walls sparkled like flecks of gold. Inside, we meandered through the gracious main rooms, past the crackling hearth in the cantina, to the windowed dining room in back. A server in a white peasant blouse, red cummerbund, and black skirt bought us smoky red chile salsa and chips and promised a round of salty-sweet margaritas momentarily. There were maybe twenty of us at a long table, and the restaurant was buzzing with our party, families with children, and couples in the corners looking at each other longingly over their sangrias. The servers glided deftly among us all.

The man seated next to me introduced himself as John, and told me about his work at a local treatment center while earning his master's degree at Southwestern. He said he worked at what originally had been a safehouse for women suffering from serious trauma, and sadly, some had developed personality disorders as a result of their severely abusive childhoods. In adulthood, a few had also lost their personal identities to cults and were on long, difficult roads to recovery. These were the clients he was working with.

"That sounds fascinating," I remarked, dunking my chip in a little more salsa. "You know, I have a similar story."

"Really?" John replied with interest.

"When I was a senior in college, my psychiatrist misused transference and crossed boundaries with me—much like cult leaders do," I said. "Eventually, he coerced me into a sexual relationship with him."

I was surprised by my own candor. For a second, I wondered if I had revealed too much of myself too soon. John's eyes opened wider. Then he looked at me as though he were seeing me for the first time.

"Oh, my gosh, you're Carrie!"

Hadn't I just told him my name was Carrie? Then again, it was a little noisy in here.

"It's you. It's really you. I saw you on '48 Hours' about a month ago."

Oh that. This was the first time anyone had recognized me. Considering that he had seen the show, I was kind of surprised it had taken him so long. Then again, I'd grown my hair out from the layered bob I had during the filming six months ago.

"They were constantly advertising your story during the World Series!" he went on. "Hunter, the director of counseling where I work, asked me to watch that show with her."

His voice lowered to a reverent whisper as though he couldn't believe he was actually talking to me. "When we saw that you had relocated to Santa Fe and were looking for a job, Hunter and I looked at each other and said, 'We have to get her to come and work here! We have to find her!' We just didn't know how to reach you."

At that moment, it was as if all the raised glasses and spoonfuls of dessert in that dining room froze in midair. The restaurant clatter and chatter were replaced by stillness and silence. My voice and John's seemed like the only sounds.

"Carrie, please," he pleaded. "You could help so many survivors. Please, come work with us as a counselor in this milieu."

Once, I thought I had turned my back on the psychology profession forever. I hated the elitism, I hated the pathologizing, the detached, clinical approach, the Freudian model—all of it. But this felt different. This felt right.

I didn't need to think about John's request a second longer.

Wise Woman of Darkness and Light

~42~

Twenty-three years have passed. It's spring. As I peer out the window of my little adobe studio overlooking the Santa Fe River, I can see that the waters are rising with snowmelt from the nearby mountains. Unlatching the window and cranking it open a bit, I hear the refreshing sound of the little waterfall a few feet away. My heart swells with gratitude. The river may be a mere brook most of the year, but I am blessed to have this secluded workspace in a wooded compound on the outskirts of town.

It's Tuesday. As I listen to the water rush over the rocks outside, I page through my red appointment book to see what the rest of my week looks like. Last weekend, I got so immersed in the workshop I was teaching that now I need to get reacquainted with the rest of my life. Let's see . . . on Wednesday, my last client's appointment is at 3:30, which should give me time to make it to my daughter's lacrosse match after school. Then, my husband has his Saturday night piano gig which I usually went to. As a mother, wife, art therapist, and educator, there is so much to juggle. I make a cup of tea and collect myself before my first client arrives and my day begins.

When a client comes to me in session, needing direction and unsure of where to begin, I encourage him or her to "lead with the victories," that is, to start by recounting what is working in life, what they're proud of. It's an approach I use myself too.

Last weekend's workshop went better than I could have imagined. I began the class on self-care and boundaries for fourteen therapists by having them illustrate how they feel when they're energized, engaged, and doing their best work with their clients. Then I asked them to make a second drawing, illustrating the all-too-common experience of healers like us when they feel drained, overwhelmed, and just "off." In the discussion that followed, we explored how the sacred work of therapy feels when the therapist is in a weakened state.

I queried the group: "What is the ultimate boundary violation for a therapist?"

Several chimed in at once: "sexual contact with a client."

"Yes, that is the most egregious violation," I said. "It is shown to be so damaging to a client's welfare that today, it is a felony in twenty-three states."

It wasn't always, I thought to myself, gratified to look around this room of professionals, most of them women. Briefly, I mentioned that I myself had been coerced by my therapist as a college student over thirty years ago, but I kept the dialogue focused on the participants and the profession, not me. If everything I had endured was for some higher purpose, this might just have been it. I felt no tension in my body, no discord, only groundedness, only truth, as I spoke again.

"Intellectually, we all know that sexual contact with a client is ethically wrong. Yet it happens. To prevent it, we must understand *how* it happens.

"First, consider the client. The clients at greatest risk for exploitation are those who have low self-esteem, need validation, are confused, are feeling alone, are impulsive, have a history of childhood trauma, are having relationship problems, or have a psychiatric disorder. That said, what do you notice about this list of characteristics?"

"Well, it sounds like just about everyone we treat," chimed in a middle-aged, male social worker. Heads nodded and eyes widened.

"Exactly. In fact, a research paper by Linda Mabus Jorgenson on countertransference and sexual exploitation by therapists shows how easily exploited our most fragile clients are. When the client feels adrift emotionally, he or she is most likely to cling to the therapist for guidance. And that's what we're here for—in the beginning. But over time, it's our job to strengthen our clients, so they can weather these stormy seas on their own. The therapist who becomes preoccupied with being a savior or a protector has lost control of himself or herself and is no longer contributing to the client's journey of empowerment."

I scanned the room, making eye contact with each individual. "Has anyone ever had a client come to you in session and reveal interactions with their former therapist that made you cringe?"

Ten participants raised their hands.

"Well, the research shows that more than 50 percent of psychologists interviewed shared that they have treated at least one patient who had been in such a sexually inappropriate relationship with a therapist."

I paused and let that one land. The room was silent.

"As therapists, we have enormous power to either help or harm our clients. Over the course of your career, it is very likely that you will need to report a boundary violation by another therapist. The more we can police our own profession, the fewer clients will be abused, and the more the public will trust us."

There was a look of humility and knowing on the face of each therapist, and I could tell that each of them knew what I know myself: It takes tremendous emotional strength and personal responsibility to be a leader of lost souls.

I wrapped up the session by having each student complete a life-balance wheel worksheet, using a circular diagram to evaluate their levels of satisfaction in eight areas: business/career, finances, health, family and friends, romance, recreation and fun, personal growth, and physical environment. Many confided that they thought their lives were more balanced until they saw obvious gaps on their wheels. We acknowledged that as healers who have been trained to be there for others, too often we become accustomed to barreling through life with our emotional fuel tanks only half-full.

The professionals in the class left with action plans focused on creating greater balance and personal happiness. I left with a sense of completion, a full heart, and a job well done.

Hearing the river flowing outside brings me back to the present. I look at my appointment book again. A new client is scheduled to arrive in about twenty minutes. So far, I've only talked to her on the phone, this lost woman in search of herself, hoping to find guidance on her journey through darkness.

I go through my daily ritual of lighting my candles—one a votive to the Divine Mother Mary, another an aromatherapy candle that will soon fill the room with the calming fragrance of lavender. I still my mind and invoke the powers of healing that will support me as I lead this lost woman. My own journey has taken me to the lap of many masters: Jesus, Mary, Quan Yin, Gaia, the Angels, the Holy Spirit, and, more recently, the spirit of the river, trees, and birds outside my studio window. I know I must keep my heart and mind open to help this woman find her own divine allies.

I hear a knock and open the door.

"Hi," she says, her eyes full of the mist of unshed tears. She is young, about thirty-five, and attractive. Her pretty, blonde hair looks as if it hasn't been combed for days, and her shirt is wrinkled. She anxiously shifts her weight from one foot to the other and twirls her hair in her fingers.

"Hi, I'm Carrie. Welcome. Please take a seat wherever you want."

She eyes the cozy room with its stuccoed walls and earthy tiled floor to find my sofa and chairs sprinkled with throw pillows of turquoise, red, and gold, flanking a broad coffee table offering art supplies of many forms: oil and chalk pastels, markers, sequins, glue sticks, and papers of all colors and sizes.

For a moment, she brightens, "Oh, yes, I came because I heard you do art with your therapy clients. I'm dying to find my creativity again," she says, a tear dripping down her cheek.

I am a bit taken back by her immediate transparency. Not all souls come into therapy so willing and open, but this one is ready. She is obviously flooded with emotion and starving for self-reflection.

I take my own seat in the round-backed wicker armchair. She nervously sits opposite me in its mate, with the olive green chenille throw and beaded peacock pillow, the coffee table between us.

I remind myself that the client before me is probably lost in her own internal darkness and has come to me to find hope and light. Like Persephone—Queen of the Underworld and, later, the Goddess of Spring—I must help her develop eyes of knowing in the dark so she can find her way to the surface and a new life. To do that, I must get a sense of where she is, and where we need to go from here.

We chat for a moment, and I suggest she start by drawing a picture of how she feels right now.

She gingerly places the drawing board on her lap and picks up a sheet of black paper.

The woman sniffles. "Everything feels so black right now."

Her fingers gravitate to the red, blue, and maroon chalk pastels, and she quickly, almost violently, conjures up an abstract picture.

I look at the all-too-familiar image on the paper: pointed shards placed haphazardly on the page, drops of red blood dripping from the broken pieces.

She plucks tissue from the blue box on the coffee table and dabs her eyes, then leans back in the chair and heaves a big sigh.

"Everything I thought was real is shattered. . . . My husband and my best friend . . . I caught them in bed together . . . They're obviously not who I thought they were. Now I don't even know who I am anymore."

Her body shakes, and I can sense how the ground has fallen out from under her, swallowing her into a pit of despair. Her captors are her depression and the husband who betrayed her. She is mired in the most toxic feelings she has ever had.

"Now, draw a picture of what you want to feel, who you want to become, as you heal from this."

She looks at me with her big, blue eyes, silently searching for guidance. Then she stares toward the window as a Western blue jay lands on a branch. She doesn't seem to notice it. She takes a deep breath and gets to work. I can't help but think that the jay seems to be looking through the window at her and me. My heart warms. *Ah, one of her spirit guides . . . and so soon.*

As the bird flies off, my eyes settle back on the woman's right hand searching through the palette of pastels. She lands on yellow and puts a little dab of yellow chalk on a fresh sheet of black paper. Her breathing slows down, and her countenance softens. She makes swirling motions, and her picture opens up with yellow, then flesh tone, then aqua symbols that seem to dance with each other. Now, she's picking up her pace, becoming more enrapt in her creation. She surrounds the marks with black, red, and blue shards that seem to give way to the brighter colors as they come into focus in the center of the paper.

"I used to love to dance, you know . . . Kind of like these aqua lines. I used to love to dance." She bursts into tears.

As her tears flow and her soul speaks, I can almost see the cloud of despair lift for just a moment. I feel my own feet on the floor, grounded in the earth while I watch a speck of light start to pulse inside her, hungry to be witnessed. I am blessed to watch yet another initiation. I know this won't be easy. True initiations never are.

After the woman leaves, I complete the paperwork for her intake process and my preliminary notes. I'm confident I can help her.

In our Western culture, we are hungry for rituals of initiation. In our quest for civilization, we have eradicated most rites of passage from modern life, but such an archetypal experience cannot be stifled. It just springs up in other forms. Often, modern-day initiations are accidental or traumatic, making us feel like victims rather than willing participants. Still, they force us to look inside for our true light, our true wisdom, and in so doing, find our highest selves. Just as in a shamanic journey, the initiate experiences a psychological dismemberment—of beliefs, of identity.

It's a daunting journey, and not one to be taken lightly. Not everyone survives. But many do. I did. And now, just as Persephone returns to the Underworld each winter, I, in the middle of my career, have made the descent and resurfaced again and again, with client after client.

Today, I am past the age Dr. Anthony Romano was when Earle Plumhoff filed a lawsuit against him for gross negligence, wanton recklessness, and malpractice. Was Tony an out-of-balance healer who turned to his patient for the love and validation he craved? Or was he a narcissistic perpetrator who calculated the whole affair from the beginning? Or was he both? I will never know. I haven't laid eyes on him since the night I saw his image on "48 Hours," many years ago.

Because of that man, I fell deeply into the void, the Underworld, and for what seemed like an eternity, he held me as his captive. It's not a path one would consciously choose. Perhaps the path of Persephone, the archetypal goddess of ancient Greece, is only for those who are called to it on a soul level. It certainly felt that way for me. And I have been forever changed.

Since then, I have become Demeter, the divine mother who will stop at nothing to protect my daughter, and all daughters, from those who would use their innocence against them. I am no longer Persephone—and yet I am always Persephone. Now, as my own daughter nears adulthood, and I my crone years, I feel myself beginning to identify with Hecate too, she who travels between worlds and witnesses all crimes, especially those against women and children, as I spend day after day, session after session, working with people who have been betrayed, manipulated, abused, raped.

Delving further into the myth, if Hades had not tricked Persephone into eating the pomegranate, she would be free forever from the Underworld. Instead, she eats the seeds of the most abundantly seed-filled fruit on Earth, and is eternally compelled to return and re-emerge. To me, the seeds of the pomegranate represent what I learned at Sheppard Pratt and the things that nourish us on the journey from trauma to healing, such as compassion, presence, resilience, inner authority, trust, belief, renewal, and awareness that the light is always more precious after a brush with darkness.

My experience with soul-ripping trauma, as both an initiate and a witness to the initiations of others, has led me to the conclusion that, if embraced, trauma recovery is a spirit path toward wholeness and wisdom.

I say goodbye to the river and close up my office for the day. Then I drive home to my little adobe in the country at the base of the very mountains that appeared in my dream more than twenty years ago.

I open the front door to hear the keyboards as my musician husband bangs out "1999," rehearsing for a party in honor of the birthday of the late musician Prince. My heart swells with both sweetness and sorrow.

I dump my satchel on a dining room chair, then tiptoe across the house to his studio. With my hand on the doorknob, I listen for my cue, then burst in, singing:

If you didn't come to party, don't bother knocking on my door!

I shimmy my way over to him as he sings back:

I've got a lion in my pocket, and baby he's ready to roar!

We laugh. He tickles the keys absentmindedly while we chat about our day. "Oh, and I already chopped the veggies," he says, "so all you have to do is cook the rice and stir-fry the rest."

I leave him to his rehearsing and head into the kitchen. On the way, I look out the sunroom window to see my beautiful maiden of a daughter playing outside with her beloved dachshund puppies. The daffodils are in bloom, the tulips rising.

It has taken me thirty-five years to recover from the trauma I experienced at the hands of the doctor who was hired to heal me, and then to evolve into a healer myself. Painful and powerful, it has been my life's work and purpose and brings me back to the divine message I heard as a girl swinging from a tree, the message that perplexed me as a young woman, and that I now fully understand:

"Everything that happens in your life is created by *me* as a test to see how you will respond, what you will choose. I will be watching and noticing. . . . You are not alone."

Epilogue

More than thirty years later, I still shudder to think of all the joy and justice I would have missed if I had succeeded in my suicide attempt at age twenty-four. It has been a long journey back to health, and writing this book has played a significant role in making peace with myself. With every word I wrote, I wept with compassion for the young maiden who was imprisoned by shame and self-doubt.

After the legal proceedings of the late 1980s, I came across the concept of soul curriculum, an empowering way to find meaning in the dark chapters of our lives. According to this view, a larger part of us—connected to the whole, the divine, the godhead, the quantum field, whatever we call it—designs what will happen in our lives before we are born, just as a teacher designs a course curriculum, then guides students through the process of learning it. The triumphs, the tribulations, the lessons—are all orchestrated to shape us into our best selves. When I reviewed my life through this lens, it fortified my early mystical knowing that, "Everything that happens in your life is created by *me* as a test. . . . I will be watching and noticing. . . . You are not alone."

I am now certain that healing must be holistic, encompassing body, mind, and spirit. Our current medical model is inextricably tied to the pharmaceutical industry and emphasizes symptom suppression over healing. At age twenty-six, when I was properly diagnosed with chronic candida brought on by four years of antibiotic use for acne, the lethargy, allergies, panic, depression, and collapse of self-esteem I experienced the summer before I met Dr. Romano finally made sense. With that groundwork in place, my physical and emotional healing could take root.

Today, as a counseling professional, I frequently recommend that my new clients also begin seeing a holistic doctor—whether it be naturopath, integrative doctor, or acupuncturist—to determine where their bodies may be out of balance, resulting in emotional imbalance as well. All too often, overuse of antibiotics and/or birth control pills causes mood swings, anxiety, or depression. Further, health insurance favors pharmaceuticals over holistic medicine, leaving many patients concluding that long-term medication is their only choice. Judiciously used, psychiatric medicine can be life saving, but frequently, deeper imbalances go un-addressed, resulting in limited healing.

My personal journey also brought to light how our society conditions us, particularly women, to surrender our intuition, and hence our authentic power, and instead put blind faith in a doctor or other authority figure. For my own part, once I found myself in a hospital surrounded by professionals with the same credentials as the man who had abused me, I had a hard time trusting anyone. However, when I began art therapy, spontaneously creating images that expressed my inner truth, I realized that doctors were not my guides. Rather, my drawings were my compass rose, I was my own guide, and doctors only helped me along a path I mapped out and determined. Through this process, I gained awareness, clarity, and strength—and my doctors and attorneys were able to support me in that.

Although not true for everyone, my healing process demanded taking action in the world: alerting the Maryland Licensing Board, suing for malpractice, testifying before the Maryland General Assembly, sharing my story with journalists, and finally writing this book. As my wise feminist therapist, Leslie Krohn, encouraged me back in the '80s, "the personal is political."

I gained deeper understanding of my purpose when I interpreted my life path in the context of the archetypal myth of Persephone, Queen of the Underworld and Goddess of Spring. Persephone's story granted me the wisdom that I am not the first person—nor the last—to be abducted, to descend, and to return, and it is this very experience that forges the indelible bond of empathy between my clients and myself.

Another integral part of the healing process is, quite simply, time. Upon decades of reflection, paired with significant social change, I've come to see how the official licensing board not only failed me and my doctor's subsequent victim but also how it failed him. Dr. Anthony Romano should have had his license suspended and been sent to rehabilitation treatment for his sex addiction. Instead, he received six months of mandatory supervision and went on to harm another patient. Today, many licensing boards are more vigilant, and efforts have been made to treat, not just discipline, doctors who cause harm. As a counseling professional, one of my areas of expertise is teaching self-care and boundaries for mental-health professionals, in the hope of preventing the isolation that can lead even experienced practitioners to cross the line.

Above all, in my own experience as both a healer and a patient, I've witnessed how trauma can serve as a powerful initiation to the actualization of the soul's purpose. For me, that meant leaving no stone unturned, no feeling unfelt, and no belief unexamined. Even though victims are not responsible for the abuse by our perpetrators, we must assume 100 percent responsibility for our healing. No one else can do it for us. And in doing so, we become the masters of our souls.

Blessings,
Carrie Ishee
Santa Fe, N.M.
2019

Afterword

Psychiatrist Stephen Levine describes his patient Bea, who had repeatedly expressed intense and persistent erotic feelings toward him in therapy.[1] She once presented him with a necktie at Christmas, which he accepted "after much conflict." Two months later, after delaying her normal appointment so that her next session occurred on Valentine's Day, she gave him a box of chocolates and an expensive pen. Despite her acknowledging the love and desire for a sexual relationship that were embedded in these gifts, Dr. Levine refused them. Bea was mortified and upset for weeks over her humiliation. By holding the line and allowing the patient to express her love in a safe environment, he allowed this recently divorced woman who could not feel sexual interest in her husband to eventually feel safe with a man. "And this," she said as her therapy terminated, "has been worth everything to me."

Psychologist Carl Rogers[2] described the need for balance in professional-client relationships by asking four questions:

- Can I *be* in some way which will be perceived by the other person as trustworthy, as dependable or consistent in some deep sense?
- Can I let myself experience positive attitudes toward this other person—attitudes of warmth, caring, interest, liking, respect?
- Can I be strong enough as a person to be separate from the other?
- Am I secure enough within myself to permit him his separateness?

A Severe Violation of Trust

In these guideposts of Levine's and Rogers', we have the core of one of the two major themes of Carrie T. Ishee's book, the question of what can happen when the critical balance between closeness and separateness, between the eroticism of human connection and sexual exploitation, is not properly maintained.

Carrie began her therapy with Dr. Anthony Romano as a college student because she was suffering from panic attacks and depression. In many ways, he was initially helpful to her. But in the course of treating her, he did many things that many professionals would consider inappropriate in a therapeutic relationship. He isolated her from other aspects of her life by encouraging her to separate from her parents and take a leave from her college studies. He insisted that she had problems with her sexuality that she had never felt or expressed.

Gradually, he developed an increasingly personal relationship with her, disclosing his own personal struggles to her, inviting greater familiarity, and seeing her outside the practice setting. Their relationship eventually led to sexual intimacy, which continued for some time. It became increasingly apparent to her, however, that this intense personal relationship was no longer helping her and was, in fact, isolating her from other positive influences in her life.

This progression of closeness has often been referred to as the "slippery slope."[3] Many of Dr. Romano's behaviors may have been considered inappropriate in their own right, but each one also brought him and his patient closer to sexual involvement. As this progression continued over months of therapy, the sex ultimately seemed like just a small additional step and was thus much easier to rationalize.

Did Dr. Romano plan from the outset to seduce Carrie into a sexual relationship? Perhaps. However, it is also possible that what happened was at least partly a consequence of his own loneliness, of his great respect for Carrie as a person and as a budding therapist whom he invited to join him in his practice one day, and of her own emotional feelings for him.

His behavior, as Carrie reports it, reminds me of the physically deformed and emotionally deranged Phantom of the Opera, who begs of Christine Daaé, his musical protégé, "Say you'll share with me one love, one lifetime. Lead me, save me from my solitude."[4]

We may never know Dr. Romano's motives and plans for his intimate relationship with Carrie. As Dr. Levine points out, however, a therapist's role is to encourage the independence and growth of his patient, not to foster her dependency on him, either personally or professionally. We know that the medical profession strictly forbids sexual intimacy with patients, as do virtually all health professions.[5] It does not matter who initiates a sexual encounter, whether the patient consents or not, what her psychiatric diagnosis is, or how long the sexual relationship lasts. Sexual intimacy with a patient is unethical. Period. Disciplinary sanctions may vary for a variety of reasons, but the standard is firm.

Carrie's depression reached the point that she attempted to take her own life, and was saved only by someone finding her near death in her apartment. After spending a number of months in an excellent private psychiatric hospital, she was encouraged to take legal action against Dr. Romano because of his clearly unprofessional behavior.

As Carrie began to put her life back together, she also became involved in Maryland's Treatment Exploitation Recovery Network (TERN). She discussed her case on CBS's "48 Hours," and she testified before the Maryland General Assembly supporting passage of a bill establishing a twenty-four-member Task Force to Study Health Professional-Client Sexual Exploitation.[6]

It was at that time, in the early 1990s, that I had the opportunity to meet Carrie and hear her story. I had become involved with this issue ten years earlier through my membership on and chairmanship of the Maryland Board of Examiners of Psychologists. Just from working on the disciplinary cases with which we were confronted, I realized how difficult it was for victims to come forward or even to learn what legal resources were available to them. It also became clear that we were not doing enough as professionals to teach our students about professional-client boundaries or to appropriately address allegations of misconduct. During that time, Barbara Foster (now Barbara Francis), an assistant attorney general with whom I had co-authored a book chapter on this issue,[7] introduced me to another TERN member, through whom I eventually met Carrie.

Soon after the task force bill was passed, Carrie moved to New Mexico and we had no contact until she asked me to read her book and to write this afterword. I am honored to have been asked to do so, and I am delighted to see how well she is doing now.

Meaning and Fulfillment Out of Adversity

Our twenty-year separation brings me to the second major theme of this book. Most of all, it is a book about the triumph of the human spirit. Even after a serious breach of trust that almost ended her life, Carrie was able, with the help and support of a number of other people in her life, to rediscover the talents and strength of character that she always knew she had and to build a healthy marriage, a family, and a professional identity that has helped her fulfill many of her life's goals.

Carrie knew from her early years that she was bright, both artistically and musically talented, and physically attractive. She excelled in her studies, and she was, during her therapy with Dr. Romano, accepted into a psychology doctoral program. She had a very supportive family. However, both her continuing depression and her deep personal involvement with her therapist led her to question herself in many ways.

During and after her hospitalization, her expressive nature began to emerge, as did her self-confidence. She eventually met Chris, her musician husband, who was willing to move to Santa Fe with her to start a new life, family, and career.

Carrie kept journals through most of those years, and these have enabled her to slowly and carefully craft this insightful and moving account of her victimization and remarkable recovery. I have been struck by her knowledge, her perceptiveness, her level of relevant detail, her sensitivity, and even the balanced way in which she now sees both her former therapist and the health professions as a whole. She has seen it from both sides, and she understands both the problems and the progress in the field. As I read through the book, I found myself eager to begin each new chapter.

This book is a wonderful contribution and will be useful not only to helping professionals who are interested in learning more about professional-client boundaries but also to all helping professionals. All of us are susceptible to being seduced into a serious boundary-crossing, not so much by our patients but by our own neediness, isolation, and life stresses which may lead us to deny the reality of what we are doing. There may even be situations in which we feel that we are somehow above the need to comply with professional standards. Dr. Romano knew all the time that he was violating an ethical standard, just as you or I may be well aware that we are violating a speed limit just before we are pulled over.

Some victims of sexual exploitation might have spent their lives being angry and obsessed with "changing the system" in an effort to seek justice as they define it or to see their offender severely punished. If these things did not happen to their liking, they may have continued going through life with a single-minded anger, which might only perpetuate their victimization.

What Carrie did was to focus on her own strengths and accomplishments and the people who were meaningful to her. She has worked to improve things in the professional community. She has not done it as a condition of survival but rather in the context of a fulfilling, balanced lifestyle. For this reason, her story can be an inspiration to anyone who feels she or he may have been exploited in any manner.

What Have We Learned in Three Decades?

The issue of professional-client boundaries, and sexual misconduct in particular, saw a lot of attention in the 1980s and '90s, stimulated mostly by consumer advocacy but also by the concern and involvement of a number of health professionals, legislators, journalists, and attorneys committed to addressing the problem. Task forces were formed to study the issue, laws were changed, excellent books were written, videos were produced, research conducted, and programs developed for both education and rehabilitation of offenders.[8]

These things did not happen in isolation. They occurred over the same period that attention was also being given to other forms of sexual abuse, including rape, date rape, sexual harassment in the workplace, and gender discrimination as a whole. The number of women in the health and legal professions was increasing sharply during this period. There has been a broader emphasis placed on professionalism and humanism in medicine and on the importance of self-care of the health professional.[9] Colleague assistance committees were set up to work with health professionals in distress. Initially, these groups focused mostly on substance abuse, but their mission has tended to broaden over time.

Despite these developments, there is still much to be done. Education on professional boundaries is still inadequate, both at the pre-degree and continuing education levels. Enforcement of ethical standards regarding professional-client intimacy varies substantially among states and among professions.

We see stories of sexual misconduct in the news media almost every day, whether they involve clergy, university faculty, athletic coaches, high school teachers, politicians, or health professionals. These stories often underscore the difficulty we still have as a society in understanding and addressing allegations of sexual misconduct.[10]

Professional sexual misconduct is not likely to end, any more than murder has been ended by capital punishment or gun control efforts. There are some people who don't understand the consequences of their actions, who are blinded by denial, or who simply don't care. However, I would like to think that we can minimize such violations through more and better education, more-conscientious discipline and, when warranted, more-effective rehabilitation measures.

Mostly, the issue of professional sexual misconduct needs to be seen and discussed as a more-open issue,[11] so that people can begin to understand the harm it can do, not only to the patients and clients who are victimized but also to the offenders themselves and to public confidence in their professions. This book is an excellent contribution toward that objective.

S. Michael Plaut, Ph.D.
Gainesville, FL

References

1. Stephen B. Levine, *Sexual Life: A Clinician's Guide.* (New York: Plenum Press, 1992): 226–29.

2. Carl Rogers, "The Characteristics of a Helping Relationship." *Personnel and Guidance Journal* (September 1958): 6–16. http://onlinelibrary.wiley.com/doi/10.1002/j.2164-4918.1958.tb01147.x/abstract

3. Larry H. Strasburger, Linda Jorgenson, and Pamela Sutherland, "The Prevention of Psychotherapist Sexual Misconduct: Avoiding the Slippery Slope." *American Journal of Psychotherapy* 46 (1992): 544–55.

4. George Perry, *The Complete Phantom of the Opera*, (New York: Henry Holt & Co., 1991)

5. Marilyn Peterson, *At Personal Risk: Boundary Violations in Professional Relationships.* (New York: W.W. Norton & Co., 1992): 25–27.

6. Catherine D. Nugent, Joseph P. Gill, and S. Michael Plaut, eds., *Sexual Exploitation: Strategies for Prevention and Intervention. Report of the Maryland Task Force to Study Health Professional-Client Sexual Exploitation.* 1996. (Available from Department of Health and Mental Hygiene, 201 W. Preston St., Baltimore MD 21201); S. Michael Plaut and Catherine D. Nugent, "The Maryland Task Force to Study Health Professional-Client Sexual Exploitation: Building Understanding and Facilitating Change Through Collaboration," *Journal of Sex Education and Therapy* 24, (1999): 236–43.

7. S. Michael Plaut and Barbara H. Foster, "Roles of the Health Professional in Cases Involving Sexual Exploitation of Patients." in *Sexual Exploitation of Clients by Health Professionals* edited by Ann W. Burgess and Carol Hartman, (Philadelphia: Praeger, 1986): 5–25.

8. Steven B. Bisbing, Linda Mabus Jorgenson, and Pamela K. Sutherland. *Sexual Abuse by Professionals: A Legal Guide.* (Charlottesville: Michie, 1995); Joseph D. Bloom, Carol C. Nadelson, and Malkah T. Notman, editors. *Physician Sexual Misconduct.* (Washington, DC: American Psychiatric Press, 1999); Nancy A. Bridges, "Managing Erotic and Loving Feelings in Therapeutic Relationships: A Model Course," Journal of Psychotherapy Practice and Research 4 (1995): 329–39; Andrea Celenza, *Sexual Boundary Violations: Sexual, Supervisory, and Academic Contexts.* (Lanham, MA: Jason Aronson, 2007); Federation of State Medical Boards. *Addressing Sexual Boundaries: Guidelines for State Medical Boards,* (Dallas: Author, 2006). Glen O. Gabbard, editor, *Sexual Exploitation in Professional Relationships*, (Washington, DC: American Psychiatric Press, 1989); Gregg Gorton, Steven Samuel, and Sam Zebrowski, "A Pilot Course for Resi-

dents on Sexual Feelings and Boundary Maintenance in Treatment," *Academic Psychiatry* 20 (1996): 1–13; Maxine A. Papadakis, Carol S. Hodgson, Ariane Teherani, and Neal D. Kohatsu, "Unprofessional Behavior in Medical School Is Associated With Subsequent Disciplinary Action by a State Medical Board," *Academic Medicine* 9 (2004): 244–49; S. Michael Plaut, "Sexual and nonsexual boundaries in professional relationships: Principles and teaching guidelines." *Sexual and Relationship Therapy* 23 (2008): 85-94; S. Michael Plaut, Janet Klein Brown, Mira Brancu, Rebecca C. Wilbur, and Katherine Rios, "Characteristics of Health Professionals in a Mandated Ethics Tutorial after Violating Sexual Boundaries With Patients." *Journal of Health Care Law and Policy* 16 (2013): 353-74. Gary R. Schoener, "Preventive and Remedial Boundaries Training for Helping Professionals and Clergy: Successful Approaches and Useful Tools." *Journal of Sex Education and Therapy* 24 (1999): 209–17.

9. Mira Brancu and Lisa Page, "Recognizing Boundary Violations as an Issue of Self-Care: A Graduate Student Perspective," *The North Carolina Psychologist* 60 (2008): 5, 12; W. Brad Johnson, Jeffrey E. Barnett, Nancy S. Elman, Linda Forrest, and Nadine J. Kaslow, "The Competent Community: Toward a Vital Reformulation of Professional Ethics," *American Psychologist* 67 (2012): 565–66.

10. MaryClaire Dale, "Legal Expert Links PSU, Catholic Church Scandals." *The Seattle Times,* (July 2012) 13. http://seattletimes.nwsource.com/html/sports/2018683222_apuspennstateabuse.html; Soumya Karlamangla, "Sexual misconduct allegations against California doctors rise sharply since #MeToo era began," *Los Angeles Times*, August 12, 2019. https://www.latimes.com/california/story/2019-08-11/sexual-misconduct-allegations-california-doctors

11. S. Michael Plaut, "Understanding and Managing Professional-Client Boundaries." In *Handbook of Clinical Sexuality for Mental Health Professionals, 2nd Edition.* edited by Steven B. Levine, Candace B. Risen, and Stanley E. Althof, (New York: Brunner-Routledge, 2010): 21–38.

Study Guide for Professionals

1. What progressive boundary violations (the "slippery slope") did Dr. Romano engage in that eventually led to sexual intimacies?
2. Describe and dissect the areas of transference and countertransference you witnessed in reading the book.
3. Do you think the licensing board did enough to discipline Dr. Romano for his boundary violations? What was the result of its actions?
4. What might Dr. Romano have done instead when he realized his feelings were getting in the way of helping Carrie?
5. What stood out to you in the legal proceeding regarding Dr. Romano's behavior?
6. What stood out to you about Carrie's access to her own power and wisdom that an effective therapist would have highlighted and nurtured?
7. What would you do if a client in your office shared such a story of involvement with a previous therapist?
8. What would the clinical challenges be in working with such a client?
9. Have you ever felt drawn to a client in a way that could have affected your clinical judgement? What did you do to work with the energies present in the room?
10. What might you need to add to your own self-care practice to prevent using clients for your own needs?
11. Why do you believe there is an established boundary line regarding intimacies with a client?
12. How was art-making important for Carrie's healing? Why do you think this was particularly important given what she had experienced with Dr. Romano?

13. What did Carrie do to begin trusting herself again?
14. How do gender roles and social conditioning play into what happened to Carrie in therapy?
15. How do you see the power differential present in the therapeutic relationship as a potential set-up for violations to occur?
16. How can you as a therapist keep your own power issues in mind when helping people in distress?
17. How can you give the power back to a client rather than gathering it for yourself?
18. What are the most important lessons of *Seduced into Darkness*?

About the Author

Carrie Ishee has been a student of healing, human potential, and consciousness for more than 35 years. Her quest to know herself began in college when a severe health crisis compounded by her psychiatrist's seduction and sexual abuse shattered her physically, emotionally, and spiritually.

After doctoral studies in clinical psychology, she worked as a behavioral therapist, pursued a master's degree in art therapy, and later completed a two-year training program in life coaching. Her work today is focused on helping victims such as she once was break free from suffocating shroud of trauma to create lives of meaning, purpose, and passion.